A Palate In Revolution

A PALATE IN REVOLUTION:
Grimod de La Reynière
and the
Almanach des Gourmands

Giles MacDonogh

Robin Clark
London   New York

First published by Robin Clark Limited 1987
A member of the Namara Group
27/29 Goodge Street, London W1P 1FD
Copyright © Giles MacDonogh

British Library Cataloguing in Publication Data

MacDonogh, Giles
   A palate in revolution: Grimod de Là
Reynière and the Almanach des gourmands.
   1. Grimod de La Reynière, Alexandre
Balthazar Laurent 2. Gastronomy –
France – Biography
   I. Title
   641'. 01'30924   TX637

ISBN 0-86072-109-4

Typeset by Reprotype Ltd, Peterborough
Printed and bound in Great Britain at
The Camelot Press Ltd, Southampton

Contents

Preface i
The Makings of a Gourmand 1
Exile: The Political Education of a Gourmand 29
A Gourmand in Paris 43
The Eclipse of a Gourmand 97
Grimod's Food 109
A Gourmand Miscellany 159
Notes 225
Bibliographical Note 235
Index 237

Note on Illustrations

The frontispieces to the eight *Almanachs* (1803-13) are reproduced in order of publication.

Preface

'*Le plus lettré des Gourmands, le plus Gourmand des lettrés*',* Grimod de La Reynière died on Christmas Day 1837. This modest first work in English will therefore commemorate the 150th anniversary of his death. While I make no apology for giving the founding father of gastronomy a better press in this country, I cannot lay any claim to having produced an exhaustive work. Readers who wish to know more must go to Grimod's most recent French biography – *Le Gourmand Gentilhomme* by Ned Rival (Le Pré aux Clercs, 1983). Equally in French, there are modern reprints of both the *Manuel des Amphitryons* and of the first volume of the *Almanach des Gourmands*.

A great many people have been helpful in the course of preparing this book; many of them were kind enough to research some small piece of information while I waited at the other end of the telephone. I am especially grateful to the following: John Blackett-Ord, Roderick Blyth, Tim Clarke, Jill Cox, Helen Glanville, Caroline Hobhouse, Tim and Stephanie Johnston, Philip Mansel, Jennifer Paterson, Sophia Sackville-West, Katharine and Charles Sheppard, Simon Wallis and the staffs of both the British Library and the Bibliothèque Nationale in Paris. Very special thanks are due to Piers Cumberlege who gave up a number of weekends to read the proofs. All the translations from French are by me unless otherwise stated, and despite all the assistance I have received, my mistakes are all my own too.

---

*Charles Monselet, *Les Oubliés et les Dédaignés*, Alençon 1857.

The Makings of a Gourmand

Bibliothèque d'un Gourmand au XIXᵉ Siècle.

I

Alexandre-Balthazar-Laurent Grimod de La Reynière was born in Paris on 20 November 1758. On his father's side he was the fourth generation of a dynasty of noble tax farmers, originally from the gourmand city of Lyon. One of the most hated offices in Ancien Régime France, the *fermier général,* or tax farmer, bought a concession from the King permitting him to collect taxes from every milieu in the realm. In theory, it saved the King the expense of collecting them himself; in practice, it meant the money, rather than going into the King's pocket, ended up in that of the farmer, which in turn made for a multiplication of taxes in order to procure some direct revenues for the crown. It is not difficult to see that this situation contributed directly to the foment which brought about the Revolution in 1789.

Though Grimod liked to suggest the founder of the line was no more than a clever pork butcher who saw his chance in supplying the armies of the Maréchal de Soubise, the reality was quite different.[1] Grimod's great-grandfather, Antoine Grimod, was in fact the son of a rich Lyonnais notary. Antoine the Younger, the first tax farmer and *secrétaire du roi,** died only a year before Grimod's birth, aged over a hundred.

Antoine's second son, Grimod's grandfather, acquired the *seigneurie* or manor of La Reynière which, following the contemporary practice, he added to his name. (The custom is not wholly dead in this century – one has only to think of Giscard d'Estaing.) Gaspard died in 1754, leaving a fortune of fourteen million *livres* and his office of *fermier général* to his son Laurent. According to the author of the *Almanach des Gourmands,* his grandfather died 'on the field of honour, suffocated by a *pâté de*

**'A title without functions, but greatly endowed with privileges and, as a result, highly sought after.'* (Marion, *Dictionnaire des Institutions de la France aux XVIIe et XVIIIe Siècles,* Paris 1923). The title conferred full nobility.

foie gras'. It was a fitting heredity for the man Sainte-Beuve was later to call 'the father of the table', and as Grimod's essay 'The Useless Soldier' narrates, Gaspard was an unabashed gourmand. Sadly though, we must deny him his honourable death, as the *pâté de foie gras,* that great set piece of French *gourmandise,* did not see the light until some time between 1779 and 1783, when it was prepared for the Maréchal Marquis de Contades, Governor of Alsace, by his Alsatian *cordon bleu.* Jean-Pierre Clause.

Grimod's father, Laurent Grimod de La Reynière, was born in 1734. Though Louis XV granted him the right to inherit his father's lucrative office when he was only seventeen, Laurent was less suited by nature to the business of finance than his ancestors had been; it must however be said that at the time of his marriage to Grimod's mother, he was reported to be worth in the region of sixty million and one of the richest men in the kingdom. By inclination, Laurent preferred artistic pursuits and amused himself by copying the works of Van Dyck, Rubens, Poussin, Greuze and Watteau. In 1787, the French Royal Academy of Painting paid him the compliment of making him an honorary associate member. His portrait by Van Loo shows an effeminate figure, and his timorous nature was well borne out by contemporary accounts. He had a preternatural fear of thunder and loud noises and would sit out a storm in a vaulted basement room, the door blocked by a mattress soaked in oil, while a servant stood outside beating on a drum at every thunderclap. No one on earth could prise him from this cellar until the sky had once again assumed a more clement appearance. While not wholly inheriting his own father's business acumen, he was no less a gourmand. A frequently repeated story tells of Gaspard's descent on a provincial inn and his noting with joyous anticipation the seven fat turkeys gobbling in the yard. The tax farmer obtained rooms from the innkeeper, but when he enquired about dinner he was told roundly that there was nothing left to eat.

'Nothing left to eat,' replied the Parisian, 'what are those turkeys that I saw outside?'

'The young gentleman from the capital ordered them all to be roasted for his evening meal, sir.'

Gaspard was anxious to meet this young man with so prodigious an appetite that it even outstripped his own, and asked the innkeeper to introduce him. To his great surprise, the man brought before him was none other than his son Laurent.

'*Sire*,' he said in justification, 'it was you yourself who told me that there was nothing good on a fat turkey; I had intended to eat only the oysters.'

His father, recognizing the nascent gourmand in the young man, was comforted: 'Though you are a little extravagant for a young man, I cannot say that you are unreasonable.'

The Grimod family had for years pursued a policy of marrying within their own social circle: other financiers and tax farmers. Though noble by Antoine's acquisition of the charge of *secrétaire du roi* in Lyon at the beginning of the century, as financiers their social position was even lower than that of the 'robe' (nobles whose origins at least lay in the magistrature). Gaspard changed all that in 1749, when he married his elder daughter, Françoise-Thérèse, to Chrétien-Guillaume de Lamoignon de Malesherbes, later president of the Cour des Aides, Chancellor of France and the ill-fated defender of Louis XVI.[2] Though from the 'robe', Malesherbes was one of the most distinguished jewels in its crown. The cost of these ill-assorted nuptials was a dowry of half a million *livres*, not to mention other details of the marriage contract, attractions which well made up for the undistinguished lineage of the bride.

On 1 February 1758, it was the turn of Laurent to make a good match. The choice fell on Suzanne-Françoise-Elisabeth de Jarente de Sénar, twenty-three-year-old daughter of the Marquis d'Orgeval. At first, the noblewoman had refused to leave her convent at Pentémont for this unappetizing suitor from the world of high finance. The convent in question, today occupied by the ministry responsible for former servicemen, was situated on the left bank between the rues de Bellechasse and Grenelle. Its mission was above all to educate the children of the higher nobility, and to serve as their *pension* till such day as a suitable husband could be found. The de Jarente family belonged to one of the most ancient houses of Provence, but like so much of the Provençal nobility (many of whom were prominent figures in the Revolution and the Terror) lacking in sufficient funds to match their pretensions. As Grimod was later to put it, his mother arrived with a dowry of 'twenty-three *livres* and a name more ancient than illustrious'. The truth, as we shall see, was slightly different. There was no doubting their illustrious name however: the de Jarente or Gerente family went back to the eleventh century, and had been on the Crusades at a time when the

Grimods were, in all probability, pork butchers.

When the time came, and Suzanne-Elisabeth had been convinced of the advantages of the match, the unequal distribution of wealth between the bride and groom had to some degree been remedied. Mlle de Jarente had an uncle, Monsignor Louis Sextius de Jarente de la Bruyère, Bishop of Digne and later of Orléans, counsellor to the King on all his councils, Abbot of Saint Wandrille, Saint Honorat and of the ancient Abbey of Lérins in Provence. The Bishop was the very epitome of a high-living, Ancien Régime prelate, a big spender, sociable by nature and the possessor of a third share in a dancing girl with the Prince de Soubise and the Chevalier de Boufflers. De Jarente settled 160,000 *livres* of rents on his favourite niece, made her his heir and, for good measure, moved into the newly wedded couple's town house.

Still, despite the luxury of her surroundings and the considerable change from the muted atmosphere of her former retreat, Madame de La Reynière was not happy. Nor did the quality of the table appear to have much distracted her from her thoughts of *mésalliance,* for if Chamfort is to be believed, at Laurent's table 'you may eat but you won't digest'. Time and again, we are told, she returned to the dream of her convent years, of presentation at court and of the 'grand habit' that she would have worn at Versailles. As the descendant of a family noble before 1400, she had every right to that honour, but as the wife of a *nouveau riche* financier she did not. Madame de Genlis, the rather precious governess of the children of the Duc de Chartres, later the revolutionary Philippe-Egalité and father of King Louis-Philippe, said of her: 'She never ceases to bemoan her fate in secret, as everything around her reminds her of her misfortune. It is not done to talk of the King in her company, nor of court dress; doing so risks throwing her into violent emotions which she is quite unable to hide and one is obliged to change the subject.' Madame de Genlis, who later rented land from the Abbey of Pentémont for the 'nursery' of her Orléans charges, cruelly caricatured Grimod's mother as the snobbish Madame d'Olcy in her novel *Adèle et Théodore.* Nor was it the only such jibe. A curious satire called *Une Bibliothèque de la Cour et de la Ville* published on the eve of the Revolution, is composed of bogus book titles; under Madame La Regnière (*sic*) the work is entitled *Les Généalogies!*[3]

Later her son summed her up thus:

> My mother, being issued from a great noble house, has never ceased to bewail her fate since taking my father's name. Fearing someone might forget her lineage, she has never admitted anyone into her society who is not of her rank, and who did not give her every assistance in grinding my father's nose into the mud by showing him up for what he is.

Great though her disappointments must have been, she was to receive a terrible shock which can only have confirmed her in all the misgivings she felt about her marriage. Ten months after her wedding she went into labour with her first child – the only one to survive infancy. To the horror of her husband and herself, Alexandre was born deformed. At the end of his left arm was a sort of claw like that of a bird of prey, and on the right there was a pincer, joined by a membrane as on a duck's foot. The noble godparents who were to have attended his baptism were put off on the pretext of the child being so ill that he was unlikely to survive the week. Instead Grimod received his first sacrament in the company of Marie-Charlotte Borgne, the widow of a tailor and a servant at the Hôtel de La Reynière. The other godparent that day at Saint Eustache was one Claude Ruty, an illiterate parquet rubber.

This unfortunate accident sounded the knell to any possible improvement in the marriage. The parents soon had it put about that the disability had come about by the child's having been inadvertently dropped into a pigpen, the inmates, those 'Kings of Base Beasts', then eating the little boy's hands; the obvious intention was to remove any stain from the child's heredity. As he grew up, Grimod had false hands fitted and Monselet, one of his earliest biographers, informs us that they were 'made out of iron and springs, and covered with white [pig?] skin gloves'. He learnt, nonetheless, both to write and draw well. In later life he developed a nasty habit of heating his iron hands on the stove and inciting unsuspecting persons to warm their hands in the same way, telling them it was safe to do so.

Soon after Suzanne-Elisabeth's marriage, a friend asked Malesherbes whether he thought she would be happy with her Midas. 'That will depend on the first lover she takes,' replied her brother-in-law. Madame de La Reynière was not slow to take up the challenge posed by the number of glittering blades who met in her salon, a circle in which her unfortunate husband was scarcely tolerated. ('Who is that curious figure from Callot?' asked a haughty courtier one day, gesturing towards a man lingering by the door. 'Pay no attention to him,' replied Madame de La Reynière, 'it's my husband.')* Her first lover was the Marquis de Lugeac, the commander of the Royal Horse Grenadiers. He was followed by a *fermier général,* M de Caze and the Chevalier de Méra. Madame de La Reynière, however, soon became embroiled in a long-standing affair with the Bailli de Breteuil, a distant cousin of Louis XVI's minister of the same name and the Order of Malta's Ambassador to Versailles. It was to last until the years immediately prior to the Revolution, and cause more than *ennui* for her son.

To compensate for her *mésalliance,* Suzanne-Elisabeth entertained every night in her house in the rue de la Grange Batelière, and from 1778 at the sumptuous town palace that Laurent had built on the corner of the Place Louis XV (now Place de la Concorde). To escape from his wife's society, Laurent bought himself the Château de La Tuilerie in Auteuil, nicknamed the 'invisible château', as its huge surrounding park hid it from the road. Laurent lived there from 1774-82, but he was in no way safe in his retreat from his wife and her guests, as the château's position on the main road to Versailles made it highly strategic in Suzanne-Elisabeth's mission to distract the court from the King's palace. In later life Grimod remembered how Morillon, the distinguished family chef, used to cope with the carriage-loads of parasitic courtiers who alighted at La Tuilerie in the hope of an excellent dinner:

> It was ten o'clock and supper was about to be served to the three members of the household, when suddenly ten or twelve carriages arrived one after the other in the courtyard announcing the presence of a further fifteen or twenty people for dinner. Fortunately the cook knew what to do, and had a good number of entrées in reserve already earmarked for such an eventuality, and at ten-thirty an excellent supper for twenty-five was laid on the table.

---

*Jacques Callot (*c.* 1592-1635). Engraver most famous for his striking depictions of the horrors of the Thirty Years War and for his engravings of grotesque beggars and dwarves.

La Tuilerie had two other gourmand owners before becoming a convent: Président Thiers and the extraordinary Doctor Véron, a man whose appetite and varied talents would have fully recommended him to the *présidence* of the Jury Dégustateur.[4]

In 1778 Laurent began building his splendid *hôtel particulier* at the foot of the Champs Elysées. The *échevins,* or aldermen, of the city had specified that the building should exactly duplicate the elevation of Chalgrin's Hôtel de la Vrillière on the right-hand side of Gabriel's celebrated composition. Laurent's architect took no notice of this stipulation, and the faithful copy which exists today is the work of the French and American architects who rebuilt the Hôtel de La Reynière as the United States' Embassy in the 1930s. Laurent's architect was Nicolas Barré, though the work was carried out by Jean-Jacques Thevenin. The curious married life of the La Reynières was fully borne out in the plans of the new edifice, for it was possible for the two of them to carry on their lives without ever encountering one another. The apartments of Monsieur and Madame were separated by a huge salon, which doubled as an entrance hall. Some of the features which elicited the most admiration from contemporaries were the polygonal dining-room, the bathroom set in a miniature Pantheon and the splendid interiors by Adam's friend and seminal influence, Charles-Louis Clérisseau,[5] undertaken in a Pompeiian style, no less fashionable in France in the 1780s than it was in the Britain of the Adam brothers. The house formed the setting for Laurent's collection of paintings which included a 'Jew's Head' by Rembrandt, the 'Holy Family' by Poussin, two Greuzes, two Bouchers and three Lancrets: 'La Balançoire', 'La Danse', and 'Les Plaisirs de la Pêche'. The panels of the life of Hercules by Etienne de la Vallée, called 'Le Chevalier Poussin', have since found their way into the collections of the Victoria and Albert Museum in London.

II

Traditionally, small children of the period were farmed out to wet-nurses during their earliest infancy. There is no reason to believe that Grimod did not suffer this fate given the little affection his mother apparently felt for her deformed child. At her death, Suzanne-Elisabeth left her son a locket containing a lock of hair belonging to a little brother who died in infancy. M Rival has suggested that the writer probably had no idea of the existence of this *cadet*, who may well have absorbed a disproportionate amount of his mother's love during his brief life. Grimod's first memory of childhood was the setting up of the statue to Louis XV in the *place* of that name in June 1763, when the little boy was four. The statue was soon decorated with a famous quip, attesting the waning popularity of the Bien-Aimé in the hearts of some Parisians.

Oh! la belle statue! Oh! le beau piédestal!
*Les Vertus sont à pied, le Vice est à cheval.**

On 15 April 1769, Grimod entered the Collège du Plessis, where his formal schooling began. The college had been founded as part of the university in 1317 but from the seventeenth century the establishment had declined into an academy for younger children. Up until that time he had been in the care of a tutor, a 'brutal gambler' whom Grimod had detested. At the Collège du Plessis he was still under his titular charge, but found means to escape him. For four and a half years, he later told his friend, the novelist Rétif de La Bretonne, he was happy at school: 'I adored my studies and never once did I suffer the slightest punishment from either the professors or the college.' On 14 November 1773, Grimod transferred to the Collège de Reims, by that time part of

---

*Oh, the lovely statue! The lovely pedestal!
Virtue walks slipshod while vice rides a charger.

the Collège Louis-le-Grand. He remained there until 1775, with his normal studies taking place at the former institution while he went to Louis-le-Grand for his philosophy and rhetoric classes.

On 14 August 1775 Grimod left his parents for the first time. Late nights of study had had a deleterious effect on his health. The journey took him to Switzerland via the Bourbonnais, the Lyonnais, the Dauphiné and Savoy. In Switzerland itself he stayed briefly in Geneva before settling in Lausanne. On the way the young man stopped at the Grande Chartreuse, where he was tempted to become a monk. Strangely enough, in the years when he was incarcerated by *lettre de cachet* in the Abbaye de Domèvre he was still able to regret his decision not to do so. Lausanne proved to be a nine-month idyll almost as seminal to Grimod as it had been twenty years before to Edward Gibbon, and their experiences were in no way dissimilar. Grimod remained in the city from 10 December 1775 to 26 September of the following year: 'That year was the happiest of my life,' he wrote from Domèvre in May 1787, 'free, independent, constantly invited out and fêted, in love, but not enough to make me unhappy, enjoying an existence and a consideration, rare for one of my age, which flattered my self-esteem and my vanity, while I pursued pleasant studies which were wholly chosen by myself ...' The object of his amorous attentions was a certain Suzanne T— but it was not long before she did make him unhappy. At first he was agreeably struck by the liberty of contact reigning between young people in the Swiss city, but later when the young Swiss woman spurned him he was to write one of the first of his caustic offerings on the subject of women; 'As girls they are false, shamming and difficult to get to know, as women they cease to hold themselves back.'

Grimod returned to Paris in November 1776. The little Bailli was increasingly in residence at the rue de la Grange Batelière and Grimod opted to spend much of his time at La Tuilerie while he read for the Bar. At first this choice of career must have seemed attractive to his parents, who realized that the magistrature was a more effective entrée to higher social circles than finance could ever be, but Grimod refused to become a judge, facetiously adding that 'as a judge, I could find myself in the position of having to hang my father, while as an advocate, I would always be able to defend him'. In 1780, Grimod was doing his pupillage at the Grand'Chambre of the court at Châtelet, the equivalent of the criminal court. He was full of optimism about his choice of career; the democrat in him was at its highest point: 'Is there a freer or more beautiful career than that of an advocate and an orator? He depends on nobody and ignores the strictures of ministers, defending constantly the unhappy and the oppressed good people of the world.' But behind his lauding of the Bar was a feeling of independence from his family and the vast hereditary wealth that would one day be his. Grimod, above all, wished to make a name for himself: 'I would find it repugnant to be nothing more than my father's son. For the present I am *Maître de La Reynière,* advocate at the Paris Parlement. I have an office, clients, memoranda to publish, who could ask for more?'

His other passion of the time, and one which was to obsess him all his life, was the theatre, and the young student would often mingle with the theatregoers on the *parterre* of the Comédie Française, 'the only amusement worthy of a remotely educated man'. According to Desnoiresterres, the author of the first full-length biography of the gastronome, Grimod also found it a useful way of escaping his tutor in order to stray into the Palais Royal, the headquarters of Paris's pornocracy of the day, and a way to make up for some of his more bitter disappointments in love. The creator of this passion for the theatre in the young Grimod was, in all probability, Mademoiselle Quinault, nicknamed *'du-bout-du-banc'*. Mademoiselle Quinault was given this epithet to differentiate her from her elder sister who retained her maiden name despite having married the Duc de Nevers. A friend of Voltaire, d'Alembert, Marivaux, the Comte de Caylus, Duclos and d'Argenson, Mademoiselle Quinault had made her début aged fourteen at the Comédie Française in 1714. Her strange nickname derived from the fact that it was an honour to be admitted to her company even 'at-the-end-of-the-bench'. Although an intimate friend of his mother, she became a sort of adopted grandmother to the young Grimod, whose famous supper in 1783 was said to be a tribute to the old actress, who died that year. From 1777, the stage-struck Grimod began to contribute articles on the Parisian theatre in the *Journal des Théâtres*. Though only nineteen, Grimod proclaimed his mission to 'defend taste and truth'. It would appear that the truth was found to be in poor taste, for the *Journal* collapsed after only fourteen issues. But Grimod was not slow in finding a new outlet for his theatrical critiques and he became the correspondent for the Swiss *Journal*

Helvétique de Neufchâtel. His articles led to an accolade precious to the young writer: he was received into the Academy of the Arcades in Rome, a literary club which had counted Voltaire and Fontenelle among its members.

Encouraged, perhaps, by his success in literature, the young Grimod became increasingly *enragé*. Much of this took the form of ridiculing his parents by a number of harmless pranks. In one story recounted by Paul Delacroix, Grimod installed himself in the *cour d'honneur* of the family *hôtel* with a basket full of salads and vegetables and began to peel them with a joyful dexterity. When his mother flew into a horrified rage at his conduct, Grimod riposted: '*Madame ma mère,* the great difference between a lettuce and the greater part of the people we know, is that a lettuce has a heart.' One day the young lawyer rounded up all the beggars he could find in the vicinity of the family home and arranged them on either side of the path leading to the front door. When his father arrived at the gate Grimod gestured towards his unfortunate following: '*Monsieur,* charity, I beg of you, for these poor devils who have been or are about to be made destitute by the *fermiers généraux*.' Japes of this sort led to the cutting off of Grimod's substantial allowance, but the writer knew well how to embarrass his parents. One day he was dining with a friend. At the end of the meal, Grimod offered to take the friend, a fellow advocate, to his next appointment. Arriving at that place, Grimod asked the man how long he would be. The colleague replied that his business would take him only a few minutes. The writer informed him that if that were the case he would wait outside in the La Reynière coach and take him on to his next appointment. The increasingly puzzled friend informed Grimod that he was going to the court where he would be busy for several hours. 'In that case,' Grimod told him, 'I must charge you a crown.' The colleague was thunderstruck to find that his friend was using the family coach as a taxi and the story went round Paris with predictable speed. The next day Grimod *père* reinstated his son's allowance.

It was about this time that a serious crisis developed between Grimod and his mother. The young man, who found 'no crime as vile as that of adultery' and was increasingly sickened by his mother's openly parading the Bailli, had begun increasingly to distance himself from the family hearth, spending his time in his office in the rue Chauchat or in the little *entresol* he had rented on the Île de la Cité, ostensibly to be near the court. Madame de La Reynière hit upon an unscrupulous scheme to draw her son back to her skirts. Grimod had a fondness for a young cousin of his, a certain Angelique de Bessi. Madame de La Reynière was aware of her son's weakness and brought the girl over to live with her in her apartment in the family home. The ruse was eminently successful; Grimod ceased his roving and returned to the hearth, where he was to be seen in constant communion with his young cousin. His mother, however, had been less than frank and had kept from her son one vital piece of information. Mademoiselle de Bessi was betrothed to an insignificant officer worker – Charles Mitoire, who was in the service of Grimod's father. The marriage was duly celebrated in November 1779.

The scene that followed has come down to us in the version recorded by Rétif de La Bretonne in *Les Françaises* where Grimod is characterized as Reinette. According to Rétif the episode led to a deeper resentment against all 'womankind' and a profession of celibacy which in turn led to his signing his early philosophic works *'célibataire'*. But the more serious contention which Rétif advanced was that Grimod from that moment 'ceased to honour his mother'. Furious at his mother's conduct, Grimod accused her of being the cause of his infirmities; as the young man's tone became increasingly insolent, the Bailli intervened, hitting the defenceless son. The action was to distance the two La Reynières yet further, as Suzanne-Elisabeth took the side of her lover in the following war of words. Grimod wrote to the Bailli in a tone of majestic bitterness, though sadly Breteuil's reply is not recorded. 'You evidently thought that my being born without hands meant you could gratuitously insult me, and threats being insufficient, you opted for force. I am sorry that someone came between you and me, I should have been delighted to see how far the Grand Seigneur would go once he had lost all sentiment of reason or restraint.' The argument led to Grimod's being banished from the house. 'You congratulate yourself, I suppose, on having had me banned from the paternal hearth by your presence and your insults ... but no honest soul could applaud the conduct of a man who sought to embitter the relationship between a mother and her son and sow the seeds of discord in a family.' Grimod showed himself to be under no illusion when it came to his mother's sentiments: 'It is the cruel truth that my mother has never loved me. And the primary cause is my natural infirmity, of which she is the sole cause. The other reason, perhaps, is the rather too marked distaste I have exhibited for all those things she idolizes: grandeur, birth, fortune and dignity...'

Though the bitterness towards his mother and towards Breteuil was to continue until the end of her life, Grimod was annoyed by the version of the events recounted by Rétif in *Les Françaises,* and was at pains to point out that his emotions towards his mother were as dutiful as the next man's. The problem, it seems, was rather more in the physical repugnance she had for him:

> I recognized your portrait of me as Reinette and saw the story of my tussle with Madame Mitoire, or all that was recountable of it. I think the picture you paint of my relationship with my parents is a little overdone and could lead to even greater opprobrium being directed against me. The most malicious of enemies could not have done better work and above all the phrase 'he ceased to honour his mother' fuels my domestic quarrels and could do me great harm! If my opinions and way of acting are different from those of those to whom I owe my life, I have never stopped having for them all the respect that is due to them in every way...

The wound caused by Angelique de Bessi was never to heal and, in the person of the Bailli de Breteuil, Grimod had made himself an enemy who was later to contribute directly to his incarceration in the Abbaye de Domèvre.

III

From 1780 onwards the lawyer and critic began to get a name for himself in Parisian literary circles. At the age of twenty-one he became a member of a dining-club, La Société des Mercredis. The club, as its name implies, met every Wednesday for a sumptuous dinner. At first they used the restaurant Villain in the rue Neuve-des-Petits-Champs, but later the club used the Restaurant Le Gacque in the Tuileries. Dinners started at four, seventeen members being convened under the presidency of M d'Aigrefeuille, Knight of Malta, and at that time the Prosecutor of the Cour des Aides in Montpellier.[6] He was more famous as one of the two *officiers de la bouche* to the gourmand *archichancellier* of Napoleon's court, Cambacérès. There has even been a suggestion that d'Aigrefeuille pandered not just to the latter's highly developed gastronomic preferences; Cambacérès was rumoured to be homosexual. The club, which survived till 1813 or 1814, gave titles to each of its distinguished members drawn from their appearances or their tastes. D'Aigrefeuille, for example, was Maître Dindon – Master Turkey – because of his ruddy skin and smug air. Geoffroy, the Professor of Eloquence at the University of Paris and a noted journalist, was called Maître Homard – Master Lobster – because of his criticisms 'pinched'. Maître Turbot was the vaudevillist René Alissan de Chazet, the author of a light-hearted piece in 1803 called *L'Ecole des Gourmands* which satirized the life of Grimod.[8] The latter chose the name Maître Ecrevisse – Master Crayfish – gamely mocking his deformities with the allusion. The club continued to exist throughout the stormy years of the Revolution, having always as the centrepiece of its dinners a huge braised turkey (perhaps in honour of the president?) It was the longest lasting of all the clubs in which Grimod participated. According to Desnoiresterres, the theme of the meetings was reactionary politics: 'There, in their cups, the members abused the modern age and spoke nostalgically of vanished splendours.'

This was more than likely at the end of the club's life, but at the beginning this was improbable, as the Revolution had not yet upturned society, and Grimod, at least, was rather to the left. Apart from jealously guarding the secret of its braised turkey, the 'most lovable and most gourmand of clubs' possessed the secret of an aphrodisiac called *linimentum vitilitatis,* though Grimod tells us that it would be 'superfluous for most of the members'.

Inspired by the gentle literary tittle-tattle of the Wednesday Club, Grimod decided to start his own circle in the form of a breakfast club meeting twice a week to discuss literature. Rétif de La Bretonne left a long description of the working of these breakfasts in *Monsieur Nicolas:*

> The object ... was to bring together everyone of talent, whether from the capital or from the provinces. They consisted of *café-au-lait,* tea and slices of bread and butter with anchovies. They began at eleven o'clock and concluded at four with a sirloin or leg of mutton weighing fifteen or eighteen pounds. Only cider was served with the meat. Freedom with decency was the rule. The guests could bring anyone they liked with them, up to two, three or four persons. The coffee was weak and one could drink as much as one liked without danger. The ration was twenty-two cups per person. Two Marysas, with taps for mouths, faced the room, one containing coffee and the other milk, so that each guest could help himself as he saw fit ... We began with conversation which revolved around every kind of subject. Then manuscripts were read, poets recited their verses, dramatists declaimed their plays and anticipated the effect they would produce. It was a veritable academy. Citizen Pons of Verdun read us the first cantos of a fine poem, which he ought to be persuaded to finish. It is true that Fardeau read his epigrams there, but they wounded no one and we laughed to tears over them. Never was there such a free and varied entertainment; one made a host of agreeable acquaintances, and easily rid oneself of those who were not so. The young man's parents disapproved of these breakfasts, and perhaps they were right; but for us and the public, we could not but approve of them extremely. They came to an end when he was confined at his family's request in '86.*

---

* Translation: R. Crowdy Mathers, 1930.

Rétif's account is inaccurate in a number of places but it gives an impression of the magnificent 'at-homes' of a distinctly literary-minded young man with money to burn. Instead of cider, for example, Grimod served *verjuice,* the juice of unripe grapes, as drunkenness was altogether taboo. As he himself said of the breakfasts in his first successful book, the *Lorgnette Philosophique* of 1785: '...these philosophic breakfasts are characterized by the hatred of wine and sots, the love of letters and of coffee'. The number of cups drunk by each member was seventeen, something of a magic (or possibly Masonic) figure for Grimod. A. M. Clavaux, who managed to put away thirty-four cups, was instantly made Perpetual President of the club, which brought together a number of prominent figures from the literary world like the two Chénier brothers,[9] the Trudaines,[10] Sebastien Mercier,[11] Fortia de Piles,[12] Saint Prix,[13] Larive,[14] the Comte de Narbonne,[15] Beaumarchais[16] and that 'modern Alcibiades' the Chevalier de Castellane.[17] In the corner, presiding over the famous regulations, was the bizarre figure of M Aze, wearing a full-bottomed wig, and giving the impression of writing minutes.

M Aze was one of the most eccentric figures in Grimod's weird menagerie, and his relationship with him lasted right down to the former's death in 1808. Moreover, so strong was Grimod's affection for the man that, as he put it, he never put bread on a tablecloth without asking M Aze. Jean-Baptiste-Philippe Aze was born in Paris in 1725 and began life, as his father had done before him, as a butcher. Aze, however, swapped his butcher's hook for a burin and became an engraver and a goldsmith as well as dabbling in countless other occupations and having an honorific ceremonial role in the processions of the church in one of the Parisian parishes. He owned a tiny estate near Senlis, which by some happy accident was a *fief seigneurial,* allowing Aze to keep pigeons, which he sold in the poultry market – La Vallée. Aze was not only the author of twenty children but, it was always claimed by Grimod, of four quarto volumes of rules of conduct which Grimod regularly invoked till the end of his days without ever producing the manuscript.

Grimod met Aze when the latter set up a stall to sell the works of other goldsmiths in the great hall of the courts of justice, where he was wont to repair to another stall between cases to feast off a *fricassée* of kidneys. Entering Aze's shop Grimod began bargaining for a pair of gold chandeliers which had been made for the

Empress of Russia. Their long friendship developed out of this sale, Grimod constructing a reasoned system of philosophy out of the nostrums of this father of twenty. And the former's admiration for the elder knew no bounds when he demonstrated a method of cooking a huge sirloin, suspended on a cord before the hearth.

Although it was his famous supper which earned Grimod lasting fame in the eyes of his fellow Parisians, he had managed, even before that evening, to create an aura of scandal around himself. His 'revolutionary views', or his preferring the company of curiosities like M Aze to the more dignified world of his mother or even his father, were scandalous enough in themselves. Rétif produced an example of his repartee at the end of the final volume in which he had so mischievously printed all Grimod's correspondence to him. A certain duke in his mother's circle was heard to utter some jibe at the expense of financiers as a breed; Grimod took up his father's cause with alacrity: '*Monsieur le Duc*, I divide the court into three groups. The first and smallest group is that of honest people, the second is made up of nobodies who do neither harm nor good, and the third is composed of scoundrel oppressors of the Nation, scandalously enjoying the revenues of the state. Now, you know well, *M le Duc*, that you are in neither of the first two categories.'

Young Grimod had embraced the people's cause. While in exile in Domèvre he gave a frank exposition of his opinions in response to the cruel parody of the *Songe d'Athalie* which had been printed under his name: 'Seeing my father's wealth as being the rightful property of the Nation ... I adopted proletarian manners.' Later on in the same text he makes a slightly contradictory statement; 'I renounced my illustrious maternal lineage and began to style myself "*bourgeois de Paris*".' Some of his left-wing principles were aired in a small book he had published at the time, the *Lorgnette Philosophique* – 'Consideration is given to various occupations only in inverse proportion to their usefulness. We despise the baker who feeds us, we flatter the *Turcaret** who robs us, and we respect the great lord who oppresses us.' Part of Grimod's proletarian style of the day was to spend the early mornings roaming the Halles, the central market, observing the manners of the people and, one imagines, the price of fish, for

---

**Turcaret:* title of a play by Lesage (1709). An unscrupulous plutocrat.

doing his own shopping was another part of his youthful rebellion. He must have cut a curious figure, dressed in the *toupet* which made him famous throughout Paris and wearing a mechanical hat which he could lift to passing ladies without even moving his arms. The *toupet* was so bizarre, giving him, by all accounts, the appearance of a hedgehog, that it was commemorated in a popular song.

Changez-moi cette tête,
Cette Grimaude *tête,*
*Tête de hérisson.**

Grimod's wig became the pretext for a bloody duel which took place in the Champs Elysées. The incident which provoked the combat took place on the parterre of the Comédie Française during a performance of *Armide*.[18] Someone gave Grimod a rough shove and the latter remarked loudly: 'Who's that pushing there? It must be some wig-maker's boy.'

'I'm pushing,' replied M de Cases, an officer and son of a tax farmer like Grimod himself (could this possibly have been the son of Suzanne-Elisabeth's lover?) Grimod's adversary continued, using the *tu* form to stress his digust: 'Give me your address. I'll be round tomorrow to comb your hair for you.'

The duel took place in broad daylight. Grimod's bullet removed de Cases' eye and went through the back of his skull. He died a few hours later.

---

*Change that head for me, that hackish head of a hedgehog.

IV

Diogène moderne,
Un fou que chacun berne,
Croit tenir la lanterne
Et tranche du Caton.
Contre la raillerie
Sa cervelle aguerrie.
Affiche la folie
Et prêche la raison.*

On 1 February 1783 Grimod gave the famous supper which had every tongue in the capital wagging with a thousand different versions of the events. In the *Lorgnette Philosophique* Grimod described the effect the meal had on Paris, which may not have been wholly accidental as his *Reflexions sur le Plaisir* were published the next day, and quickly went through three editions. 'Damis [i.e. Midas] gives a dinner of fourteen services and invites seventeen people. He lights four hundred candles. Could anyone credit the fact that a feast of this sort should obsess all Sirap [Paris] for fully six months and cause twenty pamphlets to be written?' The dinner, all idea of 'hype' notwithstanding, was given in honour of Grimod's new mistress Jeanne-Renée-Françoise Loyson, known as Madame de Nozoyl, a bit-part actress and the daughter of a prosperous jeweller. Nozoyl, who came in men's clothes to the feast, was to prove a long-standing embarrassment to Grimod and his family, Grimod having settled an irrevocable income on her in an unwise moment, and set her up in a love-nest opposite the Procope, then a literary coffee house.[19]

---

* Modern Diogenes, a madman whom everyone sends up, who believes himself our guiding light and sets himself up as Cato. While his brain declares war against this ribbing, he appears to be mad, yet preaches reason.

So many versions of the events of that night exist, that it is difficult to know which to believe. M Rival has been through them all and has probably come closest to separating fact from fiction. Even the invitation, in the form of a *faire-part* for a funeral, has been recorded in many forms, though a copy of the original is preserved in the Bibliothèque Nationale in Paris. This is to some degree as a result of later pirated editions. The invitation ran:

> Maître Alexandre-Balthazar-Laurent Grimod de La Reynière, esquire, advocate at the Parlement, Member of the Academy of the Arcades in Rome, free associate member of the Paris Musée* and Editor of the dramatic sections of the *Journal de Neufchâtel,* requests the pleasure of your company at a supper, which will take place at his domicile in the rue des Champs Elysées, in the parish of Madeleine-la-Ville-Evêque, on the first day of February 1783.
>
> Every effort will be made to receive you according to your qualities, and we flatter ourselves that you will be fully satisfied, and we might dare to add that from this day forward you will never want for oil or pork.
>
> We assemble at nine-thirty for supper at ten.
>
> You are requested this instant to bring neither dog nor valet, the meals being served *ad hoc* from trolleys.

This curious invitation was crowned in the case of the seventeen guests by a catafalque surmounted by a cross. The funereal reference, it was believed at the time, referred to the death of Mademoiselle Quinault, a loss which Grimod's mother, who passed for being one of Madame Quinault's greatest friends, had not apparently bothered to notice (a fact observed by the antagonistic Madame de Genlis). In middle age Grimod wrote of her as 'a woman of great wit, who had a sharp and original way of saying the most trivial things, which was matched by an excellent heart and great facility for dealing with the world of high society'. Grimod's nineteenth-century biographers recount the story of the young man's having ensured his free use of the parental home by telling the horrified Grimod *père* that he was about to give a firework party ('to the Devil with your rockets and bangers, sir,

---

* The Musée: an organization for the dissemination of knowledge, of all sorts, which doubled up as a club. Its motto was: 'Liberty, Equality'.

can't you go and let them off elsewhere?') But as M Rival has correctly observed, it would have taken far less than that to remove the self-effacing Laurent from the scene. The dinner was stage-managed by Dazincourt, the acting-teacher of Marie-Antoinette, and following a contemporary affection for the antique, which was equally present in the paintings of the fashionable David, the supper was set to imitate a Roman *coena*.

On entering the *hôtel*, the guests were greeted by two guards in armour, whose role it was to verify the invitations: 'Have you come for Monsieur de La Reynière, the People's Bloodsucker, or for his son, the Defender of the Widow and the Orphan?' In the hall the guests were obliged to put down their arms, hats and decorations before being ushered into a darkened room by a man dressed up as the Chevalier Bayard *(sans peur et sans reproche)* with a lance in his hand. The knight led the new arrivals before a sort of judge wearing a wig and a square bonnet who noted the qualities of the guests on official paper. This was M Aze. When all the guests had arrived, Grimod entered the room, dressed in his advocate's robes, and asked the assembled company to follow him into a pitch-black room. A few minutes passed then twin doors opened to reveal a room lit by 365 lights *à l'antique*. The room was draped in black and a catafalque set up in the middle of the table. A balustrade went all the way round the room, guarded by two halberdiers.

Four young men were placed in the corners of the room equipped with censers. The supper having begun, the guests found the dishes on ambulant trolleys, a demonstration of Grimod's horror of valets, to which he gives voice many times in the *Almanach des Gourmands*, the eight volumes of which were to represent the sum of his views on the table of his times. Nothing is known about the meal which followed except that the first course was composed entirely of pork and the second was cooked in oil.

'How did you like those meats?' Grimod asked after the removal of the first service. 'Excellent weren't they? Well, they are supplied to me by the butcher himself, who is a cousin of my father. His name is — and his shop is to be found in rue —. As he is a relation of mine, I should be grateful if, from now on, you were to buy your meat from him.'

At the end of the second service there was a similar performance: 'The oil was supplied by another cousin of my father's who is a grocer. I recommend him as strongly as I do the pork butcher...'

Grimod's father, according to Desnoiresterres, had an eccentric habit of painting his house with oil, doubtless thinking it a way to ward off lightning. Grimod was evidently playing on his father's harmless folly. As the evening wore on (the supper did not end until seven in the morning), the public were admitted to watch the festivities from the balustrade, and were offered biscuits and refreshments to keep them going through the night. It appears that the Bishop, Grimod's uncle, was of their number, though somewhat brusquely manhandled by the halberdiers. According to Grimm, Madame de La Reynière made a brief appearance on the arm of her lover. In the story Grimod is reported to have recited the verses of the Abbé Delille:

*Et ces grands débris se consolent entre eux.**

Not all the guests were prepared to stomach this sort of insolence, especially a number of fellow lawyers who were present. Of the others at the feast, there were the men of letters, Vigée and Lebrun; the officer Champcenetz [20] (one of the two authors, with Rivarol, of the *Songe d'Athalie*, the parody of Racine attributed to Grimod which launched an attack on Madame de Genlis); Fortia de Piles; the painter Neveu[21] and Dazincourt[22] the actor. One of the lawyers was so upset by the evening that he got up to leave, proclaiming: 'They will send you to the madhouse and strike you from the list of members of the Bar.' Grimod responded by locking the doors to the apartment and preventing any further guests from leaving. Coffee and liqueurs were taken in an adjoining room lit by 130 candles while the guests were entertained by a magic-lantern show and some experiments with electricity performed by the Italian physicist Castanio. M Rival tells us that many of the guests fell asleep.

One of Grimod's more recent friends was not present that evening, Nicolas-Edmé Rétif de La Bretonne (1734-1806). This writer, described by one recent historian as 'Balzac's pithecanthrope', had been warming himself at the stove of the Widow Duchêsne in the rue Saint Jacques, when Grimod had run into him on 22 November 1782. He was then almost exactly twice Grimod's age. The author of a large number of huge novels

---

*And these great relics console themselves together.

describing, in generally autobiographical detail, the seamier side of the capital, Rétif had made his name by publishing *Le Paysan Perverti*, a book which went through many editions in a number of languages and apart from *Monsieur Nicolas* (which was translated in the thirties), the only one of his works to be published in English. As we have seen, Rétif soon became an *habitué* of Grimod's literary breakfasts and, as they became closer, many of Grimod's earlier writings betray the mark of Rétif. Grimod agreed to restage the famous dinner for the elder man's benefit. Rétif gave a full account of the evening in *Monsieur Nicolas*. Some of the details are a little confused. The other guests of honour were Sebastien Mercer, the author of the *Tableau de Paris*, the Trudaine brothers and Pelletier (de Saint-Fargeau?)

> We were invited for midday, and while awaiting supper we were plied with manifold delicacies, all of which were calculated to edge the appetite for more solid nourishment. Also we were treated to a demonstration of the phenomena of electricity by M Catiano [*sic*] the Italian, and afterwards to a shadow show, admirably executed. Thus we were entertained until suppertime. At eight o'clock we were served with soup. This was necessary to reproduce the first repast, which was the true Roman *coena*, combining dinner with supper. Twenty-eight different courses followed, each one ceremonially borne in preceded by two flutes and a master of ceremonies holding a lance, with which he beat rhythmically. Also there were two unbearded boys, dressed in Roman fashion in albs similar to those worn by our choirboys, who walked in front on either side of the dish bearer, and two female servants, exactly matched, to take away the empty plates, whom legend transformed, as regards the first supper, into two young girls, one dark, the other fair, wearing flesh-coloured tights and buskins. They were followed by the gentleman carver (who was the master of the feast himself), conspicuous among the others for his stature. The procession walked three times round the table, after which the dish was lowered and placed into position by the lance-bearer, helped (rumour said) by the two young girls, since the silver dishes of M de La Reynière's father were enormous. There were twenty-eight guests, and the master of ceremonies had announced that we should have only one

dish besides the soup. And this is what we expected, or at most that the dishes would differ only in seasoning. Therefore we exclaimed aloud when the second one appeared and there were twenty-eight, that is to say one for each guest. The dining-hall was lighted by 365 candles in honour of the 365 days in the year. The waiting maids' hair served, in Roman fashion, as napkins for greasy fingers.*

Costly entertainment, childish pranks, an expensive and unsuitable mistress and a state of war between parents and child under the family roof were all contributing factors to the shameful exile to which Grimod was condemned in April 1786, one which was fundamentally to alter his view of the world. But these were not in themselves sufficient to unleash Breteuil's furies; Grimod was to play one last prank which led to his incarceration at Domèvre. Briefly then, the facts are these: One Deville, anxious to send up a poor poetaster with the spiritual name of Fariau de Saint-Ange, sent the latter some gushing verses and a letter purporting to come from the lawyer and frequent guest at Grimod's literary breakfasts, Duchosal.[23] Saint-Ange, thrilled with his laudatory verses, had them printed, at which a furious Duchosal objected. Saint-Ange showed him the accompanying letter, which was also signed by him. Duchosal made a complete disavowal of both texts, and there the matter might have rested had not Grimod seen possibilities of extending the farce one afternoon in the Procope. His production was a bogus legal brief setting out Duchosal's case against Saint-Ange. Nor did it remain there; the document was heavy with polemic and mockery directed at a number of people. The tract went into three editions.

All Grimod's colleagues were furious, not least Duchosal, who threatened to have Grimod's name removed from the list of members of the Bar. Fariau de Saint-Ange threatened legal action. Contemporary accounts suggested that Laurent bought him off with 12,000 *livres*. The Lieutenant-Criminel, the Marquis de la Salle, threatened to horsewhip the young man. Meanwhile, his family decided that the best solution was to get him out of Paris. Malesherbes, in public a great campaigner against the infamous *lettres de cachet* by which young people could be

---

* Translation: R. Crowdy Mathers, 1930.

arbitrarily imprisoned upon request from their parents, which he was about to invoke against his nephew, suggested he abandon the law and be banished to a convent. Beaumarchais, being two-faced in more ways than one – for the great exponent of liberty in *Figaro* was also Grimod's congratulatory host on the night before his banishment – suggested that the man be sent to the lunatic asylum at Maréville,* while the Abbé de Jarente came up with the idea of Domèvre. The family having taken the latter's advice, the vengeful Bailli was despatched to his cousin 'the horse-minister', as Grimod called Breteuil, alluding to Caligula, and had the *lettre de cachet* duly signed.

Grimod woke on the morning of 10 April 1786 after having spent the previous evening in the company of Sebastien Mercier and Beaumarchais, *both* of whom had congratulated him on his pamphlet. To his surprise he was informed that a *berline* awaited him in the courtyard to take him to Lorraine and exile at the Abbey of the Canons Regular at Domèvre-sur-Vezouse, thus concluding the first part of his bizarre existence.

Joseph Joubert[24] summed up the mentality of the young Grimod in the following words:

> [he was] a young man more wise than singular, for in the end his singularity was merely the desire to get closer to the life of the common people while pretending he was born to mediocrity. It was part of his philosophy to lead his life with the same frugality as he might have enjoyed had he not been the son of a millionaire; one is aware how much people from high society feel it is in their interest to belittle the conduct of one for whom life is a cruel satire. They spared him nothing in trying to make him drink the cup of ridicule down to the dregs. But this young man rejected it with a noble force, and it has spilt on the clothing of those people so anxious that he should drain it.

---

*This form of torture appears to have its origins in pre-Revolutionary France.

Exile: The Political Education of a Gourmand

Les audiences d'un Gourmand.

Though the fun-loving Grimod had been effectively imprisoned at His Majesty's pleasure, not to mention that of various other interested parties, life at Domèvre was not arduous, nor was imprisonment as dire a state as it was to become under the Revolution. The Vezouse was brimming with fish, and it is tempting to think that Grimod had an approach to life within his cloistered walls similar to that of those gourmand Cistercians in his story 'Abbot for a Day'. Moreover, the venerable Abbot, Joseph de Saintonge, was a worldly man, an ex-officer who allowed his charge leave to visit Nancy, transformed into the cultural centre of the east by King Stanislas, the enlightened Polish monarch who had been created Duke of Lorraine upon the marriage of his daughter Marie Leczinska to Louis XV. Back in his well-appointed cell, Grimod wrote copy for the *Affiche des Evêchés et de Lorraine*. He was also able to receive visits from his secretary Barthe, Mercier and his friend the Comte Fortia de Piles, who was garrisoned nearby. Still, this company was not enough for Grimod, who had been spoiled by a thousand attentions in the Parisian literary scene he had embraced so wholeheartedly.

This despair is reflected in the letters he wrote Rétif de La Bretonne during that period. We must thank Rétif for having published this remarkable collection at the end of his work *Le Drame d'une Vie*, though Grimod had less cause to be pleased with his friend for the political exposé he brought about in so doing. The first letters bear a certain optimistic note, when Grimod imagined that he would soon be liberated from his cell, though he complained strongly of Rétif's making literary copy out of his misfortunes: 'You have contrived to reopen a wound from which my heart will continue to bleed for a long time, and that an interval of nine stormy years had been unable to staunch.' The *célibataire* had become a celibate, and the experience of absent female company, even that of Nozoyl, had reminded him of the pathetic *dénouement* of his passion for Madame Mitoire. His mood turned frequently to misogyny in his reflections on the past: 'If women ... alone may grant us real pleasure, that happiness is intricately balanced against the evils that come about in frequenting them; and if I've had a few happy instants in my life, I have owed them more to friendship than to love.'

A year after his exile, and with no indication as to the length of his sentence, Grimod's letters betray a tone of increased despair. Rightly furious with Beaumarchais, he vented his spleen on Mercier as well for not coming to see him when he had said he would. Until he was finally struck off the register of advocates, he even continued to receive letters from his clients, while his attitude became increasingly philosophic. 'I have neither the virtues to be a judge, the talent to be an administrator nor the baseness to be a courtier; with the little allowance my parents give me in Paris they could get rid of me when they wanted. I'd buy an estate somewhere and plant cabbages while I meditated on human folly.' When still no reprieve was forthcoming, Grimod thought of purchasing an office in the Metz Parlement or court, presumably hoping that his giving in to their old desire that he should enter the magistrature would cause them to relent, especially as Metz was at a safe distance from the capital. Grimod's compromise failed to pluck the parental heartstrings, and the writer once again experienced feelings of chagrin. A gleam of hope came to Grimod when he realized that his thirtieth birthday (20 November 1788) would announce his legal majority, and though he '...desire[s] as much as anybody that the issue be settled within the bosom of the family, they should not be unaware of the fact that I am reaching the age when the law allows me to act without their advice, so if they still wish to come out of this business with any credit, they should act promptly.' But Grimod, despite his profession, seems to have had little idea of the position he was in as one sentenced under *lettre de cachet*. His parents' response seems to have been to make serious enquiries as to the scheme originally proposed by the Janus-featured Beaumarchais:

Would you believe that, far from speeding up my release, they are working to prolong my exile? What do you say to that? They are going to swop my prison for a dungeon. You will shiver when you learn that there is now a question of transferring me to Maréville, a house of correction near Nancy, reserved for lunatics, and those people who gravely upset the order of society? ... This is how they thank me for nine months' impeccable behaviour; it is thus that I will sacrifice the best years of my life to enforced rest, uselessness and opprobrium.

Grimod's family and their advisers may have seen a risk in the former's majority, for the news of the intended transfer arrived three days after his twenty-ninth birthday. Grimod derived some comfort during his adversity from the *gourmandise* of the monks and from Rétif's writings. 'I love to see my name flying to posterity through your writings.' However, a new ill befell the troubled prisoner of Domèvre. He heard of the parody of the *Songe d'Athalie* being circulated in Paris.

A libel against Madame de Genlis has been published in my name, on whom I have never allowed myself to express an opinion, let alone publish one. The pamphlet is not in my style, nor is it my sort of work, but my enemies will not miss out on the opportunity to maintain the fraud, and to hold me responsible. They give me yet another grievance, and this time an actionable one.

Grimod had, however, permitted himself one jibe at Madame de Genlis and her precious educational theories: 'I don't at all like the idea of women becoming tutors, and I agree wholeheartedly with the good Molière, that a woman should limit herself to knowing the difference between a doublet and a pair of breeches.'

Grimod's answer was to publish a denial, *Dèsaveu du Sieur Grimod de La Reynière Touchant la Parodie d'Athalie,* in which he was particularly outspoken on the subject of his mother's snobbery. From his mother he develops the theme to encompass all her sex: 'I have always regarded women as being as foreign to morality as they are useless to society.' Otherwise he confines himself to stating his passion for letters and to slipping in a reference to his irreproachable conduct. Later, to his great regret, he discovered that Rivarol and de Champcenetz were responsible.

Though his attitude to the monks of Domèvre was genuinely appreciative, he had not yet lost his republican ardour. Rétif believed, later on, that Grimod's period of incarceration had modified his left-wing views. In reality it seems to have been the events of the Revolution, the terrible brutality of which weaned the younger man off his passion for the people's cause, and during the Domèvre years he was even able to reproach Rétif for mixing in courtly circles.

> It seems to me that Madame de Beauharnais' [the mother-in-law of the future Empress Josephine] household would be no less agreeable if there were no courtiers received there. Men of letters have no cause mixing with such people, for they can only lose out and they should flee them and despise them. You would oblige me greatly by not mentioning my name in such company; I have never been able to give them any esteem, and their having any for me would be a great burden.

He adds of Madame de Beauharnais that her kindness and intelligence make him 'forget that she is a Countess'.

The de La Reynière parents were beginning increasingly to think of a permanent exile for Grimod from the start of 1788. At first this took the form of banning him from their part of Paris should he ever be released from Domèvre. But Grimod responded by threatening them with the courts. By March they had mooted the project that Grimod ultimately took up, that of travelling under the power of his *lettre de cachet*. Grimod was unenthusiastic at first: 'I prefer a sedentary life to one of travelling and it is too dangerous voyaging under the aegis of a *lettre de cachet* for me to be able to accept this insidious proposition.' Grimod confines himself to giving Rétif a list of dates to inscribe on the Île Saint Louis. Rétif had a curious fixation with anniversaries, the important dates in his own or his friends' lives being scratched on the stones of the island, where some were still readable halfway through the last century.

When Rétif heard next from his friend on 11 July 1788, he was in Lausanne. He has accepted his parents' offer as a *pis-aller*. Already he had taken in a number of towns on his travels; in each, the experience of a different cuisine was to be a great resource once he came to write the *Almanach*. He had gone first to Strasbourg and from there to Colmar, Basel, Constance, Zurich, Lucerne, Berne, Neufchâtel and finally Lausanne. In his travels in Switzerland, doubtless where he was not so much in danger from the *lettre de cachet,* he had set himself to study the constitutions of the different cantons. The one he most admired was the aristocratic government of Berne, which he found 'well suited to making men happy'. He found no hardship or misery, no taxes and no constraint, just the 'very image of liberty, the love of humanity matched by laws made in favour of the people'.

In Zurich, he met the famous physiognomist Lavater.[1] And in Lausanne he renewed aquaintance with an unhappily married Suzanne T–. But Grimod intended to continue his travels in France, aiming to go to Lyons, Bordeaux and Béziers 'to the house of a splendid aunt whom I've been promising for ten years I'd go and see'. Rétif had not heard from him for another two years when he received a letter from Lyon. In Lyon, as it turned out, he had been drawn once again into a theatrical world, and had found himself a mistress. He did not mention this to Rétif, but he was able to impart some good news, something which had been inadvertently caused by the Revolution he learned so much to hate. He had heard of the dismissal of the Baron de Breteuil.

> A name I cannot write without horror; and thinking that I could as well wait for news of the consequences in Lyon as in any other place, I remained here. M Laurent de Villedeuil told me that though my *lettre de cachet* had not been revoked, and could not be before the meeting of the Estates General, I could consider myself a free man and do whatever I pleased during my stay.

Thus *désoeuvré*, Grimod was free for the time being to indulge his passion for the theatre, and for its leading ladies.

He was still the millionaire's son, and stopped at Lyon's best hotel of the period, the Milan on the Place des Terreaux. His secretary Barthe promptly fell in love with the cook's wife and left Grimod to his own devices; Barthe was in the employ of the La Reynière parents. Lyon's best theatre, the Terreaux, was next door, but Grimod also participated in the sessions of the Academy and wrote a gushing brochure on the town, while penning unctuous verses to passing female thespians. One of his friends of the period was the grisly Collot d'Herbois, who with Fouché decimated the city's plutocracy during the Terror. (Despite his evident enthusiasm for the work, his ardour failed to impress Robespierre. The ninth Thermidor, however, prolonged his life a little while, until 1795 at least, when the Convention made him a scapegoat for the bread riots in Paris, and he died of fever on the way to the penal colony of Cayenne.) Grimod changed his mind about Collot after the massacres in Lyon, seeing the former actor as an embittered failure. 'This ferocious man took revenge on the people of Lyon for the countless boos he received on the stage there; he did as much for his former friends, who justly despised his insolence and his vices.'

While he was in Lyon, Grimod was able to discover at first hand the local cuisine, which still has the reputation of being the best in France. Despite complaining of a surfeit of Rhone pike, he enjoyed the *bugnes,* little Lyonnais doughnuts, and the deep-fried food of the town. He also raved about the Lyonnais ability to handle a white sauce; Parisians, neglecting the role of the egg yolk, usually transformed it into a sort of glue. The real attraction of the city, however, was Adelaide Feuchère, Grimod's mistress for twenty-four years, and ultimately his wife. Adelaide was twenty-four when he met her in August 1788. She was the daughter of a Parisian haberdasher and had made her début in the theatre six years previously, spending some time acting in French plays in Stockholm. Adelaide put up a manful resistance, as there was some question mark over her ability to adapt to Grimod's deformities. She seems, however, eventually to have reconciled herself to the writer's claws, for she bore him a child, Adelaide, or 'Mademoiselle Fafa', who died in infancy. Some of his letters to his mistress, an otherwise shadowy figure, are reproduced in M Rival's book. They betray a well-formed eroticism on the part of our gourmand, whose foreplay was by no means inhibited by his lack of manual dexterity. It is sufficient to say here that it was of the sort enjoyed by the Emperor Tiberius in his aquatic orgies on Capri.

Temporarily out of sympathy with Lyon and its citizens ('pull away the silk and you are left with a real Jerusalem artichoke'), Grimod set off on his travels again in April 1789. He took in Zurich, a short venture into Germany, Strasbourg, Metz, Nancy, Langres and Dijon. His ostensible destination was Domèvre, where the Abbot was able to inform him of the lifting of the *lettre de cachet.* The Minister had not intended him to know. Grimod also informed his correspondent that he was now reconciled with his parents: 'I am now enjoying the best of relations with my parents and often receive the tenderest letters from them. But as they love me more absent from the capital than in it, I shall not be returning to Paris'; he adds: 'It would probably be fatal for me anyhow, with my political views.' Grimod was giving the first indication that the worm had turned.

The amicable relations referred to in the letter were to be based on a solid commercial foundation; Grimod was going into business with his father. Laurent, never the man best adapted to the burden imposed upon him by his ancestry, had renounced his office of *fermier général* in 1778, in order to devote himself to patronizing the arts and a number of shady ventures which were later to place his widow and son in a fearful dilemma which dragged on for years. Grimod was to set himself up as a wholesale merchant in Lyon, specializing in the produce of the southern half of France. Ultimately, it seems, he would go into ship owning, the normal path for the rich *négociant*. Grimod took up the task with enthusiasm, travelling all over Provence and the Languedoc, trading in anything from silk to spices, attending the great fair at Beaucaire and enjoying frequent sojourns in the gentle company of his cherished aunt in Béziers. His experience in trade, though, revealed no greater acumen than his father had, and business crumbled into any number of sordid debts. Grimod did not come out of it wholly without useful experience, for if his gastronomic awareness had been tickled in the cloister, it was to be glutted in Béziers. And at his aunt's table, his political views underwent a rapid shift to the right.

Essentially, while his parents found themselves with ringside seats to watch the macabre entertainments of the Place Louis XV, now renamed the Place de la Révolution, Grimod sunned himself under a mulberry tree in Béziers, from his account a city little touched by revolutionary fervour, while he reread the ancient philosophers. As his parents shivered at the fall of every head, from those of Louis XVI and Marie-Antoinette to that of even the former's gallant defender and Grimod's uncle, Malesherbes, Grimod gorged himself at the luxurious table of the deposed Bishop of Béziers. But Grimod was not insensitive to what was going on in Paris and his fervent embracing of an antirevolutionary line was to prove too much for Rétif, who was making ends meet by working as a police spy. On 27 August 1790, Grimod wrote to Rétif,

> I am sad to observe that you are such a hot partisan of this execrable Revolution, a Revolution which has annihilated religion and property, and the glory of that empire of letters

and sciences and the arts, risking a return to the fourteenth century, or even to the time of the Goths and Vandals... do you find it so wise to have armed that riff-raff so that they may, at the first signal or the first coin, slaughter all the honest folk?

Grimod, meanwhile, continued to travel round the Midi on business, going to Lunel, where he developed a taste for the dessert wine so appreciated by the future American President Thomas Jefferson only two years before. In Montpellier he met M de Villevieille,[2] later, with d'Aigrefeuille, one of the two *officiers de la bouche* to Cambacérès, and an illustrious gourmand. They talked about Rétif. On 18 September 1790, Grimod fired the first broadside of his *gourmandise* in a letter to this *Rousseau du ruisseau* (gutter Rousseau):

> Everything which does not concern Béziers has vanished from my mind, my taste for good living is well-known, here nothing is forgotten in the desire to satisfy me. The most exquisite dinners, the finest suppers; everything good that can be fished out of the sea, and all the most succulent things that may be plucked from the earth: turbots, whiting, soles, crawfish, oysters as large as holy-water stoops... sturgeon, red partridge, which should be eaten while genuflecting, rabbits fed on scented herbs, quails as fat as chickens, aubergines, heaven-sent melons, muscat grapes... Roquefort cheese fit for a non-dethroned king, muscat wines, a true nectar served by countless Hebes, etc., and there you have, my worthy friend, a little sample of our diet. We proceed from indigestion to indigestion, the only illness which ever comes to Béziers.

From that moment on, Grimod's *gourmandise* began to get the better of him, and continued without so much as a break until 1813. Certainly the tables of his aunt and Monsignor de Nicolai, the former bishop, must have been extraordinarily lavish to turn the head of a man up till then little given to outbursts of sensualist philosophy. The city itself became a sort of Eldorado for the writer and to the end of his days the seminal influence of his gastronomic tastes was meridional.

The best meals were to be had not at his aunt's, but at the bishop's, and when talking of M de Nicolai, Grimod seems as partisan of the abuses of the Ancien Régime as he was of its indoubtable advantages.

> The Revolution, which has lightened him of 80,000 *livres* of income, has forced him to suppress his grand dinners; but he still entertains at small dinners for between eight and ten people, and his meals compare favourably with the most sumptuous. True, there are not fourteen services nor are there 339 [sic] lights, but what we eat is so good, so excellent, so perfect that it beats all comers.

He continues in this vein, talking a little of women in a way which will become recognizable, 'they are of no value at table'. Then, as if he were forgetting himself, he apologizes to the frugal Rétif for addressing him as if he were 'Sardanapalus or Lucullus',[3] but all he does is eat, and that is all that occupies his mind.

Once he had recovered from his flights of gastronomic fancy, Grimod spared a thought for the Revolution and for the system of government which it had displaced.

> Despotism favours the arts, and protects individual liberty. Look at the golden centuries of Pericles, Augustus, Leo X and Louis XIV, the latter so shamefully outraged today. One terrible glance from that king would have sent them crawling back into their element – filth – these scoundrels who have usurped his power today and who have befouled his throne .. I would die of despair if I were not rescued by my good appetite.

None the less, Grimod is anxious to hear of his friends, some of whom had risen far in the councils of the dreaded Revolution; Mercier, for example, or Pons de Verdun.[4] He wonders whether Beaumarchais is his friend or his enemy. The news of the death of his cousin, the Chevalier de Beausset, sets him off again in another tirade against democracy.

> I will never be the friend of a democrat. It is atrocious that men of letters should think as the majority do today. No one had less to complain about than they did under the old order; they said and printed more or less what they wanted, and no one thought twice about persecuting them. They were honoured, invited, given pensions far more often than they deserved... And I blush to be a member of that infamous order of advocates [he was no longer] even more

than I do for belonging to the dishonoured body of men of letters. I abjure law and letters; henceforth I shall confine myself to business.

Like a naughty schoolboy who has been convinced of the errors of his ways, Grimod pronounces himself the 'friend of order, decency and faith' and condemns 'everything that is despicable and vile; there in two words you have the Revolution'.

In his next fulmination he appears to have predicted the fate of a number of the Revolution's fellow travellers, like the unfortunate Marquis de Condorcet,[5] whose fate must have been delicious to Grimod, as he was betrayed as a *ci-devant* by his desire to eat an aristocratic twelve-egg omelette: 'Let your execrable *philosophes* rot in hell; their writings have brought about this excess, they will pay dearly for the scandalous triumph they applaud today, their blood will be the first shed in expiation and I will wash my hands in it joyously'... Moving on to the subject of religion, the gourmand continues:

> Never did fanaticism produce a thousandth part of the ills which incredulity causes today. Cursed be all atheists, deists, unbelievers and heretics! They will burn both in this world and the next, and with a light heart I will put a torch to the faggots which will consume them. You wonder whether those I have loved the best should also be thrown on to the pyre? Yes, I thirst for the blood of all those who have brought us to this pass, and if all those freethinkers were herded together, I would not let a single one live... I would rather live with a convicted criminal than a democrat.

Rétif was obviously stunned by this invective, though it might be said that he got whatever revenge he sought by having these unflattering critiques published in 1793 in the middle of the Terror. It is perhaps a tribute more to the verbosity of Rétif, than to any compassion on the part of the legislators of that unhappy time, that Grimod was not decapitated at the *trône-renversé*! In his reply, Rétif reminds Grimod of his former democratic tendencies: 'You were a democrat when nobody was...do you remember that the Cross of Saint Louis [i.e. military nobles] were the only people excluded from your breakfasts, while you admitted the grimy candlemaker's boy!'

But as the Revolution advanced in its savagery, especially with the September massacres, the storming of the Tuileries and the captivity of the royal family, Grimod moved relentlessly rightwards. He attacks Desmoulins,[6] revelling in his fate, which he had accurately predicted, the following year, and takes a final swipe at the men of letters: 'vile adulators of the scum, marching today on the bodies of those they worshipped in the past. It seems it is in their nature to grovel ceaselessly; once it was before idols, now before toads.'

I have dwelled at length on Grimod's negative reaction to the French Revolution, for it was to form the essential backdrop to his attitudes to the society to which it gave birth. Never was this father of *gourmandise* so uncircumspect again in his writings, and for good reason. He had had a narrow escape. But it cannot be said that in the years following the Terror, the crippling years of the famine, the gaudy vulgarity of the Directory or even under the Empire, did his fundamental hatred of the new order undergo any radical revision. Rather he chose to mask his vicious attacks behind seemingly harmless idioms, first the theatre, and when that failed, food.

A Gourmand in Paris

Séance d'un Jury de Gourmands dégustateurs

I

Grimod returned to the city of his birth on 14 February 1794, at the height of the Terror. His father had died a little more than a month before. He was lucky to have died in bed, as those *fermiers généraux* who had not renounced their charges had been led *en masse* to the scaffold. Grimod had been slow to move. The news that his father was dying had reached him in the spring of 1791. 'My father's health is declining visibly with every day that passes. This will necessitate my reappearing in that city of mud and blood, despite the repugnance and horror I feel for it.' His revulsion kept him in the south for another two and a half years of ambrosial delights.

The death of his father plunged the La Reynière family into a long-drawn-out crisis caused by the financier's contested will. Briefly, Grimod *père* had become embroiled in some shady business with some other businessmen in Genoa. Even the family mansion was heavily mortgaged and mother and son were to be obliged to eke out the years in genteel destitution. Grimod, as ever, blamed the Revolution although his father's obvious lack of capability must have been the primary cause. To add to their *malheurs,* at a time when heads were dropping thick and fast at the guillotine in the present Place de la Nation, and that prototype Vishinsky, Fouquier-Tinville,[1] was despatching his tumbrils with an indecent haste, Grimod's mother and first cousin were arrested and taken off to one of the city's *ad hoc* gaols.

The arrest took place only a week after Grimod's reappearance in the city; as Monselet observed, 'it was a happy twist of fate for him; he was to beg for the liberty of those who had robbed him of his own.' The ostensible cause was the presence under Suzanne-Elisabeth's roof of her niece, the Comtesse d'Ourches, the wife and daughter-in-law of known emigrés. Soon after this, Gay, Laurent's factotum, was also imprisoned, while all his business papers were seized. Throughout this crisis Grimod himself was miraculously saved (despite the French historian Funck-Brentano's assertion that he had been sentenced to death by default) for he was travelling under a passport issued in Montpellier stating that he was a tradesman domiciled in Béziers. More, the inauspicious circumstances of his birth and christening had removed the noble cachet from his birth certificate. The La Reynières had, at the time, every desire to keep his coming into the world as quiet as possible. As we have seen, his godparents would have given little indication of his parents' position, while his father's occupation had been given simply as Director of the Post Office. Grimod's papers attesting his impeccable proletarian credentials, he was able to have the house put in his charge, and was granted thirty sous a day towards its upkeep!

As far as Grimod's heart was concerned, the old wound of the Nozoyl was healed. The affection had continued even to Lyon but some malicious home truths communicated by Rétif had brought home to him the unsuitability of the liaison. Rétif, for his part, was furious with spite for the fact that Grimod had taken the part of his much-abused wife Agnès Labègue in a family quarrel of *Peyton Place* proportions.

> As regards a certain person whom you are so mad keen to promote, you have not the faintest idea, she is even baser than mad. Nozoyl who, on her way to join you in Lyon under the protection of a Parisian bookseller, made a mockery of you in front of the coach hands, inciting them to make you a cuckold as their leftovers would still be too good for you. Do you require proof? The name of the bookseller? You shall have it.

Grimod thus transferred his attentions to Adelaide Feuchère, now without child, who was still in Lyon dodging the effects of Collot d'Herbois and Fouché, who were taking the city to task for its limited enthusiasm for the social revolution:

> I agree that the street where you live is quite far from the points being attacked, but the bombs go quite far and I am assured that they are even hitting the Saint Clair quarter and sometimes the rue Buisson. It's an ugly sort of rain and one which the many parasols of Lyon are ill-equipped to deal with. They should be swopped for para-bombs!

Once the city had atoned for its sins of *lèse-liberté,* Adelaide was free to join her lover in Paris.

The Paris to which Grimod had come home was changed beyond recognition. For one thing, and for the first time in his life, he was no longer the millionaire's son who could rely on well-attested credit. His father's contested succession allowed him no income, even though the family continued to reside in the grandest town house in the capital. The only solution was to sell up the artefacts, or those they were free to sell according to the conditions imposed by his father's creditors: prints, drawings, silver, etc. Grimod wrote a journal at this time, which is now, sadly, lost. It passed briefly through the hands of the late Pierre Gaxotte, who was able to publish some extracts in the *Figaro*. Our gourmand had by no means forgotten the delights of Béziers. Reduced to penury in a time of dearth and high prices, Grimod confined himself to a form of gastronomic voyeurism, when incapable of affording the luxury object on display: '4 July 1794. Halles: artichokes. Grocer's, rue Montmarte: sugar. Greengrocer, rue Aguesseau: cos lettuces.' The next few days reveal figs, a skate, an 'exceptional eel', redcurrants, apricots, lemons, etc. On the twenty-seventh he finds a turbot, and dines with his cousin, Grimod de Verneuil, and his wife. The great events of the Revolution enter the diary in an offhand way, squashed between lettuces and fish and the quiet details of his domestic existence with Adelaide. On 9 Thermidor, the day which brought the Terror to an end with the arrest of Robespierre and his caucus, Grimod has little to report to his journal beside a trip to the Café de Foy to eat an ice. The next day the couple stayed at home; after all, there was some commotion outside in the square: 'Cannons, armed men. Executions in the square, Robespierre, Couthon, Saint-Just, Hanriot, etc. Reading, supper with Madame [i.e. Adelaide]. Went to bed at midnight.'

It is hard to know what Gaxotte left out now that the precious document has been stolen from the home of the American professor who acquired it in 1977. Grimod does not appear to have been greatly moved that the instigators of the social phase of the Revolution, those he had the least reason to like, should have been removed from the scene under his very nose. Far from being the bloodthirsty man of his letters to Rétif, there is no sign of his having rushed out to dip his hands in the blood of dead terrorists. The end of the Terror did, however, bring about the gradual release of the incarcerated members of his family and household.

Gay was the first out. 'Happy to see him free again, interesting details on his captivity.' On the twenty-second it was the turn of Suzanne-Elisabeth, whom the couple found in the house on returning from an adaptation of *Gil Blas* at the theatre. 'Joy, after supper, drawing room. Conversation about prisons (!) ... Go up to my room. Went to bed at one-thirty.' Madame d'Ourches was not released till 14 October. The Terror over, Grimod returned to the markets to ogle at the food, 'stuffed calf's head, a good turkey, a cervelas stuffed with truffles, two sucking pigs, a fine fat turkey cock, overpriced mushrooms'. At the New Year they were able to indulge in a very modest dinner for seven, of a calf's head, a leg of mutton, larks, macaronis and chocolate cream. Apart from the occasional bachelor session with M Aze, which involved a trip to the latter's *seigneurie,* the rhythm of life remained the same, 'dinner and supper every day with Madame and every Sunday with my mother'.

Many days the gourmand was obliged to *diner par coeur* or go without; money was short, supplies rare and what there was rarely worth eating. In 1810, thinking back on that time, he particularly singled out the bread: '1793 and the years which followed reduced us to a ration of disgusting black bread, which the well-brought-up dogs of the Ancien Régime would certainly never have touched.' As he walked around the city sniffing at the market stalls in Les Halles, or the central market, or La Vallée, the market specializing in poultry or game situated on the quais of the left bank near the rue des Grands Augustins, Grimod noted with regret how the Revolution had caused the disappearance of some of the more inviting features of the city under the old regime. One of these was the *table d'hôte,* a system of eating not dissimilar to that found in London in the eighteenth century, where dining was frequently undertaken at the main table of the coffee house. Diners had no choice as to what they ate, and were obliged to give up their places to the next customer once their meal was finished.

> The Revolution completely altered that system. From its first stages, all meeting-places became veritable arenas, where it was difficult to express an opinion on anything because it would immediately be interpreted politically. As all honest people were adversely affected by the Revolution, the complaints which naturally emanated from their lips

were metamorphosed into crimes against the new social order and the object of patriotic denunciations which the thousand and one research committees received with avidity. It was therefore necessary, if you did not wish to be denounced, to dine in silence, those patriots, who had worked their way into every public place, dominating conversation with their imperious manners, forcing all those people who did not think as they did to drink of the same cup of outrage. From that day on, the most respectable hotels became base taverns, polite conversation no longer reigned at the *tables d'hôte,* every service was pillaged, as no honest man could show his face there. As the appetites of the others could not be adapted to the system formerly in vigour it was necessary to close down the *tables d'hôte.* From the end of 1790, there are hardly any left in Paris.

In his perambulations round the markets, Grimod was in a position to observe the paucity of certain foodstuffs attesting a breakdown in the supply routes which had existed under the Ancien Régime, One of the staples which seems to have been most lacking was fresh fish. 'Monsters from all parts of France and Europe even, flocked to Paris in hordes; but those of the ocean seemed to want to keep their distance, and it is a fact that during the disastrous years of the Revolution, not one single good turbot, sturgeon or salmon was to be seen in the market.' The turbot he saw in the Halles on 27 July 1794 might have been forgotten in the writer's passionate reminiscence of 1812. A similar shortage had affected game. From the very first moments of the upheaval and the abolition of feudal privilege, the aristocratic control of hunting and shooting had been tossed to the winds. The result, according to the writer, was a wholesale massacre unmatched even by the frenzied workings of the guillotine. Only occasionally was it possible to find a pheasant which had 'escaped from Revolutionary justice'.

But if the Revolution had abolished the *tables d'hôte,* it had actively encouraged the system which superseded it – that of restaurants. Being essentially a man of the Ancien Régime till the end of his days, Grimod never properly adapted to these institutions which, unlike the sociable *tables d'hôte,* encouraged intimacy. More, as M Rival points out, his leaner receipts after the death of his father hardly made it possible for him to frequent these temples to the new Croesuses. The very word, 'restaurant', had not had a very long history before the Revolution broke out. The inventor was a M Boulanger, the owner of a soup kitchen, who in about the year 1765 had hung up a sign outside his premises with the legend, *Boulanger débit des restaurants divins* (Boulanger serves divine restoratives). The sign was accompanied by one in Pig-Latin: *Venite ad me omnes qui stomacho laboratis et ego vos restaurabo* (Come to me all empty stomachs and I will restore you). The word restaurant was not, in fact, original; it had existed for some time, signifying a broth or stock which might be said to have a restorative effect. Boulanger was not even permitted to sell ragoût or roast, so the first restaurant was indeed a modest affair. Boulanger decided, however, to try his luck, and began to sell mutton trotters in white sauce. As a result the caterers' corporation brought an action before the Paris Parlement. The caterers lost as the court decided that mutton trotters were not a ragoût. Boulanger, by now a famous personality in the city, began to receive all the custom he could wish for as a result of this notoriety, and added a further dish to his repertoire: poultry cooked in rock salt. By 1771, the *Dictionnaire de Trévoux* had acknowledged the contribution which the clownish Boulanger had made to the French and, in time, most other languages.

If Boulanger deserves the credit for hatching the word, the first restaurant worthy of the name was Beauvilliers, which was established under the arcades of the Palais Royal sometime between 1782 and 1786. Antoine Beauvilliers, like so many of the *cordons bleus* who joined the profession after the Revolution had driven their masters into exile, was the ex-chef of an important aristocratic household, in fact a royal one, for he had been the *officier de la bouche* to Monsieur, the Comte de Provence, later Louis XVIII. Under the Revolution, Beauvilliers became the favoured haunt of a number of politicians, including Danton. For having committed the grave fault of feeding such illustrious heads as his, it was closed down from 1793 to 1799. The real impetus to bring about the dawn of restauration came with the Revolution, when many of the leading nobles fled abroad, leaving their household staff behind them.

Grimod's friend Rétif de La Bretonne has left us with a couple of pictures of the pre-Revolutionary restaurant in *Les Nuits de Paris* which was first published in 1788. Informing us that the very word is an invention of the century, Rétif describes such an establishment at the end of the 1770s.

> I asked them to restore me [*je demandai à me restaurer*]. I was offered a rice soup, some fresh eggs, a piece of chicken or a piece of roast veal. I saw nothing here any more restorative than I had seen elsewhere. I took the soup and a chicken wing. I was served grumpily by a boy. There was no life to the place. Each *restauré* supped silently at a little round table without a tablecloth.

Not completely cured of his desire to discover this phenomenon, Rétif tried again. This time he was happier with the menu, and above all with the waitress, Julie.

> I chose the roast veal and the lentils cooked with bacon, as for six sous you only had the right to two dishes, add a sou for the bread and three more for a half-carafe of wine. The roast was excellent while the other dish flattered my rustic tastes. I had for ten sous all that my appetite and my sensuality could have wished for.

Sadly for Rétif, he was turned out after fifteen minutes, scarcely time to take stock of the effect Julie was having on his sensuality.

'Nobody will understand the Terror until the history of the famine has been written,' Michelet said. All the more remarkable, then, that the period in question should be one of such acute contrasts. Despite the going to ground of the former masters of the place, the nobility, there had instantly sprung into being a class of *nouveaux riches* able to call for pleasures which would have seemed extravagant to the most wanton of the *ci-devants*. In the streets, queues formed at four in the morning for essential supplies. There was no soap, and little or no sugar as British mastery of the seas had driven a wedge between France and its colonies in the West Indies. Bread, and what bread, was rationed, while at the same time, as Edmond Biré noted in 1793,

> Fashionable restaurants are overflowing with delicacies, exquisite wines and precious liqueurs, the cellars of the great lords have been sold off at auction and everything which has not been drunk up by the patriots has been swiped by the caterers and *limonadiers*. Thrown out on to the pavement by the ruination of their masters, the *ci-devants'* old chefs, all

the *cordons bleus* of the aristocracy, have passed from the service of princes, peers and financiers to the service of the public.

Beauvilliers had started before the Revolution. Another chef, Méot, came from the kitchens of the Prince de Condé. One night at the height of the Terror, Dumas, a member of the jury at the Tribunal Revolutionaire, suggested after a good meal that it would be an excellent joke to decapitate Méot: '*le coup du fricassé au fricasseur*'.* As Grimod described the situation so well, it did not pay to eat out if you were of a sensitive disposition. Another juror, Antonelle, celebrated the verdict delivered on Marie-Antoinette with a meal at the Hôtel Vauban of *foie gras,* thrushes, quails in *gratin,* sweatbreads, a fine pullet, *béchamels* and chicken wings all moistened by Sauternes and Champagne. Danton best summed up the envious nature of this new *gourmandise.* A sensualist of the first order, he was frequently to be seen at the tables of Méot or Beauvilliers with Fabre d'Eglantine,[2] Hébert[3] and Chaumette:[4] 'At last we have our chance to enjoy life! Sumptuous palaces, delicious dishes, exquisite wines, fabrics of silk and cloth of gold, women one never dreamt of, all this is the reward of the conqueror.' But if the self-interest of Danton provides a frightening perspective to the events of the day, the frugality of Robespierre is even more chilling; invited to celebrate Desmoulins' wedding at the Palais Royal, the 'incorruptible' announced, 'I am going home; champagne is the poison of liberty.'

The real temple of Comus of the period was the Palais Royal, that grand edifice constructed by the architect Victor Louis[5] for the future Philippe-Egalité on the eve of the Revolution. The Duke had envisaged a speculative scheme which would bring him revenue while enabling him to rebuild the palace which had come down to him from the time of Richelieu. The commercial development behind the palace allowed for a number of restaurants and cafés to be set up, while the arcades provided shelter for a good many of Paris's estimated 40,000 prostitutes. At the time the most famous restaurant in the Palais Royal was Véry, which occupied three arcades next door to where the Grand Véfour is today. Later on Véry started a new establishment on the Esplan-

---

*"Give Mr Chop the chop.'

ade of the Tuileries in a perfect imitation of the Temple of Herculaneum. Also in the Palais Royal were the Café de Foy, where Desmoulins instigated the march on the Bastille, and the Café Mécanique, where even the serving was automatic and the *limonadière* communicated with the kitchens through a speaking tube, giving Grimod more than one idea in his drive to abolish servants in the dining-room. The café was owned by a M Taurès, who was wounded for not permitting the Revolutionary song 'Ça Ira' to be sung on the premises, while his pregnant wife was disembowelled by the patriotic mob. The Café Février was also the scene of a bloody act, the stabbing of the regicide Conventuel Lepelletier de Saint-Fargeau by a royalist soldier, Pâris. On northern arcades were the Trois Frères Provençaux, ambassadors of Provençal cuisine, who introduced the Parisian to the *brandade de morue,* the *bouillabaisse,* green olives and red mullet. As Grimod said of the Palais Royal, taking in all its attractions, 'Every one of man's senses is attacked at once by tempters and temptresses of every kind.'

II

Grimod's return to the capital meant a return to club life. In the years of the Directory, and largely through his theatrical friends, Grimod was involved in a great number of more or less idiosyncratic dining-clubs. He continued to frequent the first of these, the Société des Mercredis, but we hear little of it at the time. One club which Grimod founded in 1795 was the Dîner des Mystificateurs, or the Hoaxers' Dining Club, which met at Méot in the Palais Royal. Sadly little is known about this august body apart from its intriguing list of members: Mayeur de Saint-Paul,[6] the vaudevillist de Piis,[7] the miniaturist Musson[8] and the Marquis de Sade. The degree of the latter's participation in the club is not recorded; it was presumably in the space between two spells of imprisonment. His letters to his wife give some evidence of a heightened sense of *gourmandise*. Living up to the spirit of the club's name, a prank was played on Rétif de La Bretonne, who had by now wholly fallen out with his erstwhile disciple, one imagines to a great extent as a result of the former's indiscreet publication of Grimod's virulent criticisms of the Revolution. M Nicolas was summoned as guest of honour to celebrate his election to the Académie Française. Each diner crowned his head with a laurel wreath and congratulated him. Rétif was overjoyed. Once the company had fully enjoyed the jape and Rétif had sufficiently amused them by his reaction he was cruelly deflated by being informed that it was not him but another M Nicolas, Nicolas Sélis, who had won the coveted seat under the dome of the Institute.

Another far-fetched institution was the Société des Gobes-Mouches, or the Fly-Catchers' Club. The presiding genius, 'its illustrious general, founder and President (as he takes all the titles)' was the Homeric figure of M Jourgniac de Saint-Méard, a former infantry officer in a royal regiment and a Chevalier de Saint Louis. Jourgniac was a man after Grimod's own heart who was able, at the end of his life, to consume six meals a day. The author of the *Almanach des Gourmands* never missed an opportunity to flatter the old soldier in the work – 'one of the most vast and robust appetites boasted at this moment by the gourmand city of Paris'. The club was endowed with a body of Aze-like statutes laying down the law for its gourmand members: 'Begin by feeding the body; later you may think about doing the same for the mind if you have any remaining time.' All the senses had to be developed in order to further the science; sight was important for looking at food, smell and touch had their obvious uses while hearing was deemed especially important, for without hearing you never know when the food has arrived. 'Every Gobe-Mouches,' the rules solemnly decreed, 'should regard gastronomic science as the *summum bonum*.' Those people caught talking sense were fined. Examples defined as sense were philosophy, politics or the reason for current events. Conversation was thus reduced to puns, rehashed Greek myths or jokes; anyone caught saying anything sensible was condemned to drink a glass of water. The diplomas of the club were countersigned 'Ah! Ah!', the seal being a fly in relief with the word '*Gobe*' above it and below was written '*Quid novi?*'

While the Gobe-Mouchistes mocked the contemporary obsession with the news, the Société des Dîners du Vaudeville was a more down-to-earth dining-club revolving round the theatre. Naturally Grimod, as a prominent theatrical critic, was present at its sessions and the short-lived *Journal des Gourmands et des Belles* was a by-product of the club, which later met at the Rocher de Cancale restaurant in the rue Montorgeuil. The membership was largely confined to playwrights and actresses, the latter always being an enticement to Grimod. Two of its leading luminaries were the comedy writers René Alissan de Chazet and Pierre Laujon.[9] Arthur Dinaux, in his history of French dining-clubs, recorded an amusing story of the two dramatists. One of the club's requirements was that members should compose songs to be sung after the meal (many of these tiresome productions are reprinted in the *Journal des Gourmands et des Belles*). Laujon liked to compose his under a favourite chestnut tree in the Tuileries Gardens the afternoon before the dinner, 'inspired by a pure sky and the scent of the leaves'. One day his young *confrère*, Chazet, was crossing the gardens when he saw Laujon with his back to the chestnut, humming audibly. Chazet decided to creep up on him and flattened himself against the other side of the trunk of the tree. There, able to hear the entire composition, he noted it down word by word. When Laujon left, Chazet was able to creep away unnoticed. An hour later they met again at table. After dinner came the time to sing and Chazet jumped to his feet demanding that his verses be heard first as they were the best he had ever written. His request granted, be began to sing the verses composed by Laujon. The latter's ears pricked up at this and he began to rummage in his pockets to find his notes, convinced that he must have mislaid them. But this was not the case; they were still where he had put them. More, with his notes in his hand, he was able to follow Chazet and found his song to be identical to his own. Laujon was mystified.

Three salvoes of 'bravo' greeted the verses, only Laujon did not participate in the general applause. He was silent, half from modesty and half from shock. 'What's this silence, Laujon?' asked Chazet with an ingenuous air. 'Could you possibly be jealous?... Come on, it's your turn now my friend, perhaps you can do better.' Laujon, more and more confused, hesitated then began to stammer. 'What a poor father you are,' Chazet blurted out roaring with laughter, 'someone steals one of your children and you don't even shout, "Stop thief!" Here, have your property back,' he said, passing him his notes, 'and let this be a lesson to you: walls may have excellent ears, but chestnut trees are not exactly hard of hearing either.'

III

Meanwhile, back in the Champs Elysées, an armed peace reigned in the family mansion, Suzanne-Elisabeth lodging on the ground floor while Grimod lived upstairs with his mistress. Madame de La Reynière, by now entrusted with the sole management of what remained of her late husband's fortune, gave her son a frugal income of 400 francs a month, and tried, unsuccessfully, to have him turfed out. Relations between Grimod and Adelaide had become quietly domestic; the writer had taken a decision not to have more children, the reason being given as the price of wet-nurses who would not accept *assignats* – the inflationary paper money of the Revolution – requiring coin. Rival gives an example of a modest meal in the household for February 1796: soup, two meat dishes, one *entremets* and between five and six desserts. In the evening one dessert provides their entire supper. It was quite a come-down from Béziers. As for bread, Grimod made that himself, rather than be forced to eat that which his dogs would have shunned. As far as wine was concerned, his father had left enough to supply all his needs. Indeed, it was the only part of his inheritance which he was fully able to enjoy. The inventory drawn up in 1794 lists three barrels of red wine and the same number of white, serving, one supposes as the *vin ordinaire* of the meal, while for more pleasant drinking there were about three thousand bottles of dessert wine. Grimod was well able to drive away the 'spleen' with the occasional glass of Lunel or Rivesaltes.

Madame de La Reynière, by now mistress in her own house, was therefore able to sell off some of her husband's effects. One of the moves which appealed most to her gourmand son was the renting out of the Orangery to an ice-cream maker, and by all reports a good one. Grimod never failed to praise him in every issue of the *Almanach des Gourmands*. The other sales were less heartening perhaps: the family château and all the Parisian property and, in July and August 1797, the La Reynière collection if paintings – the Rembrandt, the Teniers, Breughel, Franz Hals, Greuze, Van Loo, the Lancrets, Fragonards and Watteaus. Also under the hammer came the family furniture: Boulle cabinets, the chandeliers, prints, pastels, marbles and jewellery, all to be bought up by the Parisian *novi homines*, a collection of unattractive men who had done very nicely out of the war.

For his part Grimod found an original method of evading the bailiffs by nominally selling off all his effects bar his bed, and renting them back for a small sum. The deal involved his entire wardrobe down to his underclothes, as well as his library. The 'purchaser' was a man called Château, and even at the end of his life Grimod would not sneeze into a handkerchief without exclaiming, '*À vos souhaits, M Château*' (Bless you, M Château'). The books included a number of cookery manuals and a collection of contemporary pornography.

The house was filled with a succession of lodgers, all paying Suzanne-Elisabeth substantial rents to live in such prestigious quarters. One of the residents is given as 'Milady Kaine'(?); she was followed by a former lady-in-waiting to Catherine the Great, a Madame Divoff. This woman penned a portrait of her landlady, depicting her as a woman who received as company only *ci-devants*, priests and ladies with long noses. In her declining years Madame de La Reynière had become devout; as her son had written in the *Lorgnette Philosophique*: 'When women get so old that they are no longer able to please men, they react furiously and become devout. They must indeed count heavily on God's indulgence to offer Him what men no longer want.'

IV

The profits from the sale of his father's paintings allowed Grimod to relaunch his literary existence. The result was the *Censeur Dramatique*, a magazine dedicated to theatrical reviews of a virulent nature. Grimod remorselessly harried the Comédie Française, which since the Revolution had split into two rival companies. One of these was directed by one Dugazon, a former terrorist and a man who had played a key role in the September massacres of 1792, when he had briefly taken over from Maillard[10] at the Abbaye de Saint Germain to dispense some particularly grotesque summary justice. Altogether some 300 people were slaughtered in the prison. This stained reputation was anathema to the gentle Grimod, and the critic rarely if ever missed an opportunity to remind his readership of Dugazon's momentous career in the judiciary. The great Talma's mistress formed another butt of his trenchant wit, which led to a long-drawn-out feud with the actor himself, not unnaturally, coming to the rescue of his beloved. These attacks brought him increasingly into trouble with the censors, who demanded that in future Grimod submit his copy for perusal before publication. The organ had another role for Grimod, that of promoting a hopeless romance with a young actress at the Théâtre de Louvois, Josephine Mézeray, for whose *beaux yeux* he printed some indifferent verses. The actress was unimpressed and the lovelorn critic made something of a fool of himself in long gushing reviews of her every move and gesture.

When the bitter truth did finally dawn on him he went through another of his periodic bouts of misogyny. He wrote in the *Censeur*.

> Is there a woman, no matter how pretty one imagines she is, who can equal those wonderful red partridges of the Languedoc and the Cévennes, those goose- and duck-liver *foie*

gras which will forever render illustrious the cities of Strasbourg, Auch and Toulouse, the stuffed tongues of Troyes, the mortadelles of Lyon, Italian or Parisian brawn, Arles sausage, that delicacy which makes the person of the pig so valuable and so precious? Could one compare some painted little pretty face to the admirable sheep of Ganges and the Ardennes that melt in the mouth?... Who would dare prefer a scrawny sickly beauty to those enormous succulent sirloins which drench the carver and enchant those who eat them?

This was the first version of an often repeated passage. As Desnoiresterres observed a century ago, 'he was burning his boats'.

Grimod's limited means at the time prevented him from fully participating in the peculiar social whirl of post-Thermidorian society. Not for him the luxurious feasts of Amphitryons like Barras[11] and Ouvrard[12] or society beauties like Madame Tallien[13] or Madame Recamier.[14] Victor Hugo unjustly wrote him off as the Trimalchio of the period* but this popular myth is not borne out by the facts of the writer's poverty. Grimod did, however, have a role to play in one of the most notorious of the nightspots of the period, the Bal des Victimes. His reputation as a *farceur* landed him a job as artistic adviser to these macabre shindigs where the only people admitted were those who had lost a parent or grandparent during the Terror. It was a period which evoked sad memories for the man; he had lost not only relatives like Malesherbes and the Chevalier de Beausset, but also friends who had been caught up in the political life of the earlier days of the Revolution like Herauld de Séchelles[15] and Anarcharsis Clootz.[16] Beaumarchais, whose *Mariage de Figaro* had been seen as a profound study in the hypocrisy of aristocratic behaviour during the Ancien Régime, was even imprisoned himself and was released only at the cost of a 30,000-franc bribe. Grimod had forgiven the man who had suggested he be locked up in a lunatic asylum, though this may have had something to do with Grimod's enthusiasm for the *Barbier de Seville*. He had also pardoned Sebastian Mercier, despite the fact that the author of the *Tableau de Paris* was actively involved in the councils of the Revolution as a Deputy to the *cinq-cents*. Another writer who had reentered Grimod's life was Marie-Joseph Chénier, the brother of the tragic poet who had not survived the blood sacrifice.

---

*Trimalchio: a parvenu millionaire. Petronius, *Satyricon*.

Grimod was forced to write to survive. Justifying the abandonment of a book of reflections on the theatre, he wrote that he was 'too cold to write and the book would be too hot to publish'.

> I was a republican at a time when there was some glory in being one, when it required courage to brave the dangers of being so, i.e. fifteen years before France became a Republic ... I, whom the Revolution has deprived of 200,000 *livres* of income acquired by my ancestors, whom it has reduced to the necessity of telling actors the truth three times a month in order to nibble at a crust of bread watered by my sweat; which immolated my friends and my relations, above all a highly respected uncle whose death was possibly the most horrible crime committed in the name of the French people, who, despite all these good reasons for resentment am possibly the most tireless and passionate defender of the government when it shows itself good and just.

Though the dangers of the Terror were passed, it would be an error to believe that the administration of the Directory was any more relaxed except, perhaps, in its toleration of sexual immorality. 'People were no longer slaughtered by the hundred or poisoned by the thousand, but the stupefaction lived on and was to continue for years.' One of the ways in which the oppressive machinery of Robespierre's and Saint-Just's state had survived was in its organs of censorship, referred to by the writer as 'Olympus'. To give some examples, Corneille's tragedy *Cinna* could not be performed because of the line '*Le pire des états, c'est l'état populaire*',* while the same author's *Horace* could not be staged because of the appearance in the last act of the King of Rome. 'Can it be true,' Grimod asked rhetorically, 'that we are as little convinced of the worth of our principles that we fear the appearance of a king who died more than two and a half thousand years ago? I find it hard to credit.' Passages such as this caused some low rumblings on Olympus. Grimod however continued to be sanguine as to the future of his broadsheet, despite the opposition of the ranks of insulted Thespians.

> Up till now we have harvested no other crop from out toil than profound enmities, threats, insults and outrageous remarks... these virulent clamourings are now to be heard

---

*The popular state is the worst of states.

beyond the wings and injured pride and vanity have striven to interest Olympus in the proceedings. Dumb denunciations, intrigues, prayers and other forms of bartering, in short every means, fair or foul, has been used to bring down the wrath of the earthly Gods upon us. But this has not succeeded. Olympus has realized that it would be beneath its dignity to get involved in this pettiness; the wounded pride of a few poor players is not a fitting meal for the state.

Had he left it there, the *Censeur* might well have survived but Grimod was anxious to push his luck yet further. A passage on the particle '*de*', the brooch of nobility in France, makes one doubt the intellectual honesty of his claims to love the Revolution. 'Twenty-two million bayonettes, spears and sabres have these past four years been turned against the particle '*de*'. It has been hunted down in palaces, châteaux, factories and shops, in the courts, on the stalls and even in cottages.' The final straw came when Grimod reprinted some verses of a former Justice of the Peace and emigré Joseph Berchoux:

> *Qui me délivera des Grecs et des Romains?*
> *Du sein de leur tombeaux ces peuples inhumains*
> *Feront assurément le malheur de ma vie.*

It continued in a similar vein:

> *Et je me vis fessé pendant six ans et plus*
> *Grâce à Ciceron, Tite, Cornélius...*
> *Bientôt tous nos bandits, à Rome transportés*
> *Se sont crus des héros pour s'être révoltés*
> *Bientôt Paris n'a vu que des energumènes*
> *De sales Cicerons, de vilains Démosthènes,*
> *Mettant l'assassinat au nombre des vertus,*
> *Egorgeant leurs parents pour faire les Brutus!*
> *Les modernes enfin ont dévasté nos biens*
> *Et nous ont égorgés en citant les Anciens.**

---

*Who will save me from the Greeks and Romans? From the grave these inhuman peoples/Will certainly turn my life to misery...I have been spanked for six years and more/Thanks to Cicero, Livy and Cornelius...Soon all our bandits, transported to Rome/Will believe themselves heroes for being revolutionaries. Soon Paris will be peopled with tub-thumpers/Dirty Ciceros and base Demostheneses/Ranging murder among the virtues/Slaughtering their relations in imitation of Brutus! The moderns then have devastated our estates/Quoting the classics while slitting our throats.

On 18 June 1798, the *Censeur Dramatique* was closed down.

With his own organ outlawed, Grimod continued to write theatrical criticism for other papers like the *Feuille des Annonces Gratuites,* the *Journal des Spectacles* and *Petites Affiches.* From his articles on literature in this last he was able to put together a two-volume book entitled *l'Alambic Litteraire.* This too earned him a small thunderbolt from Mount Olympus. The meaning was clear enough: Grimod must stop using theatrical or literary reviews as a vehicle for attacks on the state. He was told to write about something harmless or give up altogether. The *Almanach des Gourmands* was the result. Though Grimod had had an interest, an obsession with food for several years, his *gourmandise* was by no means that of the accomplished gourmand depicted in the *Almanach.* To some extent he was obliged to create a new humorous style for himself to sell the book, and as for the political commentary, that had a habit of slipping in dressed up as ducks or partridges or entwined in a recipe.

That Grimod's palate was not at a high stage of development during the years of the Directory appears to be borne out by the testament of some friends from Lyon who came to dine with the writer while on a trip to Paris.

> We arrived at four having convoked for five and were ushered into a little room on the second floor. M Grimod, who came to open the door for us, seemed rather taken aback to see us arrive so early in true provincial fashion. His wig had not been done and he was horribly dirty. When his wig-maker came we used business as a pretext to have a stroll in the Champs Elysées while we waited for the chimes of five. When we returned we found him shaved, his wig dressed and powdered, and we went upstairs where we were well received by Madame [Adelaide]. We sat down to dinner, the other guests being the Bishop of Orléans, M de La Reynière's uncle, Degligny [an actor from the Comédie Française] and a famous doctor whose name I have forgotten [possibly Doctor Gastaldy]. Dinner was made up of four dishes served one after the other, and we were given half an hour at least to sample each one, there was some boiled meat, mutton, roast veal and some little creamy things that were completely off. It was after seven-thirty when we were able to escape from this damnable meal.

We should be consoled by the fact that a gourmand does not reach his prime till he is forty; nor are people from Lyon easy to please. And what of the service *à la Russe*? It was later to become the rule at the sessions of Grimod's tasting panel, the Jury Dégustateur.

V

Appropriately enough the idea for the *Almanach des Gourmands* was the product of Grimod's table-talk. The writer was dining with the publisher Maradan and the discussion turned to the failure of literature to interest the materialism and sensuality of the modern age. Would it not be a good idea then to give the public what it really wanted, a guide 'to the most solid part of their affections'? The publisher agreed. It took Grimod just twenty-five days to produce the first volume of the *Almanach*, which appeared at the beginning of 1803. The little volume, which was illustrated with a single engraving by Neveu, the painter who had been present at Grimod's famous supper of 1783, entitled 'La Bibliothèque d'un Gourmand', was an overnight success. It went through three editions and was republished in 1810, selling all in all some 20,000 copies which, considering the book was aimed at the limited number of plutocrats in Napoleonic France, was an impressive figure. The following year an edition was even pirated in Germany where it received the title of *Almanach der Leckermauler*. Attempts had been made to produce a work on a similar theme before; one such was written in verse by the same Joseph Berchoux who had penned those anti-Revolutionary verses; but where Grimod's book differed wholly from its predecessors was in its setting out to be educative. Grimod, always the man of the eighteenth century and a lawyer to the core, was to extend the codifying tendency of the time to matters gastronomic while using as his 'articles' the precepts of the aristocratic diner of the Ancien Régime.

Of the eight volumes which appeared between 1803 and 1813, the first was arguably the best. In later years the *Almanach* could become raggedy, lacking the structure of that first number. Its best element was the 'nutritive calendar' which provided the reader with a useful guide to the best way to enjoy each month and each season. Grimod later adapted this for his articles in the

Journal des Gourmands et des Belles, but his brief involvement with the magazine did not allow him to finish this updating of the original calendar. Each volume also contained, besides articles of interest to gourmands on the subject of different foods or furnishings for the table, some gourmand literature and a guide to the restaurants and food shops of the capital. In this last essential part of the work Grimod was the spiritual forefather of any modern reviewer from Egon Ronay to Messrs Gault and Millau. As with these, the threat of a further edition the following year was an incentive to improve, or suffer the consequences.

As Brillat-Savarin was later to do, Grimod suggested that readers interested in being mentioned in the guide should send him examples of their work, either literary or culinary. The response, we are told, was highly enthusiastic, and soon the cosy household of Grimod and his mistress was snowed under with elaborate dishes waiting to be sampled. The need to deal with these offerings led Grimod to found the Jury Dégustateur, a club which appealed to the not-yet-dead *farceur* in the writer while it also allowed him to resuscitate the extraordinary M Aze and his four quarto volumes of rules. The gossips of the city soon had it put around that Grimod's jury was no more than Grimod himself sitting in solitary splendour in front of a table groaning with delicious dishes, while others suggested that the writer was saving money on his food bills by eating the fare provided by the caterers and restaurateurs of the place. An almost masonic secrecy surrounding the membership of the jury was bound to provoke such rumours. In truth the club was composed of as heterodox a mixture as one would expect from Grimod's original mind.

The president of the jury was one Doctor Gastaldy. The prototype for Piquassiette in the *Ecole des Gourmands*, Jean-Baptiste-Joseph Gastaldy (1741-1806), was a member of the minor Provençal nobility from the papal enclave of Avignon. Following in his father's footsteps, he studied first at the great medical school of Montpellier (a town which could also claim de Villevieille and Cambacérès) and later in Paris. He started his career as the assistant to his father until being named the ordinary physician to the Hôpital de Villeneuve. As a result of a miraculous cure performed on the Duke of Cumberland, he was made Consultant at the Royal College of Medicine. His English reputation came in useful when he was obliged to go into exile in 1789, leaving behind him his position and his fortune. When he ultimately returned to France he was appointed surgeon to the hospital at Charenton, then reserved for mental patients (now the School of Architecture). Grimod had, in all probability, known Gastaldy for a while. He was likely to have been the famous doctor present at the vile dinner to which Grimod's Lyonnais friends were subjected. Gastaldy's gastronomic qualifications were invaluable to the younger man in his setting up of the Jury Dégustateur. 'We have never had the privilege to meet anyone,' he wrote after the doctor's death, 'of whom it could be said that their palate had a more certain, more delicate or more infallible tact. He ate stylishly and never spent less than four hours at table; but those four hours were employed so usefully for the progress of the art that one was never once tempted to accuse that depth of leaden reflection.'

Gastaldy was finally carried off by a 'monstrous salmon'. This fish was so excellent that despite the diet imposed by his colleague Dr Jeanroy, and despite the entreaties of the Archbishop of Paris, the Cardinal de Belloy,[17] no mean gourmand himself as the inventor of filter coffee, Gastaldy dipped into the fatal dish four perilous times, and on returning to his lodgings lost consciousness. It would be interesting to know how much of the style of the *Almanach* could be attributed to this famous gullet; Grimod paid him the rare tribute of saying, 'if anyone should ever get round to publishing a collection of his decisions, it would be the first *Code Gourmand* of the century'.

This 'most perfect of stills' was succeeded in the president's chair by Grimod de Verneuil, Grimod's cousin and the former controller of the postal service in Normandy. De Verneuil had for forty years been a member of the Société du Gigot de Caen (the Mutton Leg Club of Caen). Sadly we are told nothing of the nature of the deliberations of this august body, which met in a city which is a by-word for tripe. The best mutton of Normandy still comes from the Pré-Salé (literally the salt-meadow) of the Cotentin, where the animals feed on grass impregnated with a salty taste by the neighbouring coast. Grimod de Verneuil died in 1810 (it is not related that he made his apotheosis on the back of a sheep). The vice-president was M Chagot, the owner of the Château de Villebouzin near Longjumeau, not far from where Grimod was ultimately to retire. Chagot was the owner of the Creusot works and had substantial interests in mines. Like Lecocq and Haller, he was one of those *novi homines* whom

Grimod most liked to scorn in the *Almanach*. Their presence on the jury betrays an unfortunate if understandable self-interest when it came to the writer's future. Chagot was dubbed an 'excellent rural Amphitryon', and it would seem that Grimod made any number of *promenades gourmandes* to his country house, a few miles south of Paris, receiving a substantial dinner in return for the investment made by his legs. It is a distance of thirteen miles. Nearby was another member of the jury who owed his fortune to the Revolution and his château to the sale of emigré property: M. Lecocq, who resided at the Château de Chilly, which had once been the property of the great Cardinal de Mazarin.

The *chancellier perpetuel* and keeper of the seal was the pastry cook Rouget, 'the Montmorency of the oven'. Grimod had a boundless admiration for this *patissier,* and his presence on the jury attests the writer's retaining something of his pre-Revolutionary democracy. Rouget was a useful friend and adviser; an excellent judge of his competitors, he was also adept at making up cakes and tarts to honour the swarm of actresses who were received as sister members: 'Fanchons' after Madame Henri Belmont, 'Gâteau à la Minette' after Minette Ménéstrier, 'Augustinettes' for her sister and 'Hervinettes' for Mlle Hervey. An honorary vice-president was Emmanuel Haller,[18] the son of the poet and the 'vulture' responsible for sacking the Vatican and robbing Pope Pius VI. With the Marquis de Saisseval,[19] Haller had been one of Laurent's partners in the 'damned Genoese affair' which had cost Grimod *fils* his fortune. Grimod's flattering of this ogre of iniquity, whose acts of pillage would have made him anathema to everything for which the writer purported to stand, is a clear example of how Grimod was to use the Jury Dégustateur in order to straighten out his tangled finances. It appears that Lecocq lent him money, and Haller eventually retrieved a part at least of Laurent's abstracted fortune. This allowed Grimod to breathe more freely. Though Grimod's tactics betray not a little cynicism, it cannot be said that he behaved as shamelessly as many other dispossessed or non-dispossessed *ci-devants* did at the time.

Another prominent member of the jury was Albouy Dazincourt, the former acting master to Marie-Antoinette and the director of Grimod's 1783 *coena*. Dazincourt, Professor of Declamation at the *Conservatoire*, was also a founder member of the Société des Mercredis. After his death in 1809, Grimod dedicated the seventh year of the *Almanach* to his manes. Members who were also usually present were the writer Dieulafoy; Jourgniac de Saint Méard, that great appetite whose intellectual honesty had saved him from the wrath of the September terrorists; Fortia de Piles and the Marquis de Cussy, who claimed the distinction of knowing 366 ways of dressing a chicken. A Dr Rouvière held the office of physician to the jury while Grimod's cat, '*angora blanche et superbe*' (it looks rather more like an Ardennes sheep in the engravings), was also present at the deliberations.

Women members, *soeurs*, were tolerated, one feels, rather more for their looks than their palates. The group which was habitually present was composed entirely of that breed of female Grimod appreciated the most: actresses. Even the scornful Josephine Mézeray was an honoured associate of the jury, which also received the two sisters Ménéstrier, Mesdames Henri Belmont, Ferrière, Hopkins and Desbordes. Rose Dupuis was greeted with a particularly sensational cake from Rouget's oven, playing on the 'Rose' and the 'Well' of her name. From time to time Mlle Mars, the greatest heart-throb of the period, also sat with the members of the jury. M Aze, of course, was at his table to take the minutes.

The jury met a total number of 465 times. The meetings, which lasted five hours, started at seven and went on till midnight. Each member received his or her convocation the day before. The superb printed invitations were delivered even to those people residing under Grimod's own roof, as was the case with Fortia de Piles, and they were printed by the court printer. During the sessions the dishes were served *à la Russe,* i.e. one by one. This allowed the jury to eat their food hot and to concentrate on the 'legitimation' in hand. Of course Grimod had always been in favour of this idea, and here was a chance to give it the widest possible airing. Grimod also reformed the table by his banning of servants; the dishes were brought up to the room by means of a dumb-waiter while orders were conveyed to his cook by means of a speaking-tube based on that of the Café Mécanique. In Grimod's case the tube was decorated with the head of a cook.

Those summoned were strictly obliged to come. Grimod imposed a system of fines and punishments for those who did not. The *coup du milieu* or the *trou Normand* was administered halfway through the meal to revive those jaws which were flagging. The object of the exercise was to 'legitimize' (the word was drawn from diplomacy) the products of *traiteurs* (caterers) and restaurateurs like Corcellet, Véry, Chevet or Méot, and 'to inspect those foodstuffs on sale in Parisian shops'. Each dish was served unattributed, or tasted blind, as we would say today, by a quorum of five to twelve members. Armed with the rigour of M Aze's little books, there was a charade of high seriousness to the proceedings much in the way that Grimod's earlier farces had to be treated with the greatest solemnity. The formalism of Aze's regulations, however, belies the levity conveyed by the presence of so many starlets, and Minette Ménéstrier (although she may have been forgiven by granting Grimod other carnal favours) was even able to get away with declaring before a plenary session: 'I hate truffles and I hate goose-liver *foie gras*...' Any *traiteur* or restaurateur who had been granted a legitimation could, at a cost of 1.50 francs, obtain signed and sealed a document to that effect (extra copies came at 1.25 francs). The recipient could then display the certificate in the window of his shop or restaurant.

The intentional frivolity of the *Almanach* produced a few long faces in abstemious quarters and one or two critical notices in the press. It also gave rise to at least two spoofs. The first of these was the *Almanach des Pauvres Diables* written by Ducray-Duminil, Grimod's former editor, for whom he had written the pieces which ultimately saw the day as the *Alambic Littéraire*. It was signed the 'Anti-Grimod'. Ducray-Duminil contrasted Grimod's opulent world of *louche* republican financiers and racketeers with the starving masses of the cities. The poor devils of the eponymous *Almanach* replaced their *foie gras*, ortolans and woodcock by beans, potatoes, chestnuts and gudgeons, 'those poor devils of the river'. Instead of Clos-Vougeot, Lunel or Rivesaltes, the poor devil washed down his meagre diet with those dreaded wines of the Orléanais, more famous at the time for vinegar than for wine, and Suresnes, that bitter little wine from across the Seine from the Bois de Boulogne which puckered the lips of generations of indigent Parisians. The *Almanach des Pauvres Diables* was taken in good faith. The next production of its type was less well received by the authorities. It came out in 1808 and was entitled *Annales de l'Inanition pour Servir de Pendant à l'Almanach des Gourmands (A Record of Starvation to serve as a Companion Volume to the Almanach des Gourmands)*. It was a long and realistic description of the famine which was still gripping the majority of the French working classes. The work earned a savage minute written in the hand of the Minister of Police, Fouché: 'This shoddy tract must be hunted down and seized wherever it is found. The Minister requires above all that the Prefect [of Police] communicate the name of the person responsible for this work.' The events which followed are not clear, and M Rival, despite his extensive excavations in the offices of Parisian notaries, seems not to have been able to offer an adequate explanation. For whatever reason, Grimod's name was submitted to the Minister and the writer was duly summoned to the latter's office. Was he responsible for the tract? Rival thinks not; he had a great deal on his plate that year what with the *Almanach,* the *Manuel des Amphitryons* and a projected *Dictionnaire de la Cuisine,* which sadly never saw the light of day. Nor was the exercise entirely in Grimod's style.

Grimod's interview with the Minister Fouché has come down to us in many versions. The following is from Michaud (Fouché had heard that Grimod had a poor opinion of the Emperor of the French):

'*Monseigneur*, this report is false, no one admires your great Emperor more than I, but perhaps I might be permitted to deplore the uses his Majesty makes of his immense genius.'

'What! What do you mean to say?' Fouché thundered in reply.

Grimod continued, 'Yes, *Monseigneur*, had he applied his genius to the progress of the gastronomic arts, who knows to what degree of perfection they might have aspired.'

According to Balzac, at this moment Fouché laughed. It was a rare occurrence. Still, however well Grimod was able to draw the flak away from himself in this business, his suggestion of fondness for the Emperor is hardly borne out in his published works. There is only one reference to Napoleon in the whole series of eight volumes of the *Almanach des Gourmands,* and that is to a representation of the warrior in sugar candy. At a time when France was enjoying its greatest military glory since Louis XIV (whom Grimod admired), and before the bloody reverses which succeeded the ill-fated Russian campaign, Napoleon's internal régime had not filled the prisons with political prisoners in the same way as the Directory had, while a firm hand had prevented a repetition of the lynch-law of the earlier years of the Revolution. Still Grimod turned his back on the régime as if seeming not to notice anything but the social graces of the *nouveaux riches*. If Napoleon is damned in the *Almanach*, he is damned by his very omission. Fouché's laugh may have been less out of character than Balzac believed: the *Almanach des Gourmands* was not to appear for another twenty-five months. The rumour had it that it was no longer in demand, but as Grimod explained when the next issue was released, the popularity of the work had in no way waned. A host of unnamed problems beset the writer and publisher; the latter did not survived the battle. The 1810 edition was released by the house of Chaumerot.

As well as in the two parodies of the text, Grimod had the pleasure of seeing himself represented twice in his favourite medium, the stage. The first of these pieces, a light-hearted comedy by Alissan de Chazet, Lafortelle[20] and Francis[21] entitled *Ecole des Gourmands,* was performed on seven nights in August and September 1804. The central character is one Gourmandin, an obsessive gastronome whose dictums bear a striking resemblance to those of Grimod. Gourmandin is busily educating his son Bibi to become an accomplished gourmand. Part of this schooling is an interesting course in geography in which towns and cities are named by virtue of the delicacies they produce, i.e. *foie gras* from Strasbourg, etc. In the course of teaching his son, Gourmandin comes out with lines like: 'One must live for the sake of eating and not eat for the sake of living,' or questions like: 'What is the most civil thing a provincial might do for a Parisian?' A well-tutored Bibi replies: 'Send him a hamper for which the postage has been pre-paid.' At other times in the piece Gourmandin makes statements like: 'An empty stomach has no ears,' or, 'Opulence at table redistributes wealth,' or, 'Life is a good meal for which Hymen is only the hors d'oeuvre.'

Bibi's homework reveals a predictably gastronomic series of books to mug up: *Le Parfait Cuisinier, Le Commentaire sur la Loi des Douzes Tables, L'Apologie du Père Goulu, Le Traité des Quatres Repas, L'Almanach des Gourmands...* 'Oh! Bon, bon,' said Gourmandin. Gourmandin decides to marry his ward (who is in love with his nephew Dorvil) and undertakes a process of reform in order to render himself more worthy of the young girl... 'I shall become abstemious if that is necessary. Yes, as long as I can expect at dinner five or six entrées, two roasts, four *entremets*, a few excellent bottles of wine and a reasonably elegant dessert! In faith, I don't need any more than that, except on the days we're entertaining.'

Grimod had to wait until 1810 to see another likeness of himself tread the boards at the Théâtre de Vaudeville. The authors of this second play on a similar theme, *Arlequin Gastronome ou M de La Gourmandière,* were the *chansonniers* Barré[22] (de Piis' partner in the direction of the theatre), Radet[23] and Desfontaines.[24] The play was performed four times, not perhaps receiving quite the attention envisaged by its authors. It was set in the gastronomic capital of France, Lyon, where Arlequin de La Gourmandière has just been elected President of the Jury Dégustateur. The story line is similar in almost all its details to the *Ecole des Gourmands*, which may have accounted for the poor welcome and the odd hiss it received that December. The chief difference was that it aired the whole business of legitimations and featured a pheasant transformed into a superchipolata. The only recorded contribution made by this frivolous piece to the history of the theatre was that it was surely one of the first where the actors were seen to dine on stage. The sight of guzzling actors provoked a savage attack. The spectators having dined, the critics thundered, it was disgusting to have to witness this agape. Grimod, however, came to the rescue of the piece in the *Almanach des Gourmands*. 'It is true that the audience enjoys little more than the aroma of these meals, where, often to the great distress of the actors, wine from Suresnes replaces that of Volnay, the Champagne or Claret indicated in the text, but for a gourmand who has dined well, to see others eating is still a pleasure.' The critic of the *Courrier de l'Europe* hit harder still, referring to Grimod as a 'once famous author' and to his style as 'grotesquely pompous'. There were evident drawbacks to fame.

The success of the *Almanach des Gourmands* encouraged Grimod to turn his hand to other projects connected with food. In the first flush of the popularity of the *Almanach*, the publishers Capelle and Renaud were anxious to capitalize on this new public awareness for *gourmandise*. Grimod too was sensitive to the fact a paper was necessary to maintain quality in the kitchen. The project was therefore entrusted to the 'Dîners du Vaudeville' with Grimod as the presiding genius. The result was a monthly magazine entitled the *Journal des Gourmands et des Belles* which appeared for the first time in January 1806. Grimod's fellows on the paper were his old friends from the Vaudeville, which meant a great deal of the copy was composed of bacchic couplets penned by the likes of *chansonniers* Gouffé[25] and Désaugiers[26] and the comedy writer de Piis. A woman writer, Marie de Saint Ursin, contributed articles on food while other pieces were assured by the Abbé Geoffroy, Maître Homard of the Société des Mercredis and the anti-Grimod, Ducray-Duminil.[27] The editorial staff met on the twentieth of every month for a huge meal at Baleine's restaurant, the Rocher de Cancale. As the publishers footed the bill for the meal it was the day Grimod ate for the other twenty-nine of the month.

The first issue was emblazoned with a portrait of the great gourmand, giving subscribers every indication that Grimod's role in the business was much more important than it was in reality. In fact the writer's contribution was more or less confined to a leader on the culinary attractions of the month in question, and one or two recipes of a more or less bizarre sort. As time went by Grimod's editorial was superseded by one signed 'Gastermann', a pseudonym for an otherwise unknown journalist called Reveillère. In that year's *Almanach*, Grimod records a growing disappointment with this first ever gastronomic magazine. 'On which the author of this *Almanach* even worked for some months ... it will probably not survive the autumn.' Apart from the cavalier treatment his copy had received, Grimod had other problems with the publishers, who sought to restrict the usual political licence to which he was used in his other publications. One subscriber who asked for an account of a dinner under the Terror received a discouraging reply, aimed chiefly one imagines at the former *representative en mission*[28] Fouché, though it could well have been meant for any other former terrorists who were still well regarded by the imperial state: 'Never has the press been less free in France, the Government seeking to stifle all memory of those unhappy days.' Contributing less and less to each number, Grimod finally retired from the paper at the end of the year: 'They will be easily reconciled to my retirement.' With Grimod gone and Gastermann at the helm, the magazine became more and more a fashion digest and a repository for drinking-songs. Grimod's only legacy was to bequeath, unwillingly, the system of legitimations.

In the year 1808 Grimod undertook two projects besides the *Almanach* for that year. The *Manuel des Amphitryons* and the *Dictionnaire de la Cuisine*. Only the former was ever published, being issued by the same house of Capelle and Renand which had caused so many upsets during his collaboration on the *Journal des Gourmands et des Belles*. The book is divided into three parts: a treatise on carving, a series of menus destined for dinners involving from twelve to sixty guests, and a third on 'the elements of gourmand good manners'. The first of these is among the most cogent of Grimod's writings; it is prefaced by a potted history of cooking in France with some typically acerbic judgements on the quality of the modern Amphitryon: 'It is not sufficient to have spent one's life rinsing glasses to become a connoisseur of wine, nor is having served plates to all and sundry enough to teach you how to manage a good meal.' There follows a detailed description of all those foods requiring carving, from the bustard to the turbot, each one affording the author an opportunity for social commentary. The second part is possibly the one of the least interest to the modern reader, a series of menus composed of formal dishes of the Ancien Régime, and as a result heavy with the formalism of the time. The last part is the nearest Grimod ever got to realizing his ambition to publish M Aze's rules and regulations. Again very little of this etiquette would mean much to the modern gourmand.

While refusing to dwell on the victories of his Emperor, Grimod is not blind to the consequences wrought by the war on the business of the gourmand and the Amphitryon. The British mastery of the seas had impeded the supply of some of the commodities most dear to a gourmand. Others, like salt cod, had wholly disappeared as the majority of this vital part of the *brandade de morue* came from Newfoundland or the little French islands just to the south, Saint Pierre and Miquelon. More serious still was the fact that the English, a race he generally loathed, had stopped the manufacture of M Richard's sturgeon pâtés: 'The English, those fierce tyrants of the sea, have declared war on the sturgeon ... Every lover [of these pâtés] has been waiting with his mouth open for more than a year.' Another disadvantage of the time was the way that tradesmen were taking advantage of the new weights and measures imposed by Napoleon to perpetrate frauds against the shopper. Otherwise Grimod confines his criticisms of the régime in power to the provocative use of the old names for streets and institutions. The Pont de la Concorde, for example, has, in his eyes, reverted to its previous form of Pont Louis XVI, while in this passage on a café in Marseille he again demonstrates his contempt for everything which has occurred in the foregoing twenty years: 'On the Place now called Imperial, which has been successively denominated Place de la Tour, Place Necker, Place de la Liberté according to time and circumstance ...' Grimod, not satisfied with that jibe, openly teasing as it must have been to the imperial censors, continues with a list of people you would be likely to meet in the said café: 'brokers, stockbrokers, businessmen, that horde of licensed pimps which has grown so immeasurably since the Revolution'.

In the final year of the *Almanach*, suspicious gaps appear in the text testifying to the operations of a censor, while in private Grimod grumbled about a succession of lawsuits he might have to face. The most significant of these gaps appears under the text on 'Reductions' which follows (theoretically Grimod is referring to the use of Madeira wine in sauces): 'This word is better known to finance than to cooking, and from the time of the Abbé Terrey, who reduced incomes by a tenth, to the Directory which reduced them by a third, we have suffered reductions in every sense, sort and form. The only thing which may not be reduced is the gaiety of the French [...for three lines].'

Still, there might well have been civil actions against Grimod, who not infrequently used the *Almanach* to settle old scores against friends who had disappointed him or against tradesmen who had abused him or any other customer. A M Grec came in for especially brutal treatment;

> We owe it to the maintenance of the gourmand police to point out this shopkeeper as a man of very poor faith. Only a few days ago, and after having sold M Francis (a dramatist and member of the Epicurean Club which meets at the Rocher de Cancale) a rotten pâté, he not only refused to take the said pâté back (changing it for some other merchandise) but refused even to recognize the pâté as being his. His insolent wife went so far as to insult M Francis in the crudest possible terms when he threatened to expose her infamy to the Epicurean Club.

M Grec took advice from a lawyer who told the tradesman that the action 'could go a long way'. Grimod published M Grec's letter but added a mischievous note, 'Not as far as M Francis' pâté might have gone had it remained in M Grec's shop; left to its own devices it was beginning to walk all by itself.'

Grimod's Parisian itinerary provided him with many such

opportunities. Like any good modern gastronomic critic, he was not anxious that the caterers and restaurateurs should rest on their laurels: '*Amour propre* is present in all professions, and in this context, butchers and pork butchers will soon be as susceptible as actors and poets...Generally it is the most mediocre artists who shout the loudest.' With this in mind, the critic was determined to debunk all but the very best, and there were few enough who did not receive some sort of criticism over the years of the *Almanach* which was intended to improve the quality of their wares. Of those who remained constantly in vogue with the writer were shops like the Hôtel des Americains, which was the Fauchon of the day, selling anything from the most exquisite wines to the most delicate of foods. In the same breath Grimod would always mention Corcellet, then in the Palais Royal, now in the rue des Petits Champs (the original sign of the shop, now in the Musée Carnavalet, is supposed to represent a gourmand in the person of Grimod himself). Corcellet has had a remarkable history, its commerce not having changed, except in location, for nearly two centuries. The other great grocer of the Palais Royal was Madame Chevet, who occupied 'a little dark corner'. Grimod also had nothing but praise for the vinegar and mustard manufacturers Maille (another survival to our own time) and Bourdin, the wine and spirit merchants Tanrade and Noël Laserre, and the chocolate maker Debauve of the rue des Saints-Pères. This last establishment is the only one to survive to our day in its original premises. Sulpice Debauve had been the dispensing chemist to Louis XVI, and at Christmas chocolate boxes still bear the Bourbon coat of arms.

Other merchants were not let off so lightly. The inaptly named Biennait, after receiving Grimod's highest esteem, replied (presumably failing to send in his products for legitimation), 'Good wine has no need of the cork.' The *rôtisseur*, as it happened, had little need of Grimod's recommendation for he had been chosen as supplier to the court. In reality Biennait had been involved in the royalist plot of 1795 and had been forgiven for his treachery only because Cambacérès had enjoyed his poultry. The *Archichancellier* had then ensured his being selected to supply the court. Grimod was without doubt aware of Biennait's royalist past.

M Biennait is now the *rôtisseur* to the Emperor, which

means that his majesty's *officiers de la bouche* (who often have grand lunches prepared for him) find it easier to go to his shop than to go to the market at La Vallée. A great many people make out that, like some over-succeeding churl, M Biennait has given himself very self-satisfied airs since he swopped his pheasant for an eagle.

Sometimes there was less justification for his attacks. A certain M Alexandre is slighted several times for having been ungracious enough to deny Grimod lunch once when the latter had walked all the way to his country house at Achères near Saint Germain-en-Laye. Talking of the retirement of the great Philippe of Chartres, Grimod writes obscurely using a Macedonian shift in order to drive his punch home: 'M Le Moine has taken over from the celebrated Philippe, a man more greatly esteemed by gourmands than the father of Alexander (a negative Amphitryon) of Achère [*sic*].' The Le Moine in question, by the way, had been the bitter rival of Philippe in the manufacture of Pâtés de Chartres. In the reign of Louis XVI, two poets, Collin d'Harleville and Nicholas-François Guillard, had been recruited by the rival parties to sing the praises of their wares.

Sometimes Grimod's familiar tone must have come as a rude shock to the simple tradespeople about whom he wrote. Speaking of a butcher called Ferrand, Grimod observes,

> Madame Simon was wholly convinced that only a living husband can console the widow, and she has done precisely what all other butchers' wives do in her position, that is marry the butcher's boy. Now instead of a husband who was lean, long, sallow and past his prime she has one who is plump, wide, fresh, rose-pink and in the flower of his age.

The Salon des Princes run by a M Nichole is found guilty of abusing the protection it enjoyed from Grimod's old breakfast companion, the 'Alcibiades of our century', the Chevalier de Castellane. M Nichole sent Grimod a calf's head *en tortue*, i.e. a mock turtle soup. Nichole's dish did not please the jury; there is even a distinct accusation of facetiousness on his part. He is warned not to try their patiences again with 'a hoax rather than a legitimation'.

The author is often agreeably surprised by what he finds. Before 'that revolutionary and devastating torrent' it was possible to get delicious *petits pains* in the rue Dauphine. To the writer's great delight they, like many other things of value, began to reappear under the Empire. Processions like that of the fattened ox of Lent were revived once the religious persecutions came to an end with the Concordat. Lent itself began to be reobserved much to the disgust of butchers, who lost business as a result. 'Only the profane are to be seen in their shops [during Lent].' Meanwhile the fishmongers were naturally overjoyed: 'They bless the return of regular worship which has brought back faithful custom' ... 'Until 1803 people obeyed the commandments of the Church in secret, if one dared to fast or not eat meat during Lent, one lived in continual fear of denunciation.' Elsewhere the itinerary attests the remarkable variety of foods available in Paris, even despite the blockade, which had sadly deprived the locals of the porter and cheddar cheese which were stocked in peacetime by Louis Millot in the rue de Montmartre. Grimod does not tell us whether Burton beer was still being pumped in the Café Anglais of the Palais Royal. From M Prévost, the Chaptal[29] of the kitchen, Grimod was able to buy the very first *galantines*, pâtés made to resemble the animal from which came most of the meat to make them. Here again was an example of the positive results of the Revolution: Prévost had been the *cordon bleu* to the Marquis de Brancas until 1789 'upturned his stewpot'. Opposite the College d'Harcourt in the Latin Quarter, Grimod found excellent Bayonne hams in the shop of M Le Moine. Le Moine employed the services of a huge tomcat to protect his hams; the cat weighed thirteen and a half pounds in its prime and after Grimod's eulogies 'received more than one visit from persons of quality'.

Grimod still spent much of his time sniffing the stalls of the Parisian markets, the principal one being Les Halles, which had been the 'Parisian Belly' since 1135. It was to remain in that position until 1969 when it was transferred to Rungis near the airport of Orly. The sadly demolished pavilions by the architect Baltard were not built until the 1850s, and the market consisted of a series of sixteenth- and eighteenth-century buildings built in and around the medieval cemetery of the Innocents. Though the installations were originally meant to serve different commodities, by the beginning of the nineteenth century the foods on the stalls had become promiscuously jumbled in such a way that it was impossible to buy an apricot without being overcome by the fumes of tripe, while the salt cod (if you were lucky enough to get any) jostled with the tuberose. The market was so ramshackle and delapidated that Grimod complained that it would be impossible to buy a cabbage without exposing yourself to losing a limb. The solution suggested by the writer was that eventually realized by Louis-Napoleon: the construction of hangars with clearly defined functions; fish in one, meat in another, etc.

The other market in which Grimod was to be seen was La Vallée, which stood on the quai des Grands Augustins near Saint Michel. La Vallée was the principal retail outlet for poultry and game, everything feathered and furred. As a correspondent, M Remuzat, remarked, the market was conveniently close to the 'Marmite Perpetuel', that extraordinary restaurant where the cooking-pot had been simmering on the hob for nearly a century as a sort of finishing-school for capons in rock salt. From La Vallée, the capons 'had only a short jump to make, to fall into the pot'.

Remuzat was one of many people who wrote to Grimod about the *Almanach* and who either conveyed useful information or complaints about Grimod's partialities. One of the strangest exchanges of letters came from a German princeling living in Freiburg-im-Breisgau who, having been stimulated by all he had read in the *Almanach*, desired Grimod to find him a French cook for his household. Grimod obliged and found him one from the kitchens of Madame Tallien, one of the *belles* of the Directory whose marriages and affairs seem to describe the Calvary of the revolutionary years as she went from a noble financier before 1789, to a terrorist during the Terror, to a Director and a war profiteer during the Directory, ending up with the Prince de Chimay under the Empire. The cook was despatched to Germany and began to reform the household of the prince, but the latter was outraged by the expense of the metamorphosis and the richness of the food. Within a week the cook was back on the road to Paris. 'I had no idea,' he wrote to Grimod, 'that the manner of cooking had so totally changed since the Revolution ... It was the sort of food to ruin my health and exhaust my pocket.'

VI

Restaurants were still booming under the Empire and a less marked division of wealth allowed for a wider cross-section of the population to eat in them, even simple labourers who had spent a profitable day 'putting aside their cabbage and bacon to eat a pullet with cress' in a restaurant. The best restaurant of the day was, without a doubt, Véry. The brothers of that name had two establishments, one in the Palais Royal, the other in the Tuileries on the Terrace des Feuillants. This prestigious position owed something, it was said at the time, to the Maréchal Duroc's[30] fondness for Véry's wife. The German dramatist Augustus von Kotzebue,[31] visiting Paris in 1804, was highly struck by the variety of the menu offered at a fixed (high) price. It was made up of nine soups, seven pâtés, oysters, twenty-five hors d'oeuvres, fourteen beef dishes, thirty-one of poultry, twenty-eight of veal and mutton, twenty-eight different fish recipes, forty-eight *entremets* and thirty-one desserts. On the wine list there were twenty-two reds and seventeen whites. The construction of the rue de Rivoli ultimately destroyed the perfect little classical temple in the Feuillants, though Véry survived longer than the other buildings which had been constructed there, 'like a monument among so many ruins'. Grimod wrote in 1810,

> Alas, this splendid monument erected by M Véry to the glory of good cheer is soon to disappear. This superb restaurant where the sparkle of its mirrors, its crystal, its porcelain, the wealth of its bronzes and sumptuousness of its silverware, etc, which rivalled the merits of its cellar and its kitchen, made for an ensemble which amounted to the most beautiful Temple which has ever been erected to the God Comus in any of the four corners of the earth.

It was in fact the only restaurant of the period to have been built specifically for that purpose and was the ordinary resort of rich foreigners, generals 'who drank more than they ate and roared with laughter', ambassadors and heads of civil service departments. After Véry's destruction the establishment continued to prosper until 1859 in its original premises under the arcades of the Palais Royal. It was there that his creator sent Lucien de Rubempré, on his arrival in Paris, to eat a meal of Ostend oysters, a fish, a partridge, some macaronis and some fruit which, with a bottle of claret, lightened him of fifty francs which would have kept him for a month in provincial Angoulême.[32] Balzac himself, despite a genuine admiration for Grimod de La Reynière,* was more of a glutton than a Lucullus. His own one recorded visit to Véry is a record of a truly gargantuan appetite. In theory Balzac had offered to take his publisher Werdet out to lunch. The latter, fearing perhaps that his writer was unwise to choose such an expensive restaurant, ordered a bowl of soup and a chicken wing. Balzac for his part had no such false modesty and swallowed a hundred Ostend oysters, twelve Pré-Salé mutton cutlets, a duckling with turnips, a brace of roast partridges, a sole Normande, without counting hors d'oeuvres, *entremets*, fruits, etc., including a dozen pears. All of this was washed down with the most famous wines, liqueurs and coffee; all disappeared without so much as the writer pausing to catch his breath. Having finished this prodigious feat of gluttony, Balzac confessed to having no money on him; 'By the way my dear fellow, you wouldn't have any cash on you would you?'

Werdet was stunned; he had been invited out to lunch and yet Balzac had not a *sou* to pay the bill.

'I must have some forty francs on me,' he replied.

'That's not enough, give me five francs.' Taking the money, Balzac called for the bill with an imperious tone. 'This,' he said to the waiter, giving him the coin, 'is for you.' Then, writing a few words on the bottom of the bill, he said, 'This is for the lady at the counter, tell her it is from Honoré de Balzac.'

The next day an outraged Werdet received a bill for sixty-two francs fifty. He deducted it from the author's account, not forgetting the five francs for the tip.

The restaurant which Grimod frequented the most and which was also a great favourite of the characters of *La Comédie*

---

*See 'The Eclipse of a Gourmand', p.106.

humaine was the Rocher de Cancale.* The restaurant originated in 1794, being the idea of one Alexis Baleine. Originally the house was situated on the corner of the rues Montorgeuil and Mandar though the restaurant moved to another part of Paris in 1845. Another restaurant calling itself the Rocher de Cancale was established also in the rue Montorgeuil on the corner of the rue Greneta. This building can still be seen today with its stucco decoration of rocks encrusted with molluscs. Sadly, it is presently a shop selling jeans. In the seventh year of the *Almanach*, Grimod gives the reader a full menu for a dinner for twenty-four which took place on 28 November 1809. The bill came to 1,000 francs with a tip of twenty-four going to the chef and thirty-six to the waiter.

Four Soups

Crayfish bisque	Julienne of asparagus tips
A soup *à la reine* of almond milk and rusks	Chicken consommé

Four Relevés for the Soup

A pike *à la* Chambord	A beef rump cooked in Madeira and garnished with vegetables
A turkey stuffed with truffles	A turbot

Twelve Entrées

Filets mignons of partridges in aspic	A turban of little rabbit fillets
Snails	Vol au vent *à la financière*
Pullet fillets spiked with truffles	Chicken wings threaded with chicory
Red partridges in game stock	Grain-fed chicken with crayfish butter
A sauté of lark fillets	Salmon escalopes in an *espagnole* sauce
Pullet escalopes in a *velouté* sauce	Filet mignons spiked with truffles

---

*Another favourite of Balzac's. The Abbé Herrera takes Esther to dinner there in *Spendeurs et Misères des Courtisanes*.

Second service
Four Grosses Pièces

A trout
A pâté de foie gras
Crayfish
A glazed ham

Four Roasts

A pheasant
Smelts
Snipe
Soles

Eight Entremets

A bowl of blanc-manger
Hashed apples
Asparagus
Truffles *à la serviette*
A bowl of orange jelly
A vanilla soufflé
Cardoons in beef marrow
Truffles *à la serviette*

From 1796, Baleine's restaurant had been the headquarters of the Dîners de Vaudeville; hence, Grimod's connection with the house was both long and close. Moreover, one of the two founders of the dining-club was Capelle, the publisher of the *Journal des Gourmands et des Belles* and of the *Manuel des Amphitryons*. Grimod gives us no indication of the purpose of the above orgy but it could have had something to do with the success of the last-named work which had been published the year previously. The Academician Laujon died after a meal at the restaurant in 1811, still humming a couplet when he expired. Apart from actors and comic writers, the famous Cancale oysters, poultry and game and those 'little hot pâtés in Madeira sauce worthy of the Gods' attracted a clientèle of Russian princes, German barons and diplomats from all over the world. It was one of first ports of call for Kotzebue who found himself in with the literary set and the actor Talma. Together they 'stormed the Heavens with champagne corks'. Grimod summed up Baleine's talents in a florid passage,

> M Baleine is now in the position to swallow the majority of his rivals, like the cetacean of the Holy Writ who engulfed the Prophets, and whose name he bears; these new Jonahs, disgorged and not digested, will be forced to proclaim the glory of the Rocher de Cancale in every corner of the earth. This restaurant is now the Rock of Tenerife in the gourmand universe.

Next door was the restaurant the Parc d'Etretat which also

founded its reputation on the sale of fresh oysters all the year round. Méot had survived its association with revolutionaries like Danton and Desmoulins, and was able once again to establish itself in the forefront of Parisian *haute cuisine* with food which was, according to Sebastian Mercier, 'hot, prompt and well made'. Méot was something of a cross between an eating-house and a high-class brothel with its sumptuous decoration and reputed features like a huge silver tub in which rich clients could be bathed in champagne assisted by suitably attractive Hebes. Indeed, Hebe was on the ceiling pouring a glass of nectar for Jupiter. An English traveller eating in the restaurant in 1802 has left us with a description of his dinner: 'Vol au vent with roes and coxcombs, fried chicken, minute cutlets, a salmi of partridges with truffles, a mackerel, splendid little peas and a bottle of Volnay'.

Whereas Méot remained with the equivalent of three stars in Grimod's book, Robert was in danger of total relegation from the guide. The original Robert had become *officier de la bouche* to Prince Murat,[33] whose first cook, Laguipière, had died of the cold before the siege of Vilna. The backsliding of the *cordons bleus* into the houses of the new imperial nobility was no rarity. Many former cooks to Ancien Régime noble families deserted the hobs of their restaurants to take up courtly positions under Napoleon or at the Restoration. The most celebrated instance was that of Beauvilliers, who returned to his old master the Comte de Provence, become Louis XVIII in 1815. Queen Hortense adopted the cook Massino, her mother Josephine employed Vedel, while the very un-gourmand Emperor himself had his kitchens controlled by Dunant. Robert the younger was not made of the same culinary mettle as his brother nor, it seems, did he possess the charm: 'When the elder Robert left his restaurant to direct the kitchens of a prince, since become a monarch, he put his restaurant into the hands of his brother. By the sole mutation the best restaurant in Paris has been transformed into an up-market soup kitchen in only a few months.'

Le Gacque was on the Terrasse des Feuillants next door to Véry until its departure for the rue d'Antin at the end of the Empire to make way for the first terraces of the rue de Rivoli; it was a restaurant for gourmands with more limited means than those who dined frequently at Véry. Its chief importance to Grimod, who as a result knew the kitchens well, was that it was the habitual meeting-place of the Société des Mercredis until that club's demise soon after 1812. This very first of Grimod's dining-clubs was on its last legs when Grimod penned the ultimate volume of the *Almanach*.

> ... this club no longer sparkles with the same brilliance as it did when we dedicated the fourth year of this work to it. A schism has entered its breast; several gourmands of the first order having left it, their places being taken by others who are not up to their capacities. Alas! How could this discord have ruptured a club which has brought together all its members in heart, intention and appetite, where all the members have lived in a more than brotherly union for over seventeen years?... M Le Gacque is more shaken than anybody, for it means twenty-six fewer dinners a year at his restaurant, and what dinners!

Le Gacque's son-in-law Henneveu ran a restaurant in the Boulevard du Temple which survived until 1860. It was called the Cadran Bleu.

It was becoming increasingly fashionable to dine in the Champs Elysées in restaurants like Le Boeuf, Du Bertret and Le Doyen. The latter, still one of the smartest restaurants in the avenue, was founded by Michel Le Doyen in 1791. The restaurant moved to its present position in 1848, having started life in a ramshackle lean-to and been then a favourite meeting-place for *conventionels*. The Director Barras was a great *aficionado* of Le Doyen. Elsewhere restaurants like Naudet, Billiote in the Place Vendôme, Berly in the rue Saint Honoré and that of Donzelle, the ex-chef of the Maréchal de Castries, in the rue de Bourgogne, were at the height of their popularity. A great spot for the nightlife of the period was the Boulevard des Italiens where there were a number of fashionable cafés like the Café Hardy where Mme Hardy invented the *déjeuner à la fourchette* so disapproved of by the old-fashioned Grimod. The writer none the less appreciated the kidneys and chops which one could have grilled at any time of day as well as her *émincés* of chicken with truffles, stuffed *andouilles* and mushrooms served in a shell which, he said, would revive the appetite 'of a dying man'. The Café Riche in the same street was famed for its simple English food, thus causing Cambacérès to say that 'you have to be very hardy to dine at Riche and very rich to dine at Hardy's'. In the 1850s Riche changed its reputation and became the top restaurant of the time. Also in the boulevard was Tortoni, which had started life as Velloni in 1798. In Grimod's day it was considered the best ice-maker in the capital. Nearby was Nichole's Salon des Princes which had outraged the Jury Dégustateur with its mock turtle. Two of the writer's favourite ports of call were Mme Guichard's establishment on the Seine at Bercy and the Marmite Perpetuel. Bercy had previously been the site of a number of noblemen's residences lying slightly to the east of the walls of Paris. As those families emigrated the site became increasingly filled up by wine merchants, which is how it remained until recent memory. The presence of the stout accessories to the trade, coopers and bottlers as well as labourers connected with heaving bottles and barrels, led to the establishment of a number of little riverside restaurants which did a lively trade in fried fish and fish stews. These still survive to a small degree along the Marne. Mme Guichard had captured Grimod's heart with her fish stew, though by 1810 he finds, as so often, that the reputation he had largely created for her had made her slack. She got off with a warning, which he hoped would be sufficient to bring her back to making decent meals.

The Marmite Perpetuel had by 1810 been on the boil since 1724, having had 300,000 capons pass through it in the course of its history. It was situated at 10 rue des Grands Augustins, a stone's throw from the market of La Vallée. Capons could be collected at any time of the day or night, and they were so excellent that beside them all others seemed no better than old boilers. In 1810 a Mme Chardon-Perrin bought the Marmite from the previous owner, M du Harme. In her hands the restaurant diversified a little, also making good *matelotes* which could rival even that of Mme Guichard. Near the Marmite was the Café Conti or Café Anglais where an English breakfast could be eaten while reading the English papers.

The Palais Royal still took pride of place among the centres of Parisian gastronomy. Apart from the previously cited luxury establishments like Véry, Méot, Beauvilliers, the place was a warren of cafés and restaurants. Before its destruction under Charles X, the interior arrangement of the Palais Royal was greatly altered by the existence of the Galerie d'Orléans, a hastily erected structure which divided off the little garden of the palace of the Orléans family from the fun-loving prostitute-infested space behind. Balzac has left us with a vivid impression of the gallery before its demolition.

This bleak heap of mud-huts, its windows sullied by rain and dust, of flat-roofed sheds covered with tatters on the outside, the filth of half-constructed walls providing a composition which resembled a gypsy camp or the shanty town of a fair, those jerry-built lean-tos which surround Parisian monuments which have never seen the light of day; grimacing features which perfectly suited the different trades that teemed beneath this lewd hangar, brazenly twittering with some mad gaiety, where from the Revolution of 1789 to the Revolution of 1830 such a huge amount of business was transacted.

In 1805 the Palais Royal contained fifteen restaurants, twenty cafés and eighteen gaming-tables. Apart from those mentioned above, the best restaurants were both Provençal, being the Trois Frères Provençaux and the Boeuf à la Mode. The three brothers were in fact three brothers-in-law from Marseille called Maneille, Barthélemy or Trouin, and Simon. The restaurant established the vogue for Meridonal cooking in Paris, selling *brandades* and the 'various ragoûts of their region'. It was one of the most fashionable in the city. It was very difficult to get a seat. The Boeuf à la Mode commemorated that famous dish 'that will be *à la mode* for as long as the Pont Neuf remains *neuf*'. It was founded by another pair of Marseillais in 1792 who were famed for their salt cod, *bouillabaisse*, green olives and nougat. The sign hung outside the restaurant continued to give offence; it depicted an ox dressed as an Incroyable.*

Still the best of the cafés was the Café de Foy occupying seven arcades of the Palais; in 1806 Horace Vernet[34] had decorated the ceiling with a swallow in the course of an animated dinner. The Café du Caveau had been patronized by musicians before the Revolution. In the Empire it had an extremely important patron in the *Archichancellier* Cambacérès who came daily at eleven for his cup of chocolate. The patronage of the second power in the land allowed the proprietors to build a rotunda in the garden which remained there till the end of the last century. Nearby was the Corrazu which had been favoured by Barras and the man to

---

*Incroyable: belle of the Directory. According to Balzac's dictionary of Paris street signs, the ox wore a shawl and a fantastic hat.

whom he referred as that 'sly little Corsican' – Napoleon. There was a dancehall upstairs with the evocative name of *pince-cul*.*
The Café Anglais still existed for those 'who liked to lunch in the [English] manner'. The Café Egyptien was decorated in that modish style which commemorated Napoleon's Egyptian campaign. Meanwhile the Café des Aveugles would seem to be an exercise in poor taste: an orchestra composed entirely of blind people from the Quinze-Vingts (the eye hospital) serenaded a group of *louche* habitués.

**Pince-cul: literally pinch-bottom.

VII

If Grimod remains the uncontested theoretician of the 'Empire Gourmand' ('a rather voluntary republic'), there were at least two practitioners who excelled in the art beyond the gourmand's wildest dreams: Talleyrand and Cambacérès. Though it must be said that there was a shrewd political logic to their tables – as Cambacérès put it: 'It is to large extent by the table that one governs' – neither man seems to have greatly resented the impositions placed on them by their Emperor. The Emperor Napoleon himself was by all accounts a mediocre eater who, realizing his limitations, told his *Archichancellier* and his Foreign Minister, 'you will receive for me'. The ill-fated German dramatist Kotzebue was informed: 'whoever wishes to fare sumptuously must not come to me but must go to the Consul Cambacérès'. For the most part away on campaign anyway, the Corsican was frightened of getting fat and never touched more than two dishes. Nor could he be tied down for long periods at table. As Kotzebue remarked, somewhere between twelve and twenty minutes was the usual latitude, hardly enough time to engulf an ortolan. During those brief moments he ate voraciously and sloppily, preferring dishes of pasta, chicken or cutlets. He also had a fondness for the Boudin Richelieu which he swallowed with the help of glasses of Chambertin cut with water.*

Charles-Maurice de Talleyrand-Périgord, Prince of Benevento, was cast in a wholly different mould. As the protector of the great cook Antoine Carême he has a claim to a distinguished place in the history of gastronomy. Carême once said of him that 'he understands the genius of cooking, he respects it and he is the most competent judge of its delicate progress'. Napoleon's

---

* Thomas Love Peacock said of Napoleon's frugal meals that they betrayed 'a simplicity which could not conceal the ambition which lurked behind the apparent moderation'.

instructions to his minister were to give four dinners a week for thirty-six, which must have provided some of the best entertainment of the period. At these dinners Talleyrand's snobbery was fully aired; according to a perhaps less than wholly reliable source, Talleyrand, who carved the meats himself like an *écuyer tranchant* of the Ancien Régime, was apt to stress social divisions in the distribution of the food. 'Monsieur le Duc, might I have the honour of serving you some beef? Would Madame la Comtesse accord me the honour of accepting some beef? Would Monsieur le Baron have the goodness to take a little beef? Would Monsieur le Chevalier permit me to offer him some beef? Monsieur, have some beef.' And for the less distinguished guests at the far end of the table, 'beef! beef!' Talleyrand was a great devotee of the theatrical side of luxury at table, and a story which has also been attributed to Cambacérès tells of a dinner during the icy winter of 1803. The weather had got so cold that the rivers and lakes had frozen. Talleyrand, seeking to gain the maximum possible effect from the scarcity of fish, had a huge salmon brought to the table. The fish was greeted with cries of pleasure and wonderment when, all at once and at a prearranged signal, the valet slipped, casting the rare salmon to the ground. 'Bring in another salmon,' said Talleyrand, and at that moment a valet brought in a fish even larger than the first. In earlier days, hearing of his excommunication for having sworn allegiance to the constitution, the former Bishop of Autun wrote to Lauzun, later Duc de Biron, 'You have heard the news of my excommunication; come and console me at supper tomorrow. Everyone must refuse me fire and water, tomorrow we shall eat only "frozen" [i.e. glazed – *glacé* means both] meats and drink only chilled wine.'*

Talleyrand was devoted to *gourmandise*, to the degree that he told an imaginably sympathetic Louis XVIII that 'he had more need of saucepans than instructions' at the Congress of Vienna. He ate very little lunch, just a bowl of soup, but he made up for it in his evening meals, where his aptly named chef, Bouchée,

---

*Lauzun, by then General Biron, died a gourmand's death. Imprisoned by the Terror, he was executed on New Year's Day 1794. The night before his execution Biron ordered a bottle of claret and a chicken. He drank the wine and consumed most of the bird. He then lay stretched out on his mattress and snored loudly. Woken by the guards the next day he ordered some oysters. When they came to take him to the guillotine, he asked if he might be able to finish the last dozen. His wish was granted, and he was taken off to his death.

formerly of the Prince de Condé's household, would prepare up to forty-eight entrées for himself and his guests. Carême had every reason to praise his protector Talleyrand, but one suspects his reasons for accusing Cambacérès of mere gluttony were more partisan than anything else.

Jean-Jacques-Régis de Cambacérès came from Montpellier like his culinary henchman Jean-Pierre d'Aigrefeuille and de Villevieille. Cambacérès was even more aware than Talleyrand of the political ends served by sumptuous dinners; while there was a possibility of discontent at home it was good to display the luxury of the court to prove nothing was amiss. It was an attitude which would have been heartily commended by Thomas Love Peacock half a century later, who equated simple food with an unattractive form of republican virtue. Writing in 1851, Peacock (whose name alone would have been delicious to Grimod) had this to say: 'We have recorded as historical evidence, that the most incorruptible republicans were austere and abstemious; but it is still a question of whether they would not have exerted a more beneficial influence, and have been better men, if they had moistened their throats with Madeira and enlarged their sympathies with grouse... The student in his cabinet is an impartial spectator and may be a wise judge, but he is never a good governor.'* At first Cambacérès appears to have crossed swords with Napoleon over his novel form of political philosophy, when the latter countermanded Cambacérès' order that rare delicacies he brought by the messengers to the Congress of Lunéville in 1801. Cambacérès was able to bring him round once the First Consul had seen how important the deliveries were to him. As the story is related, Napoleon laughed a good deal, slapped his second-in-command on the back and exclaimed, 'Console yourself my poor Cambacérès, and do not lose your temper, the couriers will continue to carry your turkeys stuffed with truffles, your Strasbourg pâtés, your Mainz hams and your *bartavelles*.'

Cambacérès was not above using his power strictly for his own ends. Magistrates seeking advancement knew that the way to his heart was through his stomach, and sent him the delicacies to be found in the vicinities of their courtrooms. Likewise civil servants travelling to distant parts of France were charged with searching out and supplying him with the treasures of the place; goose livers

---

*Fraser's Magazine.

from Strasbourg, duck livers from Toulouse, pullets from Chartres, sausage from Arles, smoked beef from Hamburg, terrines from Nérac, hams from Mainz, etc. As Grimod put it, the table which was set to accommodate these delicacies was 'the most distinguished, the best, the rarest and most sagacious in Paris in the confirmed opinion of all erudite connoisseurs'; so much for Carême's assertion that he 'merely filled his stomach'. Kotzebue was accorded the honour of dining with Cambacérès, but paid his tribute rather to the then Second Consul's steward, d'Aigrefeuille,

> a man who has obtained considerable celebrity by the dedication to him of the *Epicures' Almanach* [the *Almanach des Gourmands*]. It is said that he justly merits that distinction, though he modestly declined it. For my part, I must confess that if the Second Consul's kitchen is superintended by him, I shall myself feel tempted to compose a eulogy of him [*sic*]; for, out of seventy or eighty dishes, to taste at least one half of which I had summoned my powers, there was not one which Lucullus or Apicius would have disdained... The Consul himself helps one to many dishes, pours out a variety of wines and liqueurs, and very politely asks his guests if they choose any. Notwithstanding the great abundance of viands, very few dishes are of such a nature as to allow the guests to partake of them; but supposing a difference of taste, the principal dishes are carried about by the servants; the rest remain stationary, and the person before whom a dish stands, helps those who wish for some of it... Here you have two kinds of table wine, as many of dessert wine and no champagne.*

Cambacérès' dinners were limited to two services and dessert served for an average of twenty-five to thirty people. The slightly mean report on the wine delivered by Kotzebue is countered by Reichhardt, who said, 'in terms of choice and finesse the wines might even surpass the solid menu, which is saying a good deal!'

As Kotzebue points out, the quality of Cambacérès' table owed an enormous amount to the choice and discretion of his sidekick d'Aigrefeuille. According to Cambacérès' biographer Vialles, Grimod had originally intended to dedicate the first volume of

---

* English translation 1804.

the *Almanach* to the powerful *Archichancellier*, but 'was snubbed'. Instead he offered the honour to his old friend from the Société des Mercredis. Contemporary descriptions of the Marquis have made him a good deal less appetizing than the great table he superintended. According to one witness of the time, he looked like the antagonist of Boileau's satire *Le Repas Ridicule* – who *'semblait d'ortolans seuls et de bisques nourrie'*;* another described him as 'small, fat and querulous'. The fullest description comes from Madame d'Abrantès:

> He had a large head placed on top of his short neck. He had huge eyes of a dull pale blue, his nose was formed out of a ball of flesh which surmounted a mouth which took its form from two fat lips which he was constantly licking as if he had just finished eating a bisque; to add to this were two fat, ruddy trembling cheeks. His legs were short, fat and squat, he had a vast belly and a skinny waist.

It is difficult to know which of these men it was who took an active interest in the *Gourmands' Breviary*. Several books make out that Cambacérès actually presided at a session of the Jury Dégustateur, but this seems unlikely, given the bohemian company he would have found there, which would have compromised his official dignity. Grimod himself wrote that: 'The lively interest he has deigned to take in this work [the *Almanach*] since its inception, and the assurances he has never ceased to accord us of his satisfaction, have become the most powerful vehicle for our efforts, and the most gentle reward for our labours.' Was this persiflage only a plea for the misogynistic gourmand's protection, given some of the more risky passages in the books? This does indeed seem to have been the case, as is borne out in a letter to his aunt, the Comtesse de Beausset, written in 1803. Grimod had been summoned to dinner at the then Second Consul's: 'I shall be forced to go in order not to fall out with him, but I will do no more for the Republic as long as I can get away with it.'

Obviously his affection was greater for the steward who managed to infuriate his master by his ability to extract the turbot's tongue before the fish arrived at the table. Little fights between the two led to one of Cambacérès' most famous pieces of

---

*Seemed to be fed exclusively on ortolans and bisques.

table-talk: reproving d'Aigrefeuille for being too ebullient at an otherwise gloomy dinner, the *Archichancellier* said, 'Can't you speak more quietly; in all honesty we can't hear what we are eating.' Cambacérès died of apoplexy in 1824, a convinced gourmand to the last. He had a great fondness for Corsican blackbirds, which had formerly been sent him by Joseph Bonaparte, as well as for little dainties like hares' tails. He was very particular about his food and would eat only wild mushrooms from his home town of Montpellier and rabbits which had been fed on wild herbs from Mont-Héron in Switzerland; partridges had to be plain roast on one side and coated in fat bacon on the other so that the two tastes could be experienced simultaneously. Finally on the subject of Cambacérès, there is an amusing story recounted by Vialles of a delicious pear in the window of the Grocer Chevet in the Palais Royal. Aigrefeuille, Villevieille, the notary Noël and the bookseller Collin all had the same idea: the pear would make an ideal present for the *Archichancellier*. Vying with one another for the honour of presenting the pear, the four began to bid for it: 'a crown,' proposed Aigrefeuille, 'two crowns,' shouted Villevieille, 'two louis,' said Noël ... but at that moment a man butted in. 'Such a trifling sum is an insult to this piece of fruit. I shall offer five louis.' 'I'll double that,' said Noël. 'Fifteen louis then,' the man declared, removing the pear, which, with no further ado, he cut into four, giving a piece to each of the bidders. 'This courteous knight was Grimod de La Reynière.'

The Eclipse of a Gourmand

Les méditations d'un Gourmand.

The retreat from Moscow in 1812 and the long-drawn-out return of the straggling remnants of the Grande Armée marked the turning of the tide for Napoleon's empire. A new mood began slowly to take hold of France. Despite instructions from above to maintain the feasting and festivity, austerity became increasingly marked. It was perhaps this sentiment which provoked the last vicious attack on the *Almanach des Gourmands* which appeared on New Year's Day 1813. The critique was printed in the *Gazette de France*, one of four political journals permitted to survive the Decrees of Compiègne of 1811. The reviewer signed himself simply 'F.X.'

> Not seeing the *Almanach des Gourmands* appear last year, I assumed that both it and the *vieil amateur** had died of indigestion, but both are with us again, fatter and healthier than ever, to judge by the 360 pages of the book and the picture of the author in the engraving sitting alone at table filling his mouth with all his strength and with both his hands...

After the mocking prologue, the critic took on a more caustic tone, describing the *Almanach* as an 'apology for all vices and all the disordered passions of human nature; it would not be wise here to talk of morality or religion to the *vieil amateur*, who would only smirk at such words'.

In short the government organ was hoisting the gourmand with his own petard. The man of order, sound morality and religion was being framed as the corruptor of public morals. When, the reviewer asked, 'was *gourmandise* not a vice?' Having taken Grimod to task for his perverse thinking, right down to his estimation of the pigs of Epicurus and their expression of pure

---

*The old [food] lover. The pseudonym Grimod employed.

stoicism, the censorious government critic went on to touch a rawer nerve. The author was at the 'end of his talents', the work was a series of moral obscenities rehashed from earlier work. It was obviously high time the old gourmand swallowed his hemlock gracefully. In spite of the worsening political situation which would result, in little over a year, in the Allies entering Paris and even in the occupation of the Hôtel de La Reynière, Grimod had been at his old tricks again. Never able to resist political commentary, Grimod had included a burlesque piece entitled 'In Praise of a Tooth-pick' which compared the fortunes of two goose feathers, one of which had become a quill while the other had been made into a tooth-pick; 'By writing the *Social Contract*, did not the pen of Jean-Jacques [Rousseau] upset the basis of the old world? Has a tooth-pick ever shed any blood except that of the gums?' Grimod had been dodging the thunderbolts of Mount Olympus for many years. It seems that with this last salvo from the *Gazette de France* he decided to hang up his quill and make off with his tooth-pick.

After having been his mistress for twenty-four years, there was to be a change in status for Adelaide Feuchère. Now that the objections of fathers or uncles were removed by death, only one person stood in his way. According to the former dispositions of the *Code Napoleon*, after he had reached the age of thirty, a parent had only one veto on the marriage of a son. If the demand was duly presented by the notary a second time, the marriage had no more necessity of parental consent. Grimod must have expected the refusal of his mother which was issued on 23 April 1812, but the lordly veto was not enough to stop the *mésalliance* from being celebrated. On 13 June of the following year, Grimod made good his escape route by purchasing, for some 14,000 francs, the *seigneurie* of Villiers-sur-Orge, a little over twenty kilometres to the south of the capital. The property comprised a small château of fifteen rooms in the shadow of a ruined keep, a farm, stables, milking-sheds and a pigsty (something which was to occupy a good deal of the old man's time), kitchen gardens and vines. Grimod was aware of the fact that the château had formerly been the home of Antoine d'Aubray, the brother-in-law and second victim of the poisoner Marquise de Brinvilliers.[1] With such a connection in its history, the manor must have seemed highly tempting for the retreating gourmand. It was also a fitting place to bring up his family, for, the year before, Grimod had adopted the daughter of Madame Hervey, Anne-Victoire Ducray-Duminil. Though the gourmand strongly denied the fact, it is quite likely that this child, bearing the name of the Anti-Grimod, was in reality his daughter. When the girl married Jean-Charles-Baptist Dronsart, Grimod settled a dowry of 40,000 francs on the bride.

Grimod had been packing his gastronomic bags in Paris. On 26 May the last or 465th session of the Jury Dégustateur had taken place in the Hôtel de La Reynière. Twenty-five jurors were seated at two tables supplied with balls filled with hot water to warm the feet of the gastronomes present. As usual the standard complement of actresses were assembled in the dining-room. Josephine Mézeray, who had been excluded as a punishment for the serious offence of having feigned illness in order to go to the opera at a previous session, was back in favour for the last session. Grimod's other loves, Mme Hervey and Augusta Ménéstrier, were seated on his right. Minette was temporarily *persona non grata*. Other ladies present were Mme Bordin from the Théâtre de Vaudeville, Mlle Mars,[2] Rose Dupuis and the new owner of the Marmite Perpetuel, Madame Cardon-Perrin. The men were represented by the Marquis de Cussy, the Comte de Piles, Chagot, Alexis Baleine, Rouget and, more surprisingly, Talma and 'Maître Homard' – Geoffroy

Less than a month later, after he had locked himself up in the family home and put it about that he was ill, friends of the gourmand were dismayed to receive the news of his death: 'Madame Grimod de La Reynière has the honour to inform you of the grievous loss she has just sustained in the person of her husband. The funeral will take place today, Tuesday 7 July. The convoy will depart from the house of the deceased, number 8 rue des Champs Elysées, at four o'clock precisely.' Mourners arriving at the house found a long range of suitably decked carriages waiting to escort the bier to its destination. Inside, the coffin was laid out grimly between two rows of torches. The assembled company stood by with 'heavy hearts and light stomachs', for it was the hour for dinner in the La Reynière household, Grimod never having given in to the Revolutionary pressure to eat later in the evening ('it is thus that three or four hundred provincial lawyers changed all at once our most sacred habits and mores'). Those assembled included the chefs of all the leading restaurants of the city as well as a fair number of caterers and literary figures like Cailhava, Mercier and Geoffroy. They stood about discussing the merits and demerits of the deceased when suddenly the two leaves of the door flew open to reveal a splendid table draped in black and lit by a thousand candles. In the centre was a coffin and at the end the Prince of Gourmands himself, looking solemn and imperturbable. 'Gentlemen, dinner is served,' the valet announced. A place was set before each of the astonished mourners (according to one account every place was decorated with a small coffin bearing the diner's name). As the crowd moved slowly forward to partake of the feast they were rallied by the host with the cry, '*Messieurs*, dinner is served, it could get cold.' The meal continued late into the night. Grimod was reported to have concluded: 'This way I am certain to have dined with my friends.'

M Rival rightly distrusts the preceding account, which has similarities with one or two eighteenth-century dinners and appears to have been the inspiration for J.-K. Huysmans in *A Rebours*.[3] As for the well-aired story of Grimod's pleasure garden at Villiers-sur-Orge, he refutes it utterly on the basis of the manuscript inventory written at the time of Grimod's real death. Grimod died in 1837, a quarter of a century after he moved into his manor. It is possible that the old Adam in him took longer to die than is now supposed and the stories of Grimod's practical jokes are present in all the nineteenth-century biographies of the gourmand. According to these writers, guests were frequently set in the stocks in front of the house before being admitted. Finally through the door, they were greeted by a panel setting out the philosophy behind the torture they were about to receive. 'Cursed be those who are unable to take the jest, they are unworthy of the orgies of the Jury Dégustateur or of its country residence.' Dinners, it was said (this lends weight to M Rival's thesis), were postponed from 6.30 p.m. till nine, leaving no time for the guest to get back to Paris. Forced to stay the night, the sleeping diner was subjected to no end of japes – shaking beds, concealed trap doors, revolving rooms, etc. A cavalry officer woke to find his uniform exchanged for the skirts of a female guest and vice versa. Meanwhile about the house and garden were concealed pipes which would squirt water at their unhappy victims, much in the manner of those at Archbishop Markus Sittikus'[4] summer palace outside Salzburg. The rooms of the house were decorated with a series of legends in the hand of the Master; over the cellar was written, '*Vive le vin, vive l'amour*', while elsewhere was proclaimed the device, 'Happy is the just man who sins but seven times a day.'

Villiers-sur-Orge had been bought as a country seat, but the events of 1814 and the death of his mother a year later resulted in Grimod's living there for eight months of the year. Adelaide, for her part, seemed little attracted by the 'idiocy of rural life' and remained in her apartment in the Hôtel de La Reynière. Grimod had still intended to continue his life as a man of letters, and in 1814 he succeeded his friend Geoffroy as the Comédie Française and Odéon critic on the *Journal d'Empire*. The position had been arranged for him by his cousin the Comte de Beausset on condition that he refrain from political allusions in his articles. Grimod had thus wrested the position from the young Charles Nodier, the author of *Trilby*.[5] The entry of the Allies into Paris that spring caused the demise of the *Journal d'Empire* and its replacement by another with a more regal-sounding name. Grimod was out of a job. The Allied occupation was also brought home to Grimod in an even more direct way: the Supreme Commander, Wellington, requisitioned the Hôtel de La Reynière, occupying one of the ground-floor apartments while the shady banker Ouvrard, the very image of every one of Grimod's pet hates, took the other. Suzanne-Elisabeth, now in her eightieth year, beat a hasty retreat to the first floor, where she died a year later on 25 May 1815. She was buried in the Cemetery of the Père Lachaise. Wellington remained in possession of his apartment until November 1819 when the Allied occupation came to an end. On leaving he tipped the concierge, Basile Wattelier, a hundred francs. Ouvrard made a move to buy the house, but was unable to meet the asking price, and in the end it went to a M de Labouchère for the sum of 460,370 francs, Grimod making a particularly good sale by retaining a life tenancy of his apartment on the first floor. In practice it was more often than not the residence of Madame; it comprised antechamber, bedroom, dining-room, drawing-room, kitchen and bathroom, two rooms in the *entresol* and five servants' bedrooms under the eaves. After Grimod's death Adelaide was obliged to give up the flat and went to live in the nearby rue Godot de Mauroy. The house became, successively, the Imperial Russian Embassy, the Ottoman Legation, the Cercle Imperial, the Cercle des Champs Elysées, the Cercle Épatant (all three clubs), and finally the United States Embassy. The latter demolished the Hôtel de La Reynière, replacing it with the present copy of the Hôtel de la Vrillière.

At Villiers-sur-Orge, Grimod constructed a belvedere at his property which was to serve as an ivory tower in his retirement, used mainly, according to Desnoiresterres, to 'sleep off his bad mood and enjoy his misanthropy at leisure'. With his new wife in Paris, Grimod corresponded with her affectionately enough, sending her consignments of poultry from the yard in which he hid bottles of rare wine to avoid paying duty at the *octroi* at the gates of Paris. In the country he was free to indulge in his *gourmandise*; the Orge was full of fish: gudgeons, barbel, bleak and chub, while in his pigsty grunted the source of his perpetual fascination, the King of Base-Beasts. Rival, naturally sceptical of such stories, is forced to admit Grimod's curious interest in pigs even if he doubts some of the choicer tales told by Monselet. According to the latter, on days of celebration a pig was placed in honour at the table while a servant was charged with looking after this privileged beast, which slept on a mattress and was regularly combed, brushed and rubbed by its attendant. According to one version the pig ate at the same table as its master, having its own silver gilt service to grunt off. While out on his walks in the local countryside, Grimod was particularly solicitous when he encountered a wandering pig; removing his hat he would ask, 'Ah well, how are we then? Where are we coming from? Are we good and plump? Are we well?'

His letters to his wife in Paris bear out the obsession, the animal being referred to throughout as if it were a human being:

> Yesterday morning a young man was killed, another of them is to be killed at midnight tonight, I hope he will not have his throat cut in the château at least. That poor woman gave birth all alone, without any pain and as merrily as possible. She ate a little afterwards, her usual ordinary, some toast soaked in wine and sugar and she drank from her bottle. Mother and child are in the best of conditions.

Attached to a delivery of *boudins* (strictly speaking black or white puddings – pudding being a corruption of *boudin*; the British white pudding, however, contains no meat, the *boudin blanc* does) and sausages was a letter setting out the pedigree of the produce. 'This is to give you a foretaste of the young man who was despatched yesterday pretty early so that I would not hear his screams, his lamentable screams.' Grimod was in general fond of animals. His fondness for the Jury Dégustateur's cat is well known, as it is for that of M Le Blanc. It is related that at Villiers-sur-Orge he shared his meals with five felines.

The Restoration of the French monarchy was a disappointment to Grimod. At first he went to pay his respects to the gourmand King and patron of Beauvilliers, but the former treated him with scant courtesy. Later he came round to the idea that Louis XVIII had restored the Ancien Régime with too little regard for the remedy of its abuses, while he had little faith in the 'Charter': 'Why did he not restore everything that was good in the Ancien Régime while abolishing its abuses? The people, so weary of despots from Robespierre to Bonaparte, would have received Louis XVIII's government with open arms and we would not be at this pass.' Nor did Grimod have any sympathy for the emigrés who were so doted on by the new King: 'these bunglers who deserve the guillotine'. The ten million francs they were voted seemed to him to be an insult to those who had not chosen to desert their country in its hour of need. Perhaps he had forgotten how far he was from events in his paradise garden in Béziers? Disappointment with the last three Kings of France set in so deeply that by the end of his days he had almost come round to Napoleon: 'At least he made no effort to disguise his despotism.' Despite his antipathy to the régimes of the Restoration, Grimod played his small part in local politics, becoming for two terms a *Conseilleur Municipal*, or local councillor.

Fortunately, Grimod had two of his dearest friends as correspondents and visitors, the Marquis de Cussy and Dr Roques. Dr Roques knew of life at Villiers-sur-Orge at first hand, having stayed for a protracted period under Grimod's roof. This 'father of the gourmand church', at the age of over fifty, was on the run from one Barbeau, a jealous husband whose wife had been seduced by the doctor. Roques was the author of an excellent *Traité des Plantes Usuelles*, containing a great many anecdotes and recipes, as well as a work on the history of mushrooms. These two friends were there to console Grimod in some of the trials of his later life. One of these was the *brigandage*, the piracy, of Léonce Thiessé[6] and Horace Raisson[7] who as A. B. de Périgord produced a *Nouvel Almanach des Gourmands* in 1825, 1826 and 1827. Grimod had been encouraged himself to re-edit the work and was appalled when these young men produced one which looked to all intents and purposes to be his own work. Nor did the occasional tribute to 'our guide and grand master' succeed in pacifying the old gastronome. In the same year as this plagiarized version of his work, Grimod was faced by the publication of a far more serious work, Brillat-Savarin's *Physiologie du Goût* (translated in the most recent edition as *A Philosopher in the Kitchen*). The lawyer Brillat-Savarin[8] died a few weeks after its publication of a chill caught at a requiem mass for Louis XVI in the Basilica of Saint Denis. As a book it owes a good deal to Grimod's work, but like a good prince, Grimod deprecated himself as a kitchen skivvy beside this great chef. Grimod's self-abasement is all the more touching considering how little Brillat-Savarin acknowledged his debt to him. In only one letter does he give away having read the first volume of Grimod's *Almanach*: sending it to a friend in New York in 1804, he described it as a work 'of the rarest merit both in style and content'. Balzac, however, summed up the difference between the two writers when he described the *Physiologie du Goût* as 'a work of literature, whereas the *Almanach des Gourmands* contained only the elements'.

Doctor Roques has left us with an excellent pen-portrait of Grimod in old age which it would be as well to quote at length. Grimod had been absent from Paris and letters for so long that he was inevitably believed to be dead.

> Reading Grimod's name, our old friend Grimod de La Reynière will spring to mind, and it will be said, what a pity that this famous gourmet [*sic*] should no longer be with us! Be reassured the author of the *Almanach des Gourmands* is still of this world, he eats, he digests and sleeps in the charming valley of Longpont where we visited him only a week ago. But how he had changed! This man, once so witty, lively and original, with his unstemmable verve and sarcastic conversation, is now like one of the shadows of hell which flee at the aspect of light. If you speak to him of his *Almanach des Gourmands* or his *Manuel des Amphitryons*, he scarcely responds, he wants to die, and invokes death as the end of his torments; he knows well how to bring about his fate should it be too long in coming and yet, he is not dying, he is waiting.
>
> At nine o'clock in the morning he rings for his servants, he

complains, he screams, he exaggerates. He calls for his floury soup and eats it up. Soon his digestion begins to work and the labours of his stomach begin to react within his head, his ideas change, calm reigns, he speaks no more of death. He chats calmly asking for news of Paris and of the old gourmands who are still hale. Once his digestion has been achieved he falls silent and sleeps for several hours. When he reawakens the complaints begin afresh; he cries, he shakes, he gets carried away, he wants to die and shouts for death with clamouring calls. When the dinner hour strikes, he sits up at table, he is served and eats copiously from each of the dishes, though he says he needs nothing as his last hour approaches. At dessert his face springs to life once again, his eyebrows are raised, a little light shines in those eyes sunk deep in their orbits. How is M de Cussy, dear Doctor? Has he much longer to live? They say he is fearfully ill. They have doubtless put him on a diet, you would never have suffered such a thing, you must eat if you wish to live, isn't that true?

Finally he gets up from the table and installs himself in an immense armchair; he crosses his legs, his stumps pressed against his knees (he has no hands, merely an appendage resembling a goose's foot), and continues to ask questions, always on the subject of *gourmandise*. 'There has been a good deal of rain, there will be a fine quantity of mushrooms in the woods this autumn. What a pity it is, Doctor, that I may not accompany you on your walks in Sainte-Géneviève! I haven't the strength to walk. Aren't ceps lovely! What a sweet perfume! You will come back, won't you? We'll have some cooked for you and you will preside over their preparation.' His digestion begins, words become rarer, and more condensed, little by little his eyes close; it is ten o'clock and he is put to bed. Sleep comes to transport him to the world of dreams. He will dream of what he is to eat tomorrow.

Death came on Christmas Day 1837, at eleven o'clock in the morning. Adelaide, obliged by her husband's failing health to spend increasing amounts of time at Villiers-sur-Orge, had tucked him up in his armchair. He asked for a glass of water and, taking it in his claw, exclaimed, 'At the moment of appearing before God, I would like to be reconciled to my most mortal enemy.' With that he drank the water and died.

Perhaps he would have been happy with the fate of the hero of Marc-Antoine-Madeleine Désaugiers' verses which had crowned the *Ecole des Gourmands*:

> *Je veux que la mort me frape [sic]*
> *Au milieu d'un grand repas*
> *Qu'on m'enterre sous la nape [sic]*
> *Entre quatre larges plats,*
> *Et que sur ma tombe on mette*
> *Cette courte inscription:*
> *Ci-gît le premier poète,*
> *Mort d'une indigestion.**

It was Grimod's greatest misfortune as the first of all gastronomic writers to be superseded within his own lifetime by Brillat-Savarin. As Balzac correctly observed, the *Physiologie du Goût* reads as a work of literature whereas the *Almanach des Gourmands* is altogether too much of a *pot-pourri*. It was also his bad luck to be, as Roques described him, 'that illustrious debris of the eighteenth century' who was so much out of sympathy with the modern age. He could not understand Carême,[9] the greatest cook of his time, as he failed to conceive of the possibility of a cook embracing the roles of pastry, oven and spit with equal dexterity. But if his contribution was limited it must be said that he succeeded in doing what he set out to do: 'To save French cookery from the shipwreck of the Revolution, and to resurrect the altar of Comus on the debris of the agapes of the Jacobins' (Monselet). The first man to treat the subject 'with all the dignity it deserved', Grimod added a new form of eloquence to the French language which has in turn been adopted by every civilized language in the world. Nor will he be the last to realize the vast potential for satire and moral commentary which can be found in the battery of the kitchen.

---

*I want death to take me/In the middle of a grand meal/And that I should be buried under the tablecloth/Between four large dishes/And that it should be written on my grave/This short inscription/Here lies the first poet/Who died of an indigestion.

Grimod's Food

Le premier devoir d'un Amphitrion.

I

The French Revolution, so cataclysmic in every sphere, had a profound effect on the very nature of eating. One of its longest-lasting consequences was to alter the times of meals, creating two *déjeuners* where one had existed before, and shifting the main meal, or dinner, to the evening. The *souper*, in its heyday of the Regency, was a meal taken at around eight; in the Empire it was consumed at about midnight.

Grimod was in no doubt as to the cause of this *décalage*. It was the result of the descent on Paris of the deputies of the Estates General and their legislative successors from 1789 onwards. Having left their households behind them in the provinces, the politicians were obliged to eat out. The need to supply their hungry bellies with refreshment encouraged the growth of *restauration*, which had received an initial thrust from the emigration of the grandees, and the necessity for their *cordon bleus* of finding some other means of surviving. Grimod makes the further point that restaurant-going achieved a respectablility by virtue of the fact it resembled the British habit of eating at the tavern. In the initial stages of the Revolution at least, the anglomania of the pre-Revolutionary years retained its grip on the intelligentsia as well as on certain members of the liberal nobility.

As the *séances* of the Constituent and Legislative assemblies drew to a close at 5 p.m., the main meal of the day was necessarily delayed until the close of business. The need for nourishment in the middle of the day led to the serving of *déjeuners à la fourchette* in the restaurants and houses of the Empire. The expression, it seems, came into being around 1804 at the restaurant of Madame Hardy in the Boulevard des Italiens. Here you choose your cutlets or kidneys from the display in the window, the meat being then being put on a fork and grilled.

Obviously the new eating agenda was not established in a day and there were, for a number of years, as many variants on the theme as can be found in modern Britain, where dinner can take place at any time between twelve noon and ten at night and supper any time between seven in the evening and one o'clock in the morning. In 1800 it was said that the artisan dined at 2 p.m., the wholesale merchant at three, the clerk at four, the *nouveau riche* at five, the minister or rich bachelor at six and Talleyrand at eight. In the *Ecole des Gourmands*, a light-weight satire based on the life of Grimod de La Reynière, by René Alissan de Chazet and others, Doctor Piquassiette (i.e. 'scrounger', a non-practising doctor possibly based on Grimod's friend Dr Gastaldy, the President of the Jury Dégustateur), demonstrates the advantages of the system.

> *D'abord á midi,*
> *Tout près de Bercy,*
> *Chez un vieux curé, je dîne.*
> *Près de l'Arsénal,*
> *Chez un Général,*
> *Vers les deux heures, je dîne.*
> *Une heure après,*
> *Dans le Marais, je dîne.*
> *Un peu plus tard,*
> *Quartier Favart, je dîne,*
> *Faubourg Saint Germain,*
> *Retrouvant ma faim,*
> *Vers les cinq heures, je dîne.**

Piquassiette thus moves relentlessly through Paris from east to west, cadging meals from the clergy, the military, the merchant community, the theatrical set and finally, on reaching 'the noble faubourg', the aristocracy.

The first or *'petit' dejeuner*, the equivalent of our breakfast, was a modest affair, though we are told that it could involve chicken wings and slices of ham. In general, it was similar to the sort of meal we might take today. It could, for example, be as simple as a cup of chocolate, for the sedentary man of letters, like Grimod

---

*First at midday, hard by Bercy, at the house of an old priest, I dine. Near the Arsénal, at a General's, I dine at around two. An hour later, I dine in the Marais. A little later on, in the Favart Quarter, I dine. Feeling hungry again, in the Faubourg Saint Germain, at five o'clock, I dine.

himself. Elsewhere, the writer gives us a hint of more substantial fare, but of the same 'genre'. The choice lay between tea, coffee, chocolate, *bavaroises*, rolls or toast taken at about 9 a.m.

Grimod's personal choice has a more predictably gargantuan ring to it: 'Ten cups of tea with cream or six cups of milky coffee or four cups of chocolate, accompanied by some Brussels biscuits, toast and butter, some bread rolls as they make them in the rue Dauphine, or some of M Rouget's *flûtes**, these at their best might lubricate a gourmand's palate.'

By 1800, the second 'breakfast', i.e. lunch, had evolved into something quite lavish, something which came increasingly to annoy the author of the *Almanach*. By about twelve-thirty or one o'clock a mahogany table was covered with ten sorts of cold cut, and a number of different bottles of wine. A more elaborate meal is set out in the following menu:

Some baskets of Marennes oysters

★ ★ ★

Mutton kidneys

★ ★ ★

Pigeon breasts disguised as cutlets

★ ★ ★

Pyramids of sausages and white and black *boudins*

★ ★ ★

Pigs' trotters stuffed with pistachio nuts

★ ★ ★

A capon cooked in rock salt from the Marmite Perpetuelle

After this light lunch, in theory there was the possibility of a *goûter* or high tea. This intermediary meal had already fallen into disuse and become what it is today, children's tea. 'Since we have started dining in Paris at six o'clock in the evening there are no

---

*Today the *flûte* is a thinner version of the traditional *baguette* or French stick. M Rouget's were probably as different from these as the *petits pains de la rue Dauphine* were from modern bread rolls.

113

more *goûters*, few people besides infants and schoolchildren sit down to this meal.'

Dinner, the main meal of the day, could go on for anything between three and five hours, the latter being the fixed duration of a session of the Jury Dégustateur. Grimod was something of a reformist when it came to the ancient formality surrounding the meal, especially the order of service, which had been handed down from generation to generation since the *grand couvert* of Louis XIV. Grimod's very sensible criticisms of the ritual, which had far more to do with the aesthetic presentation of the table than with the quality of the dishes served, were little heeded in their day. In formal dinners, the *service à la Russe* was not introduced until after the second Empire.

A contemporary grand dinner was composed of four services: the first was made up of soups, hors d'oeuvres, *relevés* and entrées. There might also be a visit from some savoury flying saucer or *assiette volante*, i.e. things that must be eaten as soon as they are taken off the spit, out of the oven or off the hob; Grimod gives these examples: 'minute' cutlets, steaks, chicken croquettes, ortolans and other little birds on skewers, little pâtés, cheese *ramequins* or any form of soufflé. The second service comprised roasts and salads, with the obligatory *grosses pièces* decorating the ends of the table. In general, these remained untouched, for they were more to please the eye than the appetite and could be anything from a vast *mille-feuille* to a Nérac terrine, a heap of crayfish or a blue carp. The third service involved cold pâtés and *entremets*, either sweet or savoury; strangely M le Blanc's much lauded calf's-kidney pie is listed as a sweet *entremet*. The final service was our modern dessert, with fruits, *compôtes*, jams, biscuits, macaroons, cheeses, petits fours and sweets as well as ices. At a large, formal dinner, the first service could contain anything up to a hundred dishes. In general a colour, either white or brown, predominated, which led Grimod to categorize dinners as 'blondes or brunettes'. This colour consideration became universal in nineteenth-century cooking. One has only to think of Charles Ryder's dyed-in-the-wool father in *Brideshead Revisited* with his tasteless meals varying only in colour, from white to pink. The greatest drawback with this sort of meal was the *embarras de choix*, and the not usually reticent Grimod complains that the meal gets cold while the diner dithers. Even within the structure of each service there was an oppressive formality. For a meal composed of eight entrées, it was a strict requirement to provide two different soups, two large *relevés*, two roasts, two large cold dishes, two plates of vegetables and a mixed salad. Most appetites were wholly staunched by the end of the second service and of the *entremets*; Grimod notes, 'It is rare enough to see anyone touch them.' If they did, he informs us, it was only *par politesse*.

It is not hard to conceive of the inconveniences of the system, which allowed dishes to get cold while the confused guest endeavoured to discover whether he had sampled this or that, or the studied gourmand sought out the more prized delicacies which might have been lurking in some poorly charted area of the table before some abstemious party-pooper. There was a strict geography to the table which meant the timid were quite likely to confine themselves to whatever came within their reach, while the gourmand reached for some splendid delicacy, especially if there were a lot of people at table. Grimod pioneered his own reforms at the sessions of the Jury Dégustateur. Here each dish was presented separately, 'a true refinement in the art of good living. It is a method of eating a lot of food, hot and at one's leisure.' At the same time in another part of the city, the Hôtel Thélusson in the rue de Provence, the Emperor Alexander's envoy, Prince Kourakin,[1] was introducing his guests to the Russian method which is used in French meals today. It was not, however, made popular in the homes of the bourgeoisie until around 1870, when the great chef Urbain Dubois introduced it to his public in his two *chef d'oeuvres*, *La Cuisine Classique* and *La Cuisine Artistique*.

In another way Grimod sought to simplify the meal by reducing the role of the hors d'oeuvres to that of an aperitif. He suggests serving little gherkins, onions, Genoese beans, anchovies and pickled oysters with the *coup d'avant*. For those who had only had a three-hour dinner or who had forgone it altogether by going to the theatre or the opera, there remained that lovers' meal of supper. Grimod informs us that it started at ten and ended no later than midnight. There was no soup or *bouillie* (i.e. *pot au feu*), just a twenty-five-pound roast (!), eight entrées and six hors d'oeuvres. 'Ices are strictly necessary,' Grimod notes.

II

Grimod was rarely an inventor of the dishes he enumerates in the *Manuel des Amphitryons* and elsewhere in the *Almanach des Gourmands*. But then again it was never the primary purpose of either book to serve in the kitchen; rather it was intended more to inspire the Amphitryon than his *cordon bleu*. The concoctions which figure in the menu suggestions of the former work are nearly all the products of the aristocratic cuisine of the time of Louis XV, a fact that is borne out by their names, which pay tribute to some of the great figures of the court rather than the cooks who invented them. For a small consideration, a *cordon bleu* was open to yielding up his discovery to some lady of the court, while a subtle sensuality might connect the exquisite morsel in question with the important person whose name it bore, making Louis *le Bien-Aimé*, for example, even more kindly disposed towards a female favourite.

Very few of these aristocratic dishes are still in the repertoire of the modern cook, though there is an echo, say, in the retaining of names like Mirepoix (a basis for a number of sauces made from a *ragoût* of finely chopped carrot, onion, celery and ham) or Soubise (an onion sauce). Their eighteenth-century counterparts were elaborate things. The Soubise sauce was originally devised as a dressing for cutlets, while the Mirepoix added piquancy to quails in a pastry case. Grimod's menus read like some mid-eighteenth-century *Bottin Mondain*, with all their courtly associations: roast leg of lamb *à la* (Duchesse de) Mailly, baby rabbit fillets *à la* (Duchesse de) Berry (the rakish Regent's no less scandalous daughter), chicken *à la* Maréchal de Villeroy, soufflé *à la* Mongolfier (an omelette soufflé, with obvious allusions to lightness coming from the name of the great balloonist), eggs Bernis (the Cardinal's eggs were dressed on a purée of chicken with a sauce *à la suprême* with asparagus tips). *Mahonnaise* or mayonnaise was associated with the victor of Port-Mahon, the

Duc de Richelieu, who was credited with bringing the first bottle of Château Lafite to court (a discovery during his time as Governor of Guyenne). A fattened pullet *à la* Montmorency celebrated the famous cherries which grew on the Duke's estate. Other favourites were Chartreuses *à la* Mauconseil, and chicken fillets *à la* Bellevue, not forgetting Queen Marie-Leczinska's claim to culinary fame, the *bouchée à la reine*.

While most of these recipes would not be popular today, inundated as they often are with heavy floury sauces, Grimod does make a few simpler suggestions as to how to serve food which can be prepared in a modern kitchen. With just that kitchen in mind they are presented here not as entrées, *relevés* and *rôts*, but in a more convenient modern idiom.

Grimod was at pains to tell us that he was himself no cook. In the short-lived *Journal des Gourmands et des Belles*, where many of these recipes originate, he writes, 'Although we have never donned the apron, and though the theory of gastronomy be rather more familiar to us than the practice of cooking, we are not, however, so unfamiliar with the workings of the stove as not to be able to acquit our responsibilities *vis-à-vis* our readers.' The recipes have been presented with as few changes as possible, keeping as often as I could to Grimod's style. From time to time I have, however, made a suggestion based on my own personal experience of the dish.

SALADS

Grimod was for the reduction of the numerous dishes served as hors d'oeuvres, preferring to offer certain highly flavoured foodstuffs *en apéritif*. As vegetal hors d'oeuvres he suggests melons, figs and radishes to complement pickles, while on the more substantial side, he returns to the staple of his famous supper of 1782 by suggesting *charcuterie*, the by-products of his much-loved pigs: giblets, cutlets, sausages, black and white puddings, etc. Salads were the inseparable companion of the roast, but some of his very lucid ideas on the subject would make good openers to a modern meal. To a basic lettuce Grimod adds tarragon, burnet, beetroot, cucumber, gherkins, capers, nasturtium seeds and anchovies. Endive, a late summer salad, is simply served with a crust of bread well rubbed with garlic, which is called the *chapon* or capon. *Scarole* lettuce has no need of the capon.

Beetroot is served sliced thinly with lamb's lettuce and celeriac cut into cubes. It requires a lot of vinegar. For a highly distinguished salad, the same cubed celeriac (parboiled) is served with a sauce made up simply of a good oil, well beaten into an excellent mustard. Grimod would have recommended Maille, sadly he is not around to give an opinion of their present range. Cress is a winter salad; the dressing should have more vinegar than oil. The ordinary lettuce should not be eaten before the end of Lent; 'one must wait almost till Easter before it is worthy of our sensuality.' He suggests serving it with hard-boiled eggs cut into quarters, and anchovy fillets and a lot of (good olive) oil.

The awakening of the writer's appetite in Béziers made him one of the first ambassadors of Provençal cuisine to the north of France (along with the tomato, which made its début with the Marseillais deputies in 1789 and the Frères Provenceaux, whose Paris restaurant was the first north of Lyon to serve such southern favourites as the *brandade de morue*). Grimod's salad of little cooked onions has something of the Niçoise about it. The onions are accompanied by little gherkins, anchovy fillets, aromatic herbs, some pieces of marinated tunny, boiled egg yolks, capers and stuffed olives, 'delicious and extremely appetizing,' he adds. For fowl or game: notably fat chickens, pheasant, spit-roast partridge cut into fillets, etc, Grimod suggests the following, which could be useful for left-over meat: 'Arrange them in compartments with a chopped lettuce in the bottom of the plate [bowl]; on the other layers, arrange more lettuce...some anchovy fillets and finely chopped gherkins which enormously increase the value of a chicken salad, and make the taste far more piquant.'

SOUP À LA CAMERANI

The *Almanach* gives one or two ideas for soups of varying complication. These rarely seem practicable for the modern kitchen where few have a pot sufficiently large to accommodate a capon, half a dozen partridges and a piece of brisket weighing several pounds. One of the recipes he gives, *Potage à la Jambe de*

Bois, has been revived by the three-star chef Paul Bocuse at his restaurant outside Lyon. It must be one of the most lavish recipes for soup invented, and, I am sure, *vaut le détour*. A soup in name only is the *Potage à la Camerani*, which is more like a substantial pasta dish. It was named after Bartolomeo-Andrea Camerani, an actor at the Comédie-Italienne to whom Grimod dedicated the second year of the *Almanach*.

> Take some real Neapolitan macaroni, some excellent Parmesan cheese, some Gournay or Isigny butter, and about two dozen fat chicken livers, celery, and any sort of vegetable from the kitchen garden (carrots, parsnips, turnips, leeks, etc) .... finely chop the livers and the vegetables, cook them altogether in a saucepan with the butter.
>
> At the same time blanch the macaroni, season it with pepper and spices and let it drain.
>
> Take next the tureen in which you intend serving the soup; place at the bottom a layer of the macaroni, then a layer of the mixture followed by a layer of grated Parmesan. You then begin again in the same order, building up the levels of the construction to the height of the tureen. Place it then on a low heat and allow to simmer for a reasonable length of time.
>
> This *Potage à la Camerani* is a delicious dish, and the cause of a great many indigestions. It is the King of Soups.

MOCK TURTLE SOUP

In a rare moment of compassion towards the hated English, Grimod gives a recipe for a mock turtle soup.

> Like all races, even the least civilized, they [the English] have one or two national *ragoûts*, about which they boast, more in the spirit of patriotism than from conviction. The French adore novelties, and are always kind enough to envy those dishes which their neighbours prize, at a far higher value than their worth. Such is the case with this mock turtle soup, which has had Parisian tongues wagging for several

years now, and on the subject of which so many giddy minds engage in uninformed debate.

Many wise people, who are exempt from all prejudice as far as cooking is concerned, have asked us to enlighten them as to the nature of this recipe, that they might establish an opinion on this famous dish. We have now procured the formula through the agency of a great gourmand (an ex-naval officer, which explains a good deal), who has spent a considerable period of time in London. Here then is the recipe as given by one of the best cooks of that city and translated, word by word, from the English [sic].

Take a good calf's head, which you must boil long enough to be able to remove the flesh from the bone.

In a well-made *roux* [butter or fat, flour, water or stock], cook a veal knuckle with a bouquet garni, onions and the grated peel of a lemon, season with salt and pepper. Put in the juice of a lemon. This will make you a good sauce. Sieve through a fine muslin or silk cloth. Mix into this *coulis* the brains of your calf, which you have set aside, oysters, a little anchovy essence, a good glassful of Malaga wine, the juice of two Genoese lemons and then put in your finely chopped calf's head with a few chicken breasts.

Let the head continue cooking in its seasoning until it is truly tender. Add then a dozen chicken and meat balls, and the same number of eggballs (see below), add truffles and morels.

The eggballs mentioned in the recipe, represent the turtles' eggs. They are made in the following manner. Take some hard-boiled yolks, in sufficient quantity. Mash them well, adding a little nutmeg, lemon juice, pepper and salt. Mix the ingredients and pound them together with enough cold butter to make a quite solid paste. Make the balls about the size of a pigeon's egg and nicely round. Put them into the ragoût only a few minutes before serving.

This supposed soup is presented in England in a tureen or a turtle shell. This is lined with pastry, and the whole dish is then put in the oven to brown. The enlightened gourmand, to whom we owe the details of this recipe, suggests, however, that a French cook would be better advised to serve it in a *timbale* or in a pastry case wrought in the shape of a turtle shell, and we think he is correct in his reasoning.

Likewise he informs us that the pepper used by the English is of the red sort, but he is right in saying that this seasoning might prove too strong for the French *délicatesse*. However, as this *ragoût* has need of spices, it could still be included, though we would counsel, in small doses.

So here is the unpublished recipe for the much-vaunted mock turtle soup, which in our opinion, must be greatly inferior to the famous *Potage à la Camerani*, and just as expensive. For our part, we invite some celebrated Amphitryon (such as M Haller, for example), to have it made up in his home, conforming exactly to the recipe as set out above. If the dish is successful, he will have achieved the glory of having given French nationality to a dish which had up till then been advanced by the English every time they wished to exalt their cooking to the detriment of our own.

GARBURE

This filling soup is still common in the south-west of France, and Grimod must have encountered it while staying with his aunt in Béziers. It is a filling dish and would easily account for the main course of a modern meal. The writer gives two recipes, one with meat for feast days, the other *en maigre* for fasting.

> You will require a good meat essence, or if you do not have such a thing, a good stock. Take some cabbages and cut them into quarters. Blanch them then wash them in cold water. Drain them well by pressing, and tie up each quarter separately with twine. Line a saucepan or braising-dish with fat bacon, then arrange your cabbage on top with some small pieces of bacon, some pieces of ham or one large piece of the same, veal slices or a knuckle. Cover the whole with more fat bacon and add carrots, onions and a bouquet garni. Moisten the garbure with your stock and set it to cook on a gentle heat.
>
> When the dish is well cooked, cut some bread and simmer it awhile in your stock. Drain your cabbage through a clean cloth, pressing out any surplus liquid. Transfer the cabbage to a silver tureen, or a clay one capable of being put in an

oven, and sprinkle it with Parmesan and Gruyère mixed in equal parts. The garbure should be built up in layers of cabbage, simmered bread, cheese, etc., until you have filled the tureen. Remember that the cabbage should form the top layer, coated with a great quantity of cheese. Thus prepared, put your dish into the oven for the cheese to get crisp.

For those who do not like their soup as solid as Grimod obviously did, he recommends serving it with its stock in a separate bowl.

The lenten, or fast-day soup, obviously avoids contact with meat. It is made from a *maigre* stock, i.e. split peas, carrots, onions and celery, which you sweat in a pan with a little butter. When the vegetables begin to catch add some (vegetable) stock. Grimod recommends adding frogs' legs, carp or tench. Instead of fat bacon, use butter.

ONION SOUP *À LA* CUSSY

Most of Grimod's soups have a curiously unappetizing heaviness to them, the contemporary *potage* being a more substantial dish than the soup we think of; for those whose digestions fear a Jerusalem artichoke soup, a chestnut soup with a *coulis* of turnips or crayfish ('a good *coulis d'ecrivisses* is worthy of the table of the Gods') would be a terrifying prospect. Grimod's friend and latter-day table companion, the Marquis de Cussy, made a simple and excellent onion soup in Lent, which has been set down in the book of another of Grimod's friends from his declining years, Dr Roques. Though the soup was meant to be a penance, we are told by Roques that the Marquis always had a piece of salmon and a bundle of asparagus put aside in case the flesh should prove too weak – 'My friend La Reynière says that soup is the prologue to dinner; well a good work needs no preface.'

> Take twenty small onions, peel them and cut them into thin slices. Put them in a saucepan with a knob of butter and a little sugar. Stir them until they are golden brown then add a decent quantity of good stock and bread. Just before serving the soup, throw in a couple of small glasses of old Cognac.

STUFFED TOMATOES *À LA* GRIMOD

This also comes from Roques' *Nouveau Traité des Plantes Usuelles*. It is a simple recipe, and not very different from the *tomates farcies* that you get in most French households. At best if makes a pleasant enough hors d'oeuvre, or a main course that is easy to make and nourishing when you have not got important guests coming to dinner.

Choose large, continental tomatoes. Remove the pulp and fill them with a mixture of sausage meat (minced lamb could be nicer), garlic, parsley, spring onions and tarragon. Put them in a pie dish and cover them with breadcrumbs. Serve in this same dish when they are cooked. They can be sprinkled with lemon juice.

VEGETABLE PÂTÉS AND PASTA

Only about ten years ago, it seems, every Parisian *traiteur* was marketing his own brand of *pâté de légumes* generally lurking under some sinister green *coulis*. Grimod enthused about vegetable pâtés in 1804, which, he informs us, were invented 'a long time before' ... 'little peas, young broad beans, baby carrots and French beans at their most tender are arranged in compartments, making a dish even more delicious than the cream which forms the basis of their seasoning'. Also highly reminiscent of recent Parisian fashion is the writer's fondness for Italian pasta, vermicelli, lasagne and macaroni. Pasta had the virtue of being edible both *en gras* and *en maigre,* i.e. on feast days or fasts. Vermicelli, he suggests, are the perfect mattress for a boiled chicken. As for macaroni 'neither butter nor cheese should be spared' ... but as an economy 'one may mix, half and half Parmesan and Gruyère – only the most developed of gourmets will notice'. The latter cheese doubtless came in handy for the cheese creams, *ramequins de Bourgogne*, which Grimod so much admired from the *patissier* Rouget, and which seem to have given his digestion considerable trouble.

HERRINGS

It is unfortunate that the bloated herring should not in general enjoy a sufficiently good reputation to be admitted to opulent tables, and that the vanity of the rich should have relegated this fish to the kitchens of the populace. For, if it is true to say that this food is not among the most salubrious, or if its bitter nature is only suitable for robust stomachs, it must however be said in its defence, that it makes up for more than one of the drawbacks of its preparation. It reawakens the languid appetite, and, in the liveliest way, tickles the nervous crests of the palate. Served as an hors d'oeuvres, it will honour your entrées. Cut into small pieces and thrown into a salad, it will spice up those which are naturally too mild, like those made from lamb's lettuce or beetroot, for example; a useful resource in more than one circumstance, and one which should never be entirely proscribed. Moreover, it has one excellent virtue, which has not escaped the notice of the vinographers, that it has a singular manner of provoking thirst, and is, at the same time, highly indulgent as to the quality of the wine served. From the foregoing we may conclude, that like a great many intelligent people, the bloated herring, despite all its faults, is in general superior to its reputation.

BLOATED HERRINGS À LA DUBLIN

This has nothing to do with the Irish city of that name. Grimod is at pains to point out that the dish is of Belgian origin, and that the hitherto unpublished recipe was brought back from Brussels by a young actor called Dublin.

> ... there is a method of making an hors d'oeuvre which both adds to the qualities [of the herring] and removes a number of its defects. This dish is all at once excellent, and so easy to prepare that any food lover may give himself the pleasure curled up beside his hearth, making his own lunch on those days when, prior to a grand dinner, he requires a singular dose of appetite.

Make a case out of a doubled-over sheet of strong Dutch paper [replace by aluminium foil], which you make capable of holding eight herrings. Butter both without and within [no need to butter the outside of your tinfoil].

Take eight well-selected bloated herrings. Cut off the heads and tails and remove the skin and backbone. When you have trimmed them well, cut them in two lengthwise, making two fillets from each fish.

Arrange them side by side in the case, between each fillet putting a lump of good cold butter, which has been previously mixed with herbs. Add a quantity of chopped mushrooms – about a punnet is required for eight herrings – parsley, spring onions, shallots, a clove of garlic chopped very small and ground pepper. A dash of virgin [olive] oil may be added. Sprinkle the whole with fine breadcrumbs [fold over the aluminium foil and roll the edges], put under a hot grill ...

When the herrings are cooked, remove the case from the grill. Serve them at once with the juice of one lemon.

When this little hors d'oeuvre is made with care, it is a delicious dish ...

SALT COD *BRANDADE*

Brandade de merluche or *brandade de morue* was one of the specialities of the restaurant Les Frères Provenceaux, the ambassador of meridonal cuisine to the Parisians until its disappearance from the arcades of the Palais Royal in 1869. Some writers, however, make out that it was Grimod, taking yet another discovery from his aunt, the Comtesse de Beausset's table in Béziers, who introduced it to the north. The President, Adolphe Thiers, was so partial to this dish that he had pots of the stuff sent up from Nîmes. When forbidden to eat it on the advice of his doctors, he took to hiding the pots in between the books in his famous library, to be gobbled up at any time on the pretext of consulting some weighty tome.

Take a good piece of salt cod and soak it in several waters for a period of twenty-four hours in order to remove the salt and soften the fish. Put it in a pan full of cold water, but remove from the heat as soon as the water begins to boil. Pour off the water and remove the cod, replacing it by butter, olive oil, parsley and garlic. Melt this mixture over a gentle flame. Remove the skin from the cod and crumble the fish into small pieces, add to the pan piece by piece. You should add oil, butter or milk when it begins to thicken. Grimod adds that you can make a green version of this dish by using spinach in lieu of parsley. 'You must never stop stirring the pan, else you will have a *béchamel* instead of a *brandade*.'

This is still a popular delicacy in Provence, where it is sold in the fish shops of the market on Fridays, to be eaten with garlicky mayonnaise or *aïoli*, as a middle-class alternative to the *maigre purée Parmentier* of the peasants. Strictly speaking olive oil is more authentic than milk or cream. It is extremely rich.

MME GUICHARD'S FISH STEW

Another fish dish which delighted Grimod was the *matelote* or fish stew which was made by the quayside at Bercy, then outside the walls of Paris. And Grimod never missed an opportunity to mention the one made by Mme Guichard in the itineraries attached to the volumes of the *Almanach des Gourmands* (though in later years he had cause to reproach her for resting on her laurels). A *matelote* is literally only a fish stew prepared by the fisherman's wife. The Jardin Anglais at Bercy became a sort of *ad hoc* pleasure garden at the Revolution with the emigration of its noble proprietors, the de Malons; it has had a chequered history since. For more than a hundred years it was the home of all the cheap wine earmarked for Parisian consumption, a captive ocean of the *gros rouge qui tâche* and the *petits blancs* of the cafés. About ten years ago the wine seeped away. Bercy is now the site of a sports stadium and an opera house.

> A *matelote* is not a simple carp and eel stew, it is a masterpiece of the human mind and almost as difficult to produce as an epic poem ... It is woman's cooking which demands continual attention, eternal vigilance, extreme

patience, scrupulous cleanliness, undivided care ... A *matelote* is the sole thing of this base world – with the exception of a good joint – which must not be delayed two minutes. One may wait for a *matelote*. One must never let it wait for you.

Take an eel, a medium-sized carp, a small pike, a barbel and a monkfish. Scale them, gut them and rinse them. Cut them into chunks and arrange them on the bottom of a not too substantial cooking-pot or cauldron. Add salt, pepper, and a bouquet garni of parsley, spring onion, thyme and bay (these last two ingredients in prudent proportions), two cloves of garlic and a clove. Pour in some good red wine, just enough to cover the fish. As soon as the wine begins to boil, add a glass of good brandy. Turn up the heat and let it cook for a quarter of an hour.

Take the cauldron off the hob, arrange the chunks of fish on a plate and keep them hot. Make a sauce immediately by uniting the cooking-juices with about a quarter of a pound of butter, worked into two tablespoons of flour. Incorporate some little onions and mushrooms that you have cooked apart in some butter.

Allow to boil for two or three minutes, then pour it over the fish. Decorate the dish with fried croutons, or if you can find any in season, some crayfish.

Obviously this dish can be made with almost any combination of fish; recipes vary enormously in different parts of France where the stew is made from whatever comes to hand. In Avignon, for example, it is made from shad (one of Grimod's favourite fish) and trout; in Honfleur sea fish are used, turbot and barbel; in Ambroise on the Loire, pike and shad; in the Bourbonnais, eels, barbel, little pike, carp and tench.

SKATE- OR COD-LIVER CANAPÉS

Another fish dish the writer rejoiced in was skate-liver canapés, 'one of the canapés a gourmand likes most to stretch out on, especially in Lent'. Cod liver could be used rather than skate.

Cut some dry bread into soldiers. Dip them in hot olive oil.

> Melt some excellent butter in a pan and put in the skate [or cod] livers, some desalted anchovy fillets, a little oil, parsley, spring onion, a small glove of garlic, finely chopped shallots, capers, also cut small, salt, pepper and a pinch of mixed spice. Stir well.
>
> To make your canapés, put a bed of the fine herb mixture on each of the pieces of toast once it has cooled down, then some skate [or cod] liver and some anchovy fillets. Add a further layer of fine herbs. Finish off with some breadcrumbs.
>
> Grill the canapés for a few minutes and serve them with squeezed lemon juice.

This dish can also be made with desalted anchovy fillets. Grimod calls them 'aphrodisiac canapés'.

MACKEREL

One suspects that the frequent allusions to mackerel in the *Almanach des Gourmands* had something to do with the possible *double entendre* surrounding the name of the fish in French, where *maquereau* means pimp or a bawd (Grimod is at pains to tell us that since the Revolution the fish are everywhere well received). For the whole fish, the writer recommends they be slit along the back, stuffed with a herbal butter (i.e. one into which herbs have been worked) and simply grilled. 'But if the whole fish has no need of finery, this is not so for the fillets.'

> Part cook them in a pan with some stock and half a glass of Champagne and a little excellent olive oil, then arrange them on a dish with some *maitre d'hôtel* butter [i.e. with parsley worked into it], spring onions, shallots, salt, pepper and a little nutmeg, cover the dish and put it back on the heat for eighteen minutes. Drain off the butter, and pour in a little clarified veal stock, allow it to simmer a little while and don't forget, when serving, to squeeze the juice of an orange over the fish. The benign acidity of the fruit is well suited to the naturally gentle and sensitive nature of the mackerel.

WHITING FILLETS À LA CUSSY

Another of the Marquis de Cussy's recipes is this one for whiting fillets. It requires a truffle. If finding, or affording, this 'foretaste of paradise' proves impossible, some sort of pungent mushroom can be used. Dried Italian ceps – *porcini* – are now quite easy to find.

Cut the fillets from six large whiting [or ask the fishmonger to do it for you] and trim them. Make a forcemeat with the flesh of three more whiting of a similar size, pounding the fish with a mortar and pestle, after which you pass it through a fine sieve. Pound an equal quantity of white bread which you have soaked in milk, mix it in with the pounded whiting with an equivalent amount of fresh butter. Season with salt and pepper and a little nutmeg. Add the truffle cut into little cubes, beat in two egg whites. Place the fillets, stuffed with the forcemeat, on an oven dish and put them in the oven. Cook for half an hour.

SALMON IN CHAMPAGNE À LA GRIMOD

Sweat the whole fish in a fish kettle or a large pan [a part or steak of the fish might be more economically used], cover it with two bottles of excellent champagne and when cooked serve with baby turkey wings and a dozen freshwater crayfish cooked in the same nectar. 'As you see, this fish is something of a drunk; what's more, it will only drink the best.'

III

MEAT, POULTRY AND GAME

Grimod mentions any number of tantalizing-sounding meat dishes without giving us any details of how to prepare them. They have, in general, a period feeling to them. Take, for example, 'Loin of Veal in Cream and Breadcrumbs'; 'Quarter of Venison barded with Anchovies and cooked in its stock', 'Sirloin *à l'Anglaise* with a Sauce *Piquant*', etc. Some, on the other hand, could be straight from the menu of some go-ahead star-studded French cook,'*Emincé* (i.e. thinly sliced) Chicken in Truffles', 'Hot Pâtés with Malaga Wine', 'Hot Beef Palate Pâtés', 'Chicken and Red Partridge *Timbales*', 'Hot Pâtés with Chives', 'Veal and Ham *Timbales*', 'Veal Kidney Pies', 'Salt Cod Vol-au-Vents', 'Macaroni *Timbales*', etc., etc. The '*Timbales Mignonettes*' which he discovers on his Parisian rounds in the fourth year of the *Almanach* sound quite mouth-watering in his description '... the pastry more airy than light, filled with a ragoût which is a veritable lilliputian encyclopaedia of what is the best and most succulent product of every season ... in this one the dominant flavour is that of truffles, in that, it is fish, here ham, there game, etc. ... as varied as nature itself, as light as zephyrs, and as delicate as beauty.'

BEEF

Grimod's early passion for beef sirloin did not desert him in later days. Nor did he alter his views on the Spartan presentation of the meat to any considerable extent. At the *Déjeuners Philosophiques* the huge joint had been simply roasted, perhaps according to the method employed by the curious M Aze, i.e. suspended on a string before a naked flame. Another bizarre method advanced is that of cooking the joint in candle fat. In mentioning beef, Grimod shows a rare compassion towards the English, noting, presumably on someone else's authority, that it is worth crossing the Channel to savour the delights of an English beefsteak. Some people might be surprised to learn the reputation of England as regards the cooking of roasts, in both the eighteenth and nineteenth century – that the meat was virtually raw. Smollett found French beef 'boiled to rags', while Alfred Michiels, a Frenchman travelling in England in the 1840s, had this to say (*En Angleterre*, Paris 1844) about the *rosbif* of old England:

> I ordered something to eat. A clumsy youth brought me five forks, four knives and a profusion of little pots full of spices. There was some pimento and some pickled cauliflowers and other sauces from that side of the Channel, hardly pleasing to our tongues ... [all of a sudden] I caught sight of a mountain of beef, two waiters buckled under the weight of it. It turned out to be one of those illustrious 'roast beefs' so vaunted in the four corners of the globe. It weighed without doubt twenty-five pounds. Such a mass of flesh made me feel ill. To add to my misfortune, it had been cooked five days past, inn-keepers in the neighbourhood of London having recourse to the spit once a week during the winter months. Well, if it was burnt on the outside, it was perfectly raw inside, in such a way that you had to make a choice between eating a sort of animal coal or digesting raw flesh like a Hottentot. I cursed this English lack of *savoir-faire* under my breath, and attempted to put a brave face on this cannibal offering before me. I began to understand at last, the usefulness of the seasonings I had so recently spurned, but even with the aid of these perfidious vials, I could not go ahead with the meal. I pushed away the enormous dish and ordered something else.

Grimod had no such scruples about eating rare beef, he positively recommends it: 'Those divine sirloins from the Auvergne or the Cotentin ... these sirloins when well hung, and cooked in the English way, that is, rare, and accompanied by a stimulating sauce composed of Maille anchovies and little capers, make a first-rate dish.'

ANCHOVY SAUCE

Grimod intended this sauce as an accompaniment to roast beef. It is based on the old Roman relish of *garum*, which was made from rotting fish; in Indo-Chinese cooking a similar sauce exists, called *ngo loc*. *Garum* was generally made from the rotting innards of a tunny fish. Modern readers might agree with Pallet, who was subjected to just such a sauce in Smollett's *Peregrine Pickle*: 'Christ in Heaven! What beastly fellows these Romans were!' Grimod's sauce uses fresh anchovies and is altogether tamer.

> Wash your anchovies well in vinegar, then remove the backbones. Chop them very fine and put them in a pan with a clear veal or ham stock, pepper, salt, nutmeg and mixed spice. When the sauce begins to boil allow it to reduce to a suitable thickness. This sauce is ideal for the roast, especially a sirloin or hare cooked on the spit. Another method is to use the juice of these meats, a little stock, some coarsely chopped anchovies, capers, fine herbs, tarragon, pepper, salt and vinegar. 'When this sauce has been made well it would make you eat an elephant.'

Like *garum* the sauce should 'excite the appetite and facilitate the digestion'. He did not think highly of the rump. This is recommended for the *bouillie*, i.e. boiling-beef.

LAMB À LA SERVIETTE

Grimod believed like the rest of his contemporaries that lamb was a dull, indigestible meat and lacking in sufficient flavour to justify its early death. Possibly the definition of 'lamb' has changed over the years, and Grimod and his world were referring to milk-fed animals. None the less, in the interests of science he gives a recipe for dealing with sheep's young, though I doubt that this buttery sauce will find many imitators today. When cooking a quarter of lamb, you work together about a pound of butter, parsley, spring onions and chopped fine herbs and, on removing the joint from the spit, this 'is introduced into the burning shoulder of the lamb before carving'.

It is the adult beast that Grimod favours for his dinners, above all the meat from the sheep of the Ardennes, Cabourg, the Pré Salé, Arles, Beauvais, Rheims, Dieppe, etc. Those animals coming from the Berry or the Sologne are not considered up to scratch, the latter he finds lacking in bouquet. A good piece of mutton should be very succulent, 'long rivers of juice should issue from its flanks as you carve'. For tough meat Grimod recommends the *gigot de sept heures*, a seven-hour slow roast on a bed of Soissons beans, chicory, celery and spinach. Interwoven with parsley, the rack of mutton is called 'the philosopher's roast'; the same cut can be threaded with anchovy fillets, which might, it seems, be called the 'drunkard's roast' – 'it acquires a much stronger flavour, which obliges the diner to take frequent libations'.

One of the writer's more interesting recipes for mutton (or lamb), is the leg *à la serviette*.

> Choose the best leg a Parisian butcher can offer you. Weigh it; it should be cooked for as many quarters of an hour as it weighs in pounds, that is if you want it bloody, add another half-hour if you like it well done ...
>
> Wrap up the joint in a clean dishcloth or napkin. Fill a saucepan, big enough to accommodate the leg, with water. When the water is properly boiling, put in the joint and maintain the heat at that temperature. That is, boiling continually.
>
> When the leg has been in the water for the predetermined length of time, remove it from the pot, turn it out on a plate and serve it as it is without any other seasoning.
>
> The great heat of the water will have so firmly seized the pores of the animal, which must be well *wrapped* up and *bound* in its cloth, and its juice be so concentrated, that at the first incision you make the blood spurts out with the same velocity as the famous water-jet of Saint Cloud; it is a real flood and there are sometimes problems in saving the table from the aftermath of this succulent deluge.

For this very reason Grimod called the dish the *gigot déluvien*.

Some people may find the lamb or mutton a little stark without any sort of dressing. Elsewhere in the *Manuel des Amphitryons*, Grimod describes a quick dressing for mutton. 'The juice [of the meat] is poured over the slices with that of a lemon, pepper, salt and a little nutmeg, which goes to make a seasoning as pleasant as it is aphrodisiac.'

MUTTON CASCALOPES IN OIL

This recipe, Grimod informs us, comes from the *Ancienne Cuisine*. He refuses to go into the strange name of the dish and we can only suppose that it is in some way related to escalopes or the latter's forerunner.

> Take some fillets of mutton [lamb fillet would be more appropriate to our tastes today] and marinate them in good virgin olive oil with salt, pepper, basil, nutmeg, parsley, spring onions, shallots, a small garlic clove and two mushrooms. They should marinate for sixty minutes.
>
> Arrange the fillets at the bottom of a pan in such a way as to ensure that none reposes on top of another, cook on a medium heat, stirring constantly. When the fillets are tender, drain them and remove them from the pan. Throw into the latter half a glass of Champagne, a little ham essence or chicken stock if you have no ham essence, and some veal stock. Allow to boil. When it has done so, degrease the sauce and add lemon juice. The sauce should be thick.

VEAL

The best cut of veal is the loin, especially if the kidney is wrapped up inside it. The best time to consume the meat is in June, something which is also true of sheep, according to the *Almanach des Gourmands*, '... veal is whiter and better, mutton is more scented. As they have ceased to be fed on dry food their constitution betrays the fact.' The best veal, for Grimod, came from Pontoise in Lower Normandy, where the livestock was fed on biscuits soaked in milk to make the flesh as white as it could be.

SPIT-ROAST HAM

Spit-roast ham was popular both with Grimod and his friend, the Marquis de Cussy. Grimod recommends the use of hams from either Bayonne or Mainz, but the *new* ham, not presumably the dry meat we associate with these centres of ham production today. Rather than paying the high price of Bayonne, it is recommended to anyone wishing to try out this dish to use a gammon foreleg.

> Take an excellent ham joint, weighing from fifteen to twenty pounds [bear in mind that Grimod is thinking of cooking for a few more guests than you could decently expect to find at a modern dinner party]. Trim it and soak it for two or three days, according to its size, in order to remove the salt [this length of time would obviously be unnecessary for a gammon joint]. If you want the joint to be excellent, marinate the meat for a further half-day in two or three bottles of old wine.
>
> Put it on the spit, covering the outside with fat bacon or pig's caul. On a low heat, turn it on the spit for six hours, or more if you have a larger joint. Baste it continually with hot water which you have by you in the roasting-pan; this will remove the salt while dilating the pores, whereas wine, which seizes the flesh, would have the opposite effect.
>
> When it is almost cooked, take off the rind and lightly coat it with breadcrumbs. Serve when it has developed an appetizing colour.
>
> For the sauce, reduce the marinade, adding the juices from the cooking along with that of two lemons, remove the fat and serve hot.

With ham, Grimod displays a very rare desire to match the food with particular wines; he suggests a Rhine wine, a Pic Poul (i.e. a Rhone or Midi wine and pretty *ordinaire*) or a wine from the Roussillon (i.e. an equally full wine).

In the *Manuel des Amphitryons*, Grimod suggests using the wine of Malaga, sadly out of fashion these days, but still being produced, for the marinade and the sauce. As recorded in Dr Roques' treaty on the uses of plants, Cussy preferred to use sherry and to serve his spit-roast ham on a bed of spinach: ' "It's the moment to let the champagne corks fly," M de Cussy would cry, "this gassy wine so agreeably caresses the palate after the ham. What do you say to that, my dear phytographer? But we have a little old Médoc wine here, for those ham enthusiasts who are a trifle Grave."' The short hop from the Graves to the Médoc was not sufficient to discourage the Marquis from making a good pun. Roques tells us that Cussy, who had recently died (1837), had succumbed as a result of poor medical advice; he might have said, like the Emperor Hadrian, 'Alas, I've had a surfeit of doctors!'

CHICKEN BAYONNAISE

Grimod praised the city of Bayonne for more than just its hams. In the controversy which still flares up from time to time, the writer firmly decided that it was there that originated the mayonnaise sauce: '...*Mayonnaise, Mahonaise, Bayonnaise*... the first of these words is not French, the second points to a town with no reputation in gastronomic terms, all of which leads us to plump for *Bayonnaise*, for which the etymology derives from a city which is inhabited by a large number of inventive gourmands, and which, moreover, gives birth every year to the best hams in Europe.' Grimod's seeming levity, however, conceals a just grievance on the part of the *Bayonnais*. The traditional interpretation for the name comes from the Siege of Port-Mahon, where, it has been suggested, the besiegers were so lacking in supplies that they were reduced to eggs and oil, hence the invention of the sauce. The first recorded reference to this sauce does come from a dinner offered to the Duc de Richelieu, the victor of Port-Mahon in 1756, by the people of Marseille. But it is perhaps not for nothing that an *histoire de Marseille* is a synonym for an untruth; certainly in Bayonne, the 'golden sauce' is thought to have an older history.

Grimod was fond of a chicken *bayonnaise* as a cold entrée. With the formality of decoration demanded by Ancien Régime convention, one can only suppose that it was served from a mould and covered with truffles, capers, gherkins, spring onions and all other things he liked in profusion. The thing to remember is to mix the chicken with the sauce while it is still warm. The best results are got from boiled fowl; Grimod would have advocated olive oil.

POULARDE À LA GRIMOD

For Grimod the *poularde* or fattened pullet was far and away the best buy in the chicken line. These older plumper birds are now hard enough to find even in France. The following recipe specifies a Bresse pullet. The nearest easily available equivalent would be a free-range corn-fed chicken.

> Cut a dozen slices of raw ham of the thickness of a finger and as long as the bird to be larded, and as many slices of bread. Flatten the bird by beating it, and stuff it with a mixture of its own liver, truffles [optional], mushrooms, parsley, onions, salt, coarsely ground pepper and beef marrow and finely chopped bacon.
>
> Brown the bird on all its sides in a little butter. Before putting it on the spit [it could be as well cooked in an oven], cover it wholly with the bread slices and then the ham, cover it then with a sheet of paper large enough to hold the bird [or in a cook-bag], tie it down with string. Cook slowly with a dish placed beneath it to receive the juice, which is served with the pullet.

PIGEONS AS TURTLES

May is the season for pigeon; Grimod feels the pea was designed as its accompaniment. Failing that, a counterpoint might be established with asparagus tips, especially if you are reducing the bird to a *compôte*. There is, however, this third option in the Grimodian vocabulary, one which seems more likely to impress guests by its bizarre and slightly forbidding appearance than for its gustative qualities. The cucumbers to which the writer refers seem to be something between an outsize courgette and a small marrow.

> Choose short fat cucumbers, peel them and scoop out the middles. Blanch them briefly. Have as many pigeons as cucumbers, but pick the very smallest, scald them, cut off the head and neck, the wings and the claws, cut off the beak and clean the head. Have as many veal escalopes as you have cucumbers (and pigeons), marinate them in oil and fine

herbs, then make four holes in each cucumber (one at the end, one on each side, and one underneath) into which you put a little forcemeat [it would be wise to use the meat from the discarded pigeon carcases]. Place the cucumbers on each escalope, which should be the same length and width as the underside of a turtle. Cook them on top of a layer of fat bacon at the bottom of a pan. Season them in the usual manner and cover them with more fat bacon, moisten with meat glaze and stock. Cook on a gentle heat. When they are cooked, drain them and wipe them, as cucumbers always give a lot of juice. Cover them with a good thick *espagnole* [flour, meat stock and tomato purée]. Serve with the escalope laid on top of the cucumbers.

Thus masked, these pigeons look much like turtles. The sight of them is altogether singular.

Grimod lists a number of other ways of dealing with cucumbers which are less bizarre than the above. Stuffed *à la matelote*, they are filled with a mixture of chicken breast, york ham, truffles and fine herbs. *Au maigre*, the stuffing is concocted from fish, fish roes and mushrooms and *à la braise* they are cooked in butter and cream, the sauce being bound with an egg yolk.

QUAILS À LA D'EGMONT

Though Grimod favoured a simple method of dealing with quail, other gourmands of his own circle, notably Cussy and d'Aigrefeuille, preferred this recipe.

Truss the birds and cook them in a chicken consommé, or clear chicken stock, with rice and chipolata sausages. When everything is cooked, remove the skins from the sausages and mash them into the rice. Add a little fresh butter. Put the rice in a bowl and put the quails on top.

AN INCOMPARABLE ROAST

Grimod learned the following recipe from his close friend Fortia de Piles, sometime Assistant Mayor of Marseille. In many respects it resembles *une histoire de Marseille* (i.e. a lie), though I suppose it might be possible for a determined gourmand to bring together this ornithological collection and prepare it for the table. We print it here as a curiosity of its time.

Take a good olive stuffed with capers and anchovies that has been marinated in good virgin [olive] oil. Put it into the body of a *beccafico** from which you have cut off the head and the claws.

Put the trussed *beccafico* into a plump and fleshy ortolan.

Put your selected ortolan into the body of a lark, from which you have amputated the head and claws and removed the main bones, and which you have wrapped in a thin slice of pork fat.

Put the lark, stuffed and trimmed, into a thrush which you have prepared in the same way.

Put the thrush into the body of a quail; it should be fat and juicy and preferably a wild one from the vines, not the domestic sort.

Wrap the quail in a vine leaf, which will serve as its title of nobility and as its certificate of origin. Put it into the body of a lapwing.

Truss the lapwing well and cover it with a thin frock coat of fat, put it into the body of a good golden plover.

Put the said plover, similarly larded, into the body of a good partridge, preferably a red one, put the partridge into a young woodcock; it should be as tender as Mlle Volnais,† succulent and good and high.

After covering the woodcock with thinly sliced crusts of bread, put in into the body of a teal.

Put the teal, carefully wrapped in fat and well trimmed, into the body of a guinea fowl.

Put the equally well wrapped guinea fowl into the body of a wild duck, if you can get one. Put the duck into the body of a young pullet; it should be as white as Madame Belmont,† as pleasantly fleshy as Mlle De Vienne,† and as plump as

---

*Beccafico: of the warbler family similar to a British blackcap. In Italy, the word is used for any small bird destined for the table *(O.E.D.)*
†One of the actresses of the period, often members of the Jury Dégustateur.

Mlle Contat,* but of only middling size.

Put the pullet into the body of a good pheasant, which should be well chosen and young, but above all well hung, as a gourmand will not eat them otherwise.

Put the pheasant into the body of a young wild goose; it should be fat and well tenderized.

Put the young and lovely goose into the body of a lovely turkey hen, white and plump like Mlle Arsène.*

Finally enclose your turkey hen in the body of a good bustard.† If the fit is not exact you may block the empty spaces with good Luc chestnuts, sausage meat or any worthwhile stuffing.

Now take your roast and put it in a pot big enough to take it, lay it on a bed of onions stuck with cloves, carrots, ham, cut into little cubes, celery, bouquet garni, coarsely ground pepper, a great many slices of well-seasoned fat bacon, pepper, salt, mixed herbs, coriander and one or two cloves of garlic.

Seal the pot hermetically by luting it with pastry or some other lute. Then put the pot on a low heat for twenty-four hours, adjusting the pot in such a way as to allow the heat to penetrate uniformly and gradually. We recommend a moderate oven maintained at the same degree rather than cooking it on the hob.

When you come to serving the dish, unseal the pot, remove any excess fat if the joint requires it, and place the meat on a heated plate before putting it on the table. It is easy to imagine that the juices of so many birds, united by the gentle cooking process, and their different natures identified by their intimate confinement, gives this Incomparable Roast a wonderful taste. You have all at once the quintessence of the plains, the forests, the marshes and the farmyard.‡

---

* One of the actresses of the period, often members of the Jury Dégustateur.
† Bustard: Europe's largest bird, and the heaviest flying bird in the world. Now extinct in France (perhaps as a result of this recipe?), but still present in Spain, the male great bustard can weigh up to 35lbs. It is presumably the female that Grimod is referring to, which weighs only 11–13 lbs. (Hvass: *Birds of the World*, London 1963).
‡ Grimod gives another recipe for Monstrous Eggs, an idea which involves using three or four dozen eggs and two pigs' bladders to make one huge hard-boiled egg. It could, one supposes, be served with this Incomparable Roast.

THE *SALMIS* OF THE BENEDICTINE DOM CLAUDON OF THE ABBEY OF HAUTE-SEILLE

This recipe 'may be applied to any form of game with dark meat from plain, forest, marsh or mountain ... suitable would be the melancholic hare, the partridge, wild or domestic geese, wandering or civilized ducks, woodcock or snipe. This recipe is for woodcock, but it is just as easy to adapt it for other birds; as regards quantities, they are changeable according to the number and size of the elements involved.' This recipe might prove a successful way of dealing with grouse.

> Take three woodcock or four snipe; they should be part cooked on the spit [or in the oven]. Divide them up according to the rules of carving, then chop the wings and legs in two as well as the stomach and the crop. Arrange the pieces on a dish. On the same silver dish as you have used for carving, mash the liver and the other interior organs and squeeze over them the juice of four fleshy lemons, adding the thinly sliced peel of one of them.
>
> Replace the pieces of game from the dish that you have previously put aside. Season with several pinches of salt and some powdered spices (if none are available, some fine ground pepper and nutmeg will do), two spoonfuls of excellent mustard from the houses of Maille and Acloque* or Bardin, and half a glass of very good white wine. Put the dish on to a spirit stove [i.e. back on the hob] and turn the pieces until each one has been permeated with the seasoning and making sure that none catches.
>
> Take great care that the *ragoût* does not boil; when it gets close to doing so, baste it with a few dashes of excellent virgin [olive] oil. Lower the flame and continue stirring for several minutes ... Serve immediately, passing the plate without standing on ceremony; the *salmis* should be eaten very hot.

Grimod adds: 'It is essential you use a fork on this occasion; if your fingers were to come into contact with the sauce, you might easily eat them too.'

---

*Today just called Maille.

SAUTÉ À LA SUPRÊME FOR CHICKEN OR GAME

According to the writer, the *sauté à la suprême* was one of the few culinary contributions of the post-Revolutionary era. Indeed the *sautoir*, that shallow pan with straight sides, was, he tells us, invented in 1801. A *sauté à la suprême*, however, was no mere *sauté*; 'the *sauté à la suprême* is to the ordinary *sauté*, what a cardinal is to a simple archdeacon.' Essentially, it amounts to a way of cooking small pieces of fowl or game at table over the intense flame of a spirit stove.

> Put your *sautoir* directly on the flame at its most intense, as the delicacy of the meat is dependent on the ardour of the heat. The wings of a chicken or partridge will swell up like a balloon before your eyes, acquiring great tenderness without losing any of their flavour. Though cooked without a lid, the juices have no time to evaporate, because they are seized so rapidly. Piron's conversation,* which has been compared to a well-made firework, might easily have been likened to a good *sauté à la suprême*.

Grimod stipulates that the *sauté à la suprême* should be served with a brown *espagnole* sauce.

THE TURKEY OF THE SOCIÉTÉ DES MERCREDIS

The gourmand Société des Mercredis met every Wednesday and latterly every second Wednesday until its demise. Dinners reunited seventeen members around a table at the Restaurant Le Gacque which stood in the present rue de Rivoli, where the railings of the Tuileries Gardens are today. The centrepiece of the dinner was a huge braised turkey 'well stuffed with Périgord truffles, chipolata sausages and Luc chestnuts'. It was braised in a hot oven between two beds of veal, fat bacon, onions, carrots, thyme, bay and mixed spices, the pot being hermetically sealed. Grimod made great claims for this recipe which, he said, was the secret of cooking the bird. It makes a change from those desiccated offerings of a modern Christmas.

---

*Alexis Piron (1689–1773). Playwright.

TURKEY LEGS *SAUCE ROBERT*

Robert l'Aîné was one of the most famous cooks of the period. Until he joined the household of Murat, Napoleon's brother-in-law, Grand Duke of Berg and Cleves and, from July 1808, King of Naples, he ran the restaurant bearing his name in the rue Richelieu. The *sauce Robert* is a variant on the *sauce Soubise* of the Ancien Régime, i.e. it is essentially composed of butter and onions.

Sweat your onions in butter and add a spoonful of seasoned flour and a measure of good, preferably veal, stock. Simmer. At the last moment stir in a good measure of mustard; Grimod would have recommended Maille. Better mustards are made these days by the houses of Fauchon and Hediard in Paris.

The turkey legs should be plainly grilled.

Grimod gives one or two other hints for the serving of poultry and game. For goose, for example, he suggests cutting the eight fillets from the breast and, in a dish, adding the juice of two lemons, a spoonful of olive oil, one or two of mustard, salt and pepper. He recommends much the same dressing for duck, except that he stresses the necessity of nutmeg. Ducks should otherwise be served on a bed of olives or baby turnips, or boiled in rock salt, 'all the varieties of duck can be adapted to make countless succulent entrées, art masking the base origin of these dirty mudlarks; it is certainly true to say, that more often than one would wish, "manners maketh man".' For a partridge, Grimod uses Seville oranges. Rabbit should be cooked wrapped in fat bacon, hare should be *piqué*, i.e. have the strips of fat threaded into the meat. Leveret is served, according to the writer, with a stimulating sauce of vinegar, capers and ground anchovies.

IV

VEGETABLES AND RICE

Vegetable dishes make their entry at the end of the meal in the form of *entremets* in the third service. They shared the table then with the *entremets sucrées*, i.e. desserts, and the cold pâtés and *galantines*. In the *Almanach des Gourmands*, Grimod lists a great many ways in which vegetables were generally served at these formal gatherings. Once or twice a recipe has also come down to us. The following one is for artichokes, 'the chameleons of the kitchen'.

ARTICHOKES *À LA* GRIMOD DE LA REYNIÈRE

Cut an onion into coarse pieces, sweat them in butter until they have turned a good colour, season them with salt and spices and let them cool in the butter. In another pan, cook the artichoke bottoms separated from their leaves. When cooked, drain off the water, fill them with the onion, breadcrumbs and grated cheese. Put them in the oven to finish them off and serve without other seasoning.

ASPARAGUS TIPS *À LA* POMPADOUR

Grimod inherited this recipe from an uncle on his mother's side, a M de Jarente, Minister of State in Madame de Pompadour's heyday. '... of an exquisite delicacy, a charming simplicity, and a perfect elegance', these asparagus tips should be served with a spoon and eaten with a fork.

Select three bundles of fat Dutch asparagus, that is the white sort with purple tips. Trim them, wash them and cook them in the ordinary way by plunging them in boiling, salty water. Next cut them slantwise at a little-finger's distance from the tip. Put the stems to one side and concern yourself only with the choicer morsels, which you put in a hot cloth to dry, and keep them hot while you make the sauce.

Empty, spoonful by spoonful, an average-size pot of Vanvres or Prevalais butter,* into a silver dish, add some grains of salt, a big pinch of powdered mace, half a spoonful of refined wheat flour, and two egg yolks mixed with four spoonfuls of muscat verjuice [M Rival recommends lemon juice as an alternative]. Cook the sauce in a double saucepan. Try to prevent it from getting too heavy or thick.

Put your asparagus tips in the sauce, and serve them together in a covered dish, but draw your guests' attention to it; this excellent *entremet* should never languish on the table, but should be appreciated in all its perfection.

PEAS

'A faultless dish of peas is sufficient to establish the reputation of a great cook. The recipe we are about to give is one of the simplest; none the less a great deal of talent is required to produce it. This is the only way to eat the peas in their own juice.'

> You must use the peas as soon as they are picked. Having washed and dried them, put them in a pan with some excellent butter, some salt, one or two little lettuce hearts and a bouquet garni made up of parsley, spring onions, a little savory and two cloves.
>
> Cook it in the hot ashes [i.e. on a low heat], stirring them from time to time but adding no liquid. When they are almost cooked, taste them, then put in a good deal of butter into which you have worked some flour.
>
> When they are properly cooked, serve them with a thick sauce.

---

*Vanvres is no longer famous for its butter. A good unsalted butter is implied.

LITTLE FINGERS À LA TRAPPISTE

This recipe comes from the shortlived *Journal des Gourmands et des Belles,* on which Grimod collaborated briefly. 'The Trappist fathers were much fonder of their "little rights" [i.e. *menu-droits;* can mean "little straights" or "little rights"], than the all-too-famous *Rights of Man,* which have resulted in so much misery, and which put us on a fifteen-year diet.' Grimod's most recent biographer, Ned Rival, thinks these 'little fingers' would make an excellent alternative to the ubiquitous *petits légumes* of the *nouvelle cuisine.*

> Melt a little butter in a pan and put in an onion cut into *fillets*. Moisten with a clear stock. Have prepared some carrots, turnips, parsnips, beetroots and celery, all cut into finger lengths and blanched in a thin stock. When your onion *ragoût* is ready, put in the root vegetables and let them simmer. Finish the dish by adding a dash of tarragon vinegar.

Generally Grimod is not so specific as to the uses of vegetables, confining himself to a few suggestions, both in terms of entrées and *entremets*. Spinach, for example, can be served with gravy, butter, cream or with a *coulis,* 'virgin wax susceptible to every kind of impression... after sorrel, the habitual mattress for the *fricandeau*'.* Cauliflower can be prepared in a white sauce, with mutton gravy, deep-fried or with Parmesan cheese: 'you must choose the whitest heads; those which are off-white, or grainy, should be rejected'. Chard was a vegetable highly esteemed by Grimod. Sadly it is difficult to find in Britain. Anyone who has located a supply of it might be interested to learn that the writer thought it 'the *nec plus ultra* of human science when it comes to vegetable *entremets,* and a cook who is able to prepare an exquisite dish of chard may style himself the Best Artist of Europe'. He recommends divers ways of cooking it, with gravy, in marrowbone, or with Parmesan.

Cabbage can be safely served with boiled beef, or with an old partridge, or better in a *sauerkraut,* a dish, it seems, which had recently taken the capital by storm. Salsify is fried, or served with butter and Parmesan. Ox tails modestly conceal themselves in a

---

*A veal joint cut from the leg.

bed of carrots. Turnips are a natural counterpoint to duck. Leaks are worthy of soup only, etc., etc.

PILAU RICE WITH SAFFRON FROM THE GATINAIS

The author of the *Almanach des Gourmands* was fascinated by culinary preparations involving rice. It was the beginning of the nineteenth century when huge mounds of rice formed part of formal dinners. The following makes a good dish with lamb or chicken.

> Wash the rice well in several waters [a good starchy rice like a Basmati would be ideal]. In a pan put three measures of good stock to one of rice. Seal the vessel hermetically. When it begins to boil mix a little saffron with some stock in a cup. Put this in with the rice, reseal the pot and allow it to boil on a high heat for one hour.

V

DESSERTS

FANCHONS AND FANCHONETTES

The pastry cook Rouget, who receives such high praise for his work in the *Almanach des Gourmands,* and who was a highly respected member of the Jury Dégustateur, created the *fanchon,* and its smaller equivalent, the *fanchonette,* in honour of the actress Mme Henri Belmont of the Théâtre du Vaudeville. It was the practice of the time to fête thus the leading beauties of the day, especially, in Grimod's circle, actresses. The honour was accorded to Mme Henri Belmont for her performance in *Fanchon la Veilleuse,* a piece about a famous street singer of the eighteenth century, Françoise Chemin, *femme* Menart, nicknamed Fanchon. At the request of the jury, Rouget was obliged to make, at a later date, *minettes* and *augustinettes,* in honour of the Marquis de Cussy's mistress Minette Ménéstrier and her sister Augusta.

Make a good flakey pastry of six folds, as you would for a *galette des rois,** fill a round and buttered flan dish with it.

Garnish the pastry with *crème patissière* [twelve egg yolks, 100 grams of sugar, the same amount of refined flour, half a litre of fresh cream; perfume it with vanilla or chocolate, with coffee or almonds, add a little salt].

Cook in a cool oven. Once the tart has cooled down, cover it with meringue and sprinkle sugar over it. Allow it to

---

*A flakey pastry tart filled with almond purée and eaten on and around the *fête des Rois,* i.e. 6 January: 'the Feast of the Kings, as a result that of cakemakers, consequently, that of physicians'. In Swift's day, 'Twelfth Cakes' were similarly eaten in England.

brown in the oven. The *fanchon* is eaten lukewarm.

Grimod makes the frequent point that the true gourmand has finished his dinner by the end of the second service. This could well account for the paucity of ideas when it comes to good dessert dishes. Generally they are limited to various forms of omelette soufflé, *ramequins, blanc mangers* (this delicate dish of almond milk is about as far from a modern English blancmange as you can imagine), or *mille-feuilles*. In summer, while nature was reproducing itself, Amphitryons resting and good cooks meditating, the gourmand who was not reduced to dining in his imagination lived off vegetables and fruit. Strawberries, 'the most precocious fruit divine providence delivers to our tables', should be eaten with sugar and red wine.* The cherry is eaten *confit*, slowly baked in the oven, or pickled in brandy. He also mentions a cherry soup. Apricots should be used for marmalade, pickled in brandy, or made into paste. Apricot ice is insipid by itself and needs crushed almonds. Redcurrants are proposed for insomniacs. Raspberries should be served in a chilled *compôte* with a layer of redcurrant jelly on top. Walnuts are pickled in verjuice, 'quite pleasant but indigestible'.

Peaches are 'the most beautiful and most distinguished fruit our climate produces'; they should be cooked in water like hard-boiled eggs. The best plums are greengages, then *mirabelles*. Prunes are 'a great resource for desserts in March and April'. Raisins go to make *babas,* 'a sort of saffron-scented savoy biscuit which Stanislas I, King of Poland, introduced to France'. Apples, having a life of up to eight months, are 'one of the annual benefits of providence'; they go to make *compôtes,* can be stuffed, grilled, made into jellies, doughnuts, charlottes, pies or cooked in butter; 'the most honourable service one might render this fruit is to transform it into an apple flan *à l'Anglaise'*. Rotting medlars should be eaten after plunging them into a pan full of caramel. Almonds are used to make *blanc mangers* – 'very difficult to make well'; for the confectioner the almond is 'one of the jewels in their crown'. Hazelnuts stick in the teeth: 'People not possessing a full set of teeth would be wiser to abstain from eating them.'

Figs can be eaten with salt as an hors d'oeuvre or boiled. Dried

---

*Good red wine too. The author recalls enjoying two classed-growth 1970 Médocs in this way. As one of the proprietors put it to me, 'You see, sometimes it pays to chaptalize.'

figs from Italy or Provence are useful in Lent. Melons are eaten in a soup made with butter and milk, but the writer finds that cooking melon gives it 'a rather nasty taste'. Preferring pumpkin soup, he suggests serving melon with pepper and salt with a good red wine poured over it. Blackberries he eats with salt as an accompaniment to soup. Noting that the fruit is also used to colour wine with insufficient pigment, he says, 'it is one of the more innocent adulterations a wine merchant perpetrates'. Olives are eaten stuffed with capers and anchovies, and preserved in good olive oil. Seville oranges are the accepted bedfellows of game with dark meat (partridge, grouse, wild duck, etc.), and also 'the soul of the Bischopp [sic]', sadly there is no joke intended. Lemons are good with oil on fillets of sole. Pineapples, he concludes, are 'the most distinguished of all the fruits that grace our tables; they may not be grown here except in hothouses and with consummate care'. This line possibly inspired Balzac's ill-fated attempt to make money by growing pineapples in greenhouses in Sèvres, near Paris. The novelist was the first person to re-edit extracts of the *Almanach des Gourmands.**

Lastly, as Grimod's contemporary and imitator, Brillat-Savarin, would have said, 'a dessert without cheese is like a lovely lady who lacks an eye'. The cheese, of course, was part of the dessert, and almost all soft cheeses would have been eaten with sugar like *fromage blanc* is today. Grimod's top division consists of Gruyère, Roquefort (the supreme 'drunkard's biscuit' for its thirst-provoking qualities), Sassenage (a semi-hard, blue-veined cheese from the Isère) and Gérardmer (or Géromé), from the Vosges. It is like a larger version of Munster. After that come a further four; Maroilles, Mont d'Or, Comté and Brie. In the third division is Parmesan, a cheese supposedly popularized by Talleyrand, who started the practice of putting it in soup. Grimod notes that it is 'only used in *ragoûts,* as a pleading for macaronis and *rammequins,* and in a large number of soups with pasta'. The last category contains only one too, the Norman cheese Livarot.

The aftermath of the Revolution was a period of growing awareness when it came to cheeses. Until the dissolution of the French monasteries in 1790, certain secrets of manufacture had been held by religious communities. Certainly it has been claimed that this was so in the case of Camembert, which was unknown

---

*Variétés Gourmandes, Suivies d'une Traité des Excitants Modernes.

before 1789, and did not become popular in Paris until Napoleon III developed a fondness for it. According to legend, Marie Harel learnt the secret from a refractory priest whom she concealed from the authorities of the Terror. Livarot has a greater claim to antiquity among Norman cheeses. Talleyrand was responsible for advancing the reputation of Brie, both in France and in Europe as a whole, indeed it has been somewhat unfairly said of him that 'the sole master he never betrayed was the Brie cheese'.

The Comte de la Garde Chambonnas recounts an amusing story about Talleyrand and his cheese in his *Souvenirs du Congrès de Vienne:*

> M de Talleyrand gave a dinner; at dessert, all political issues having been exhausted, the assembled company broached the subject of the supremacy of cheeses. Lord Castlereagh advanced the English Stilton; Aldini, the Strachino of Milan; Zeltner, Swiss Gruyère; the Dutch minister, the Baron Falk, his Limbourg, which was immortalized by Peter the Great, who 'never ate any without measuring the piece with his compass...' At that moment Talleyrand's valet entered the room to inform the French plenipotentiary that a messenger was come from Paris. 'What has he brought?' the Prince asked. 'Some despatches from the Court and some Brie cheeses,' replied the messenger. 'Have the despatches taken to the Chancellery, have one of the cheeses brought to the table,' said Talleyrand. 'Judge for yourselves, *Messieurs.*' The plate was passed round the table, they tasted, they debated, and the Brie cheese was proclaimed the King of Cheeses.

GRIMOD'S WINE

Grimod was not a great drinker. In the pre-Revolutionary years he positively abjured wine-drinking at his *déjeuners philosophiques,* where the guests were required to consume seventeen cups of milky coffee; a dosage that might even defeat a modern French student; and lunchers bringing guests were asked, *'peut-il boire autant que vous saviez?'* Apart from coffee, the only other permitted beverage was verjuice, i.e. the juice of unfermented green grapes. One guest who demanded a glass of wine was forced to drink it outside the room.

This eccentricity may well have been intended to mock the heavy formality of his parents' *soirées*. The ostentatious luxury of Morillon's kitchen was starkly contrasted by the simple fare of Grimod *fils'* table; buttered bread and anchovies, doubtless to engender thirst, and for those who survived the coffee, a gargantuan sirloin.

During those lean years following his return from the provinces, Grimod had precious little to comfort him besides the contents of his father's very well stocked cellar. Having been converted to *gourmandise* by his aunt's table in Béziers, he was to be converted to wine by the one legacy of his father's he was able to get his hands on. That being said, Grimod was never an expert on wine in the same way as he was when it came to food. Some of his strictures were decidedly shaky; recommending white Hermitage and not red, for example, despite the infinitesimally smaller fame and production of the former, even at that time; or white Côte-Rôtie, which has probably never existed under that name. Grimod is of more interest when it comes to the subject of punches, or the *coup d'avant, du milieu* and *d'après*; the first two corresponding, roughly speaking, to the aperitif and the *trou Normand*, while the third has no modern equivalent as such.

The idea of associating specific wines with different foods hardly existed at all in Grimod's day. Grimod stipulates few such instances. We have seen that he recommended some pretty rustic stuff to go with his spit-roast ham; he also displayed a certain sensitivity towards good Burgundy, saying the wine was too delicate to be served with the *entremets* and should be served rather with the roast. His favourite Burgundy was the Clos Vougeot he obtained from a M Tourton, a wine merchant who had at one time bought up a parcel of the close, presumably after its sale as a *bien national* in 1790. The much despised Revolution could be excused this time, as it was in the case of M Tailleur, who had acquired his enormous stocks of old wines by plundering the cellars of *ci-devants* or emigrés. Paris was also becoming a better place for wine-buying with the construction, at the end of Napoleon's reign, of the massive Halle aux Vins on the left bank of the Seine. Even the moderate-drinking Grimod did not fail to notice the importance of 1811, the 'Comet year' and one of the greatest vintages of the century.

One food wholly dictated its vinous accompaniment, and that was oysters, which required Chablis, '…the inseparable friend of the oyster and its most appropriate companion. Chablis is one of the wines a gourmand prizes most and that with which he makes the most frequent libations.' Grimod even drafted a classification of the wines, putting at the head four wines now designated 'great growths' and another which is a 'first growth'.

Unlike the English at the time, the French drank their wine cut with water during their meals, and continued to do so well into this century, uncut wines being served at the end of the meal with the *entremets*. This naturally led to a difference in taste between the two countries, for as the expertise of the British developed in the course of the nineteenth century, they increasingly plumped for lighter, more elegant wines, fit to accompany food, while the French, seeking a brewage better suited to taking a dose of water, went for fuller, rougher wines. An example of this is found in the *Record of Visits for Château Loudenne,* where Walter Gilbey, noting the coarseness of the classed growths in 1890, writes that they were suitable only for the French table, 'where red wines are consumed at all meals, much diluted with water'. The very moderate drinking of the French had been for a long time a cause of surprise to British travellers. Arthur Young, writing fifteen years before Grimod, summed up the drinking at a French dinner:

> I have met with persons in England, who imagine the sobriety of a French table carried to such a length, that one or two glasses of wine are all that a man can get at dinner; this is an error; your servant mixes the wine and water in what proportion you please; and large bowls of clean glasses are set before the master of the house and some friends of the family, at different parts of the table, for serving the richer and rarer sorts of wines, which are drunk in this manner freely enough.*

The wine provided for the first two services was thus called *vin ordinaire* though that term lacked, then, the evil connotations it has today. Grimod tells us that the usual common wine of Paris was that of the Orléanais, and the citizens often undertook a family journey to the Loire to load up for a season. The writer calls it '...rough stuff that sits heavily on the stomach'. The other staple, as Smollett discovered, was thin Burgundy, 'sold as

---

Travels in France During the Years 1787, 1788 and 1789.

Macon', says Grimod, 'though the majority of them come from Auxerre or thereabouts'. Still, their mediocre quality was doubtless hardly noticed by those unfortunate people who were reduced to drinking the wines of Suresnes in the modern suburbs of Paris. The foulness of this wine was legendary from the seventeenth century onwards.*

In general Grimod advocated the use of white wines with the first two courses, as they were harder to falsify (he lived in sulphur-dioxide-free days), though this indulgence was not to be taken too far, especially if the white wines in question came from the Loire or even from the dreaded Suresnes: 'The small white wines of the Orléanais and above all those from around Paris, are very weak, acidic and not pleasant; they are often even sour. This is some sort of rot-gut and best abandoned to the rustics.'

Grimod's recommendations for ordinary wines contain a number of peculiarities. As reds he suggests: Langon near Sauternes, better known for white wine; Canon (i.e. Fronsac), Saint Emilion and Cahors. For gourmands, headier wines are preferable, and his list descends into an uncharacteristic earthiness: Jurançon (today a white), Grenache and Pic-Poul (simple wines from the Rhône or the Midi), Roussillon, Saint-Gilles, from around the town of that name in the Gard, Tavel (then a red wine, 'the wine of Tavelle...is very near as good as Burgundy' – Smollett: *Travels*) and Condrieu (surely never a red wine?) 'A bottle of these wines,' he writes, 'produces a greater effect on the mood of your guests than four of Burgundy or Bordeaux.' He does not inform us how, but it is certain that they would make them drunker.

The whites are no less curious: Graves and Barsac are reasonable enough, but he also recommends white Médocs, at that period being phased out by the reforming hands of viticulturalists like the Baron de Brane; the 'Napoléon du Médoc', and 'Ségur' would also seem to be a Médocain wine, from the former estates of the Marquis de Ségur (the Prince des Vignes who owned both Château Lafite and Latour). From the other side of France, Grimod proposes Beaune (Corton?), Chablis, as well as Saint Péray and white Hermitage from the Rhône. Champagne is a dessert wine; he prefers the still wines which were then produced

---

*The author recalls one year in the early 1980s when the crop was so poor in the still extant vineyards of Suresnes that the municipal council was pinning ripe grapes on the vines for the harvest festival.

in Aÿ, Pierry and Epernay.

The finer wines were served with the *entremets* at the end of the meal; '...they should always be served by the host, who sends a glass to each guest in the gaps between dishes. That is unless he prefers the easier but more expensive English method of passing each bottle round until it is finished up.' The reds are Clos Vougeot, La Romanée,* Chambertin, Saint-George (presumably the principal *climat* of Nuits-Saint-Georges), Pommard, Volnay, Nuits-Saints-Georges, Beaune, Tonnerre and the wines of a friend from there: Clos Mignenne. (In the Yonne or lower Burgundy, most of the vineyards of this area disappeared with phylloxera, leaving only Irancy and the Côteaux de Saint Bris making red wines today), Mâcon, Château Lafite, Château Margaux, Saint Julien, Saint Estèphe (most of the commune was not planted until after 1815), Pic-Poul, Tavel and Saint Gilles. The whites mentioned are Montrachet, Meursault, Pouilly and Chablis from Burgundy, Sillery, Pierry and Aÿ from Champagne, Sauternes; Graves and Barsac from Bordeaux, Saint Péray, Hermitage and Côte-Rôtie from the Rhône, Rhine and Mosel.

Grimod's real preference was for dessert wines and liqueurs, though he is frequently swayed by an excusable patriotism in his choice: 'the sweet fortified wines of Spain, Italy or even Languedoc are in general little favoured by gourmets. They find a medicinal taste in them, more worthy of the contents of an apothecary's cabinet than a wine-lover's cellar.' Despite his inclusion of Languedoc in that condemnation, he was, however, prepared to vaunt the now vanished muscat wines of Cassis and Le Ciotat above the nobler wines of Tokay, in which he found 'an extremely nasty taste of rotten apples'. Muscat de Rivesaltes he calls, 'the best muscat which exists in the four corners of the globe' and he also values the similar wines, then and now produced at Lunel and Frontignan (when they have finished gorging themselves on Beaumes de Venise, the British public might discover these equally well-made wines).

Despite his prejudices in that line, Grimod does list foreign liqueur wines among the more distinguished: Malaga, Tent (this

---

*Of Romanée Conti: 'Since the Revolution transferred these vines to other hands [than the Prince de Conti], the wine has lost much of its quality; this is because the new owner has changed the plantation in order to produce more abundant harvests.'

was an inky red wine from Alicante and popular in England, where the name Tent was a corruption of *tinto*), Sherry. Pacaret (a sweet wine from near Jerez, also then popular in England), Madeira, Clazomeni (from the town near Smyrna in Asia Minor, it was possibly made by Christians from dried grapes or sultanas), Constancia (the legendary muscatel from Groot Constancia at the Cape), Calabria (sweet wines are still made there, e.g. Greco di Gerace), Tokay (Grimod may have been one of the first Frenchmen to mention the process of 'noble rot', giving the word *Ausbruche (sic)* to the wine, now used in Austria only for wines affected by *botrytis cinerea*. Later he uses the word *trockenbee'rs' [sic]*, which would seem to confirm the use of nobly rotten fruit), Lacrima Christi, from the slopes of Vesuvius, Canary and Pedro Ximinez (i.e. sweet Sherry). With the coffee were served a whole host of bizarre liqueurs made from a variety of strange ingredients by people like his favourite distillers Noël de la Serre, and Tanrade. One man in Clermont-Ferrand had hit on the idea of a Ratafia with truffles: 'this liqueur which flies you from dessert back to the *entremets*'. As for serving, Grimod recommends thin glasses rather than thick, heavy crystal, nor should wines be decanted from their dusty bottles, for 'the true beauty of a wine lies in its age and not in the sparkling recipient which embraces it'.

Grimod was surely one of the first Frenchmen to advocate the use of the aperitif, a practice now universal in that country: 'The *coup d'avant* is almost unknown in Paris, but it is quite common in the north of Europe, especially in Sweden and Russia. It consists of a large glass of vermouth, absinthe or rum, or even a simple glass of brandy which is presented to every guest to get their appetites going.' After the soup Grimod recommends the *coup d'après,* a glass of wine drunk pure and unadulterated: 'in Paris it is held proverbially, that the *coup d'après* means a crown the less for the doctor's pocket'. It is the only moment in the course of the meal when it is permitted to drink the wine uncut with water*. Drinking *vin ordinaire* straight is a practice Grimod reserves for the *crocheteur,* a word which implies at best a porter, at worst a thief.

Between services a *coup du milieu* was served. This is the *trou Normand* (calvados) or *trou Gascon* (armagnac) which is some-

---

*In the south of France it is still the custom to *faire chabrot*, i.e. to pour a shot of red wine into your half-finished soup.

times served in French restaurants today. In theory a glass of spirits helps to revive a flagging appetite. Grimod favoured rum, Swiss absinthe or cognac for this purpose.

After dessert and to accompany the bawdy songs and bacchic couplets so dear to Grimod's heart, punches were frequently served. One which Grimod particularly liked was 'Bishop', which was popular in Britain in the age of Johnson. The English recipe uses port whereas Grimod's is more like a variant on mulled claret. The episcopal dignity of the name is a result of the purple colour of the wine, not from any other form of ecclesiastical privilege.

Ingredients:
2 or 3 Seville oranges
2 litres of old claret
5 grams of cinnamon
1 clove
250 grams of castor sugar

Lacerate the skins of the oranges without piercing them. Cut them into quarters and lightly grill them. Heat up the wine (Grimod suggests in a porcelain vessel), the cinnamon and the clove. The pot should be hermetically sealed and placed on hot ashes to brew for six to eight hours.*

Strain the liquid through a clean dishcloth, add the sugar and allow it to dissolve.

Before serving, the Bishop should be heated but never boiled. Boiling would eliminate the bouquet, leaving you with a 'common or garden mulled wine'. Grimod adds that this drink tends to affect the legs more than the head.

Despite Grimod's otherwise unsympathetic view of the English and their cuisine, his recipes for punch are all culled from English sources. The following is a rum punch.

1 part lemon juice
Some lemon peel
3 parts Jamaican rum
9 parts good hot tea
Sugar to taste

The peel should be steeped in the lemon juice for a few

---

*The jug could be set on an asbestos mat on a very low heat.

hours before being mixed with the rum. As for the sugar, Grimod recommends 'very little for sailors, a lot for ladies' ... 'This punch taken a few moments before retiring for the night, will procure them a sweet and tranquil sleep of benign dreams, as well as safeguarding them from the malign influence of cold and damp, the source of so many bouts of influenza in Paris, and one of the stoutest branches of the physician or the apothecary's trade.'

Another favourite of Grimod's is Nuptial Wine, so named possibly for its aphrodisiac qualities.

1 pint of red wine
2–3 ounces of sugar
2 glasses of liqueur

Heat the wine in a double saucepan. When it starts to boil remove it from the heat and add the sugar. Pour it into a teapot and add the liqueur. The best would be a fruit-based spirit like Cointreau or Grand Marnier. This drink 'has the virtue of improving even the most mediocre of wines'.

A Gourmand Miscellany

Les Rêves d'un Gourmand.

Balzac's *Variétés Gourmandes* was the first book to demonstrate how well Grimod's style lent itself to anthologies. It is sad that Grimod never finished his projected *Dictionnaire de la Cuisine,* as that would have naturally collated the elements of the writer's gastronomic wisdom which are otherwise scattered throughout the eight volumes of the *Almanach des Gourmands.* Eventually it was Dumas *père* who took up the challenge of producing the dictionary, and one wonders how much the author of *The Count of Monte Cristo* was influenced in his choice of subject matter by his meeting with the elderly Grimod at the Château de Brinvilliers. All in all, the *Manuel des Amphitryons* is a more successful book than the *Almanach,* and the best single-volume digest of his thought.

The following extracts have been selected from both the *Almanach* and the *Manuel des Amphitryons.*

ABBOT FOR A DAY

In the department of the Creuse, there still exists an abbey, once upon a time inhabited by the good monks of the Cistercian order, of which the name itself is sufficient to remind one of hosts of famous gourmands. The abbey is situated on the Taurion, a little stream which ought to be better known, for it feeds some excellent trout. The Cistercians knew how to do it justice for with fervour they exploited this inexhaustible mine. There, numbering only two, and presided over by a venerable abbot who ate for three, they led a quiet and delicious life, forgetting the world and its pleasures, and devoting each day to nothing more than the process of filling their skins. It is quite credible that, if the *Almanach des Gourmands* had been known at the time, these good fathers would have thumbed it more often than their breviaries.

Come what may, the order never accorded the abbacy of the place to other than a candidate distinguished by the discoveries he had made in everything that might flatter a delicate palate, one which had had years of practice and was truly worthy to belong to a gourmand. The former abbot had just died, and a number of monks aspired to that dignity, which was ultimately accorded to Father Euphratis. He left at once and arrived the next evening at the abbot's lodgings. The tenant farmers waited in the wings to show him the accounts, his brother monks to discuss the business of the house, etc. It all fell on deaf ears; he wanted trout. At supper he was served with one weighing twenty pounds. Our abbot laid in with despatch, and found it excellent. He congratulated himself on a nomination that would allow him to eat similar offerings daily. But alas! Man proposes, God disposes. The fish was not yet three-quarters eaten when Dom Euphratis began to suffocate. Vain attempts were made to save him, while he made similarly useless attempts to swallow. He died with the tail of the fish still in his mouth. The order learnt, on the same day, of his enthroning and his decease. His obsequies were magnificent, and the Cistercians returned to the task of naming a successor, who probably died of indigestion too. A death truly worthy of a Cistercian and a gourmand, two words which were at that time virtually synonymous. We heard this story from M Dolo, who guarantees its veracity. We are tempted to believe that La Fontaine knew of it when he composed *Athenée*, his pretty tale of a Glutton, and that he saw the abbot in the following lines:

> So as I must surely die,
> Only one last wish,
> Let them bring me by and by,
> The rest of my fish.

ABSTEMIOUS PEOPLE

... eternal enemies of those pleasures that they are incapable of tasting, talking of *gourmandise* like eunuchs discussing the beauties of the seraglio.

OF THE *ALMANACH DES GOURMANDS*

A debauched mind drowned in the waves of unquenchable gaiety.

The *Almanach des Gourmands* is in no degree a cookery book. Our duty lies in seeking to stimulate the appetites of our readers; only true artists can hope to satisfy them.

AMPHITRYON*

Money alone is an insufficient guarantee of a good meal.

Any well-mannered Amphitryon will offer the same dish up to three times to each of his guests. His first duty is to come to the aid of shy stomachs, to reassure them and provoke them, to spare nothing to satisfy them.

He must abhor a vacuum.

Valets should never remove a course before they have received the order from the host, and the master of the house should never give that order until he is certain that his guests have given up on all the dishes.

Their consultation with their cooks has become almost as important a duty as that of a Prince with his Minister.

---

*Note from the *Almanach des Gourmands* on the origin of the term: 'We leave to the members of the third class of the National Institute (i.e. The Académie Française, as it was called during the Empire), the decision as to whether it is only since Molière said:

> Le véritable Amphitryon,
> Est l'Amphitryon où l'on dine.

[The real Amphitryon is the one giving the dinner], that the name of Alcmene's husband has become a by-word for all those who give good dinners.' In Molière's play Jupiter descends to earth to seduce Alcmene, taking the form of Amphitryon. He gives a dinner where ultimately the real Amphitryon takes his rightful place.

APHRODISIACS

1) *Celery*: Our conscience obliges us to warn shy people of this property of celery that they might abstain from eating it, or at least use it prudently. It is enough to stress that it is not in any way a salad for bachelors.

2) *The Cock*: Doctor Gastaldy has it that the flesh has aphrodisiac qualities, which would prove not only that death in no way diminishes this animal's much vaunted temperament but also that its power is such that it can transmit a portion of its mettle to those who eat it.

APOPLEXY

To give up *gourmandise* for the sake of avoiding apoplexy would involve a remedy worse than its cure. As the old adage has it, *qui medice vivit, misere vivit*. [A man who lives for his doctor lives no life at all.]

AUGUST

Little rabbits grow into big ones, little partridges into big partridges and leverets into hares. Let us not impede their development.

BEAUTY

It is easily demonstrated that a fifteen-year-old girl retains her beauty longer than a peach, though it is true to say that this beauty fades as quickly as a dancing shadow.

BEEF

The much vaunted English ox is no more than a mass of bloated fat; ours are a thousand times cleverer and more succulent.

An inexhaustible mine in the hands of a talented artist.

The King of the Kitchen. Without it no soup, no gravy; its absence alone would be enough to starve and sadden a town.

BLONDE VS. BRUNETTE

With one or two exceptions, fair skin betokens distinguished lineage, a delicate mind, and a soft and fine skin (a quality much admired by connoisseurs, for it is as sensitive in the dark as it is in light). Ordinarily, it is a sign of softness, and of all the pleasing characteristics of the fair sex. A blonde seems humbly to beseech your heart, while a brunette seeks more to ravish it. Now there is no question about it, one prefers by far to receive prayers than orders.

Whether you think the analogy is just or not, a 'blonde'* dinner is in all ways superior to a 'brunette'.† Any cook can, without any great effort, make the latter to a passable degree, while the former is a domain of first-class cooks alone.

---

*Examples given are: *béchamels*, *quenelles*, *fricassées*, *sautés à la suprême*, *grenadins aux crêtes*.
†Examples: *civets*, *compôtes* made from roux, minced meats, bean stews, hot pots.

BREAD

The Germans are not the only European people who consume very little bread with their meals; it seems that the English eat even less. As they are even more carnivorous than the former, they would be well advised to eat more. This sort of diet is well known to be unhealthy and the cause of a great number of putrid illnesses.

BRILLAT-SAVARIN

How can such a profound and piquant talent have been so slow to reveal itself! It's quite a swansong. Did the author die of indigestion?

Beside him I'm no more than a kitchen skivvy.

BUTCHERS

Monsieur Londault of the rue St Victor has suffered a singular decline. The destruction of the University brought about his fall. His destiny was linked to that of intellectual rigour.

CANON FODDER

One of the city fathers of the metropolis of ****, an elected deputy in the so-called *constituant* assembly, and who was, moreover, the very equal of the Cistercian monk to whom we owe the recipe for the famous *salmis* which is given in the *Almanach des Gourmands*, found himself the last of ten guests at the dinner table of an Amphitryon of our modern France. The latter, having cut ten thick slices from a shivering and succulent rump, passed the plate to our hero, so that he might serve himself and pass the dish on to the other attendant diners. Our canon, despite his unimpressive stature, was a man endowed with a prodigious appetite, and thanking his host for his kind attention in carving him these slabs, kept the plate for himself, swallowing ten huge chunks in the same number of mouthfuls, and digesting them with not so much as a gulp.

The Amphitryon, who was completely stunned by an appetite which, after such a promising prologue, continued to perform wonders up to and including dessert, immediately called for drink to be brought to the canon, as he feared the man might suffocate. When this was done, he resumed his task, cutting ten more hunks of the rump for the other diners, this incident having slightly delayed the service.

CAMBACÉRÈS The frontispiece of the fifth year of the *Almanach*: 'The First Duty of an Amphitryon'

The limited space afforded by the minute format of this volume allows only to draw the broad lines of this touching scene from which we have been obliged to suppress some of the most characteristic and interesting details. Gourmands must use their intelligence to imagine them. They should remember that the largest painting on earth, the great Veronese's 'Marriage at Cana', was hardly large enough to depict gourmands at table. What would it take, one wonders, to portray the kitchen of an *Archichancellier*?

CAPON

It is not from his own choice that he has renounced the pleasures of this world to increase the joys of our own.

THE CARNIVAL

It is as difficult to imagine a carnival without pork as a Lent without salt-cod or May without peas.

The Carnival is a time of pleasure for some people, for fancy dress for others, and indigestion for all and sundry. It is without doubt the time of year when one puts on the most weight, for it is the period when the most dinners are given, and when one is obliged to do them the most justice. The most bird-like appetite will endeavour to overcome its limitations in those happy days, aiming to prove itself worthy of sitting at the same table as gourmands; for even the possessor of such a stomach is aware that abstemiousness is a sad weakness during the rest of the year, but during the days of the Carnival, it is a veritable dishonour.

During the entire length of the Carnival, jaws are in a state of perpetual motion, and one might add that they work even harder than one's feet do. Despite the passion for dancing that comes over us in that season* there are ten banquets for every ball. One may dance all the year round, but never are tables so abundant or better supplied as in those last days of carnage. Why! How people prepare themselves for the austerities of Lent by a succession of indigestions! And why should one not feel sympathy for a stomach which will be forced to fast for forty days on end?

All Amphitryons vie with one another in a sainted emulation in their attempts to assassinate their guests by the sheer force of food. Beef, veal, mutton, pork, wild boar, fallow deer, roe deer, bustards, turkeys, capons, geese, hares, rabbits, pullets, partridges, woodcock, ducks, lapwings and virgin cocks all run as fast as their legs can carry them or fly as swiftly as they might to appear in honour on our tables. The crowd is so great that the monsters of the sea cannot even find standing-room, and soles, whiting, salmon and even turbot (those princes of the ocean) are forced to wait outside, only retaking their places at the start of Lent.

---

*At the time the pre-Lenten period was one of many balls.

CARVING

An Amphitryon who knows neither how to serve or carve might be compared to the owner of a splendid collection of books who has not a clue how to read. The one is almost as shameful as the other.

The art of carving well was regarded by our rich and well-born forefathers as a complement to a good upbringing. The last tutor a young man was given was the master carver.

Amphitryons of that bygone age almost always responded well to the precepts of that last tutor; a pupil who was otherwise incapable of construing a verse of Virgil or a sentence of Cicero with his book open at the place, understood every sinew of a duck, a goose, or even a bustard.

It is above all in the practice of this ingenious art that one recognizes the possessor of an hereditary fortune.

A man who knows how to carve and serve well, no matter how little presentable he be in other ways, is not only universally admitted, but in many houses is valued above all other guests.

CHAMPAGNE

No wine is less suitable for the stomach or disturbs more disagreeably the digestion.

The sparkling wine is certainly not the best champagne. It tends to be green or tart or both ... but it is the wine the ladies prefer. Sacrifices have to be made to their tastes in the hope that we will be favoured by some pleasant prattle and the blithe bursts of a delicate erotic gaiety. In general the arrival of the champagne is the cue for a gentle liberty to begin to reassert its rights.

Foreigners, chiefly the English, appreciate champagne far more than we do. Apart from the fizzy wine, little good champagne is drunk in Paris. The rosé has gone out of fashion and the red is very poor stuff.

CHEAT, CHEAT AND CHEAT AGAIN

A Gascon, endowed with a mind greatly outstripping his meagre income, was a great huntsman, and he had every reason to be one, for had he not roamed the woods and plains his stomach would certainly have felt the deficit.

A rich neighbour resented the gradual decimation of the land caused by the ravages of the Gascon and paid him a visit in order to voice his disapproval. The Gascon replied like a true son of his race: knowing that the neighbour was marrying one of his sons in three days time, he had intended to offer him the game and fully wished to take part in the celebration of the nuptials. When the day came, the Amphitryon's cook, with instructions from his master to hold him to his promise, hurried round to the Gascon's house.

The huntsman, who had expected the visit, had so badly mutilated two foxes which he had caught in a snare, that the *cordon bleu* was easily led to believe they were a couple of hares ... But the master of the house, more of a connoisseur than his cook, was not taken in. He ordered, that notwithstanding, a complete meal to be made from the beasts; a portion to be boiled for soup, a fillet with tarragon, another in a *ragoût*, the shoulders with a game sauce, etc., etc.

When the guests were all assembled for the banquet, the most important seats were awarded to the relations of the bride and groom. Everything was so tightly squeezed that no place remained for our Gascon. The master of ceremonies, profusely apologetic, asked the latter to take his place in an adjoining room, where a servant had instructions to bring him all the dishes which had been made from the two foxes. At the first mouthful, the Gascon realized the bad turn his host had played on him, but he took pains not to let his disappointment be noticed, while he thought of a suitable excuse to leave, both in order not to be obliged to eat meats which disgusted him and to dream up some suitable means of revenge.

As soon as the Gascon was alone, he hastened to invoke the spirit of his forefathers and compatriots, a prayer which the inhabitants of Gascony never utter in vain. As soon as his exhortations were finished, he began to ferret around in the room in which he had been placed, and there behind a glass door he noticed some sort of caterer's boy, who had come to deliver some dishes destined for the feast. As soon as the boy had left, the huntsman quickly exchanged his meal for that which was intended for the high table of the banquet. He ate with despatch, not leaving a crumb capable of revealing the fraud.

The end of the marriage feast was much enlivened by the report of the Gascon's appetite. True, certain *ragoûts* had been found a trifle bitter and uncouth in taste, but as the assembled company had drunk their fill, indeed more than they had eaten, the gaiety of the occasion was unimpaired.

The dinner being finished, the Gascon was brought back into the fold. He was inwardly amused by the great interest being shown in what he had eaten and responded by praising every morsel in turn. The master of the house, exhibiting a feigned modesty which was at once intelligible to the assembled company, exclaimed, 'My neighbour is not hard to please.'

'We Gascons never are,' replied the latter. 'People pay us too many compliments in comparing our cunning ruses to those of foxes; I would like us to be seen as more docile creatures. We, after all, stay where we are put, whereas the fox will not always do what you tell him ...'

The assembled company began to look uneasily at one another; certain people made off furtively, while those who remained contented themselves with verifying their suspicions. They returned crying, 'Cheat, cheat and cheat again!' But on a wedding-day men are of good cheer, and finding the prank so amusing, they not only pardoned the affront, but invited the Gascon to celebrate with them for the full week which remained for the feast.

It would have been impossible to conceive of an indemnity more to his taste, for a gourmand knows well that the morrow of the wedding is, often as not, better than the day itself.

CHEESE

Cheese is the drunkard's biscuit.

For those who need to provoke thirst Roquefort cheese deserves more than any other the epithet of the drunkard's biscuit.

CHERRIES

It is impossible to eat a cherry without thinking of Lucullus;* his is the first Roman name (after that of Pontius Pilate) that gourmands teach their children to utter.

*It is said that Lucullus transplanted the first cherry tree from Pontus to Rome.

OF CHICKENS, ETC.

The most delicate morsel on a roasted pullet is the wing, the best on a boiled fowl, the thigh ...

As for the *sot-l'y-laisse*,* as its very name implies, it is the thinking man's gobbet.

*Literally the 'idiot-leaves-it-there', i.e. the oyster.

CHOCOLATE

Chocolate is the habitual breakfast of men of letters, office workers, and generally all those persons whose lives are more sedentary than active, using far more the resources of their minds than those of their legs.

THE CODE GOURMAND

... the table is a country with its customs and its ways like any other, and the *Code Gourmand* is made up of a host of rules, which must be observed should you not wish to be taken for a Hottentot ...

THE CONSULATE

Sheep from Beauvais, the Cotentin and from the Ardennes ran as far as their legs could carry them to be metamorphosed into cutlets and shoulders of mutton.

HIS CONTEMPORARIES

Our ancestors ate only for survival's sake; their descendants appear to survive only for the sake of eating. New fortunes are all employed in the most real and robust animal pleasures. The crowns of our millionaires nearly all end up in the central market.

CONVALESCENTS: WHITING

Whiting is the first animal nourishment permitted to convalescents; its tender and delicate flesh being one of the most healthy foods for sick stomachs, especially when there is not too much butter used in the seasoning. Whiting is suitable for all those people whose occupations condemn them to sedentary lives; in this respect it is one of the best and most discreet friends of the man of letters.

CONVERSATION

All the other peoples of Europe theorize and argue; only the Frenchman knows how to make conversation.

OF COOKS

From well-fed and well-paid valets, thanks to the Revolution, they have become in turn: citizens, pensioners and finally, *rentiers*.

Today ... having no cook means having no friends; and the person who does not have dinners can be certain of having no callers from one end of the year to the next. This would be true were he as witty as Voltaire or as warm-hearted as Beaumarchais.

In all truth one cannot be a decent cook without being at the same time a chemist, a botanist, a physician, a draughtsman and a geometer. One must also have a good nose, a keen ear and immense tact; someone not having these qualities would be continually perplexed by the hanging of meats, the seasoning of *ragoûts*, the roasting of meats, the marriage of materials or the condition of pastry. It is therefore of capital importance that a cook be provided with an extreme delicacy in all his senses and all his organs.

But the physical qualities required pale into insignificance beside the moral ones or the talent necessary for this profession. Zeal, probity, impartiality, vitality, cleanliness, the ability to judge at a glance, *sang-froid*, deep understanding and intelligence, sobriety, vigilance, rigour, patience, moderation, a passion for work, a fondness for employers, etc. This is what is required of a cook worthy of the name; taking for granted an excellent nature, a good upbringing and an unflappable wisdom. Happy the Amphitryon having such a cook! He should treat him more as a friend than a servant, keep him entirely in his confidence, support him in all the setbacks of his profession, quote him at all times and spare no expense to achieve his glory and his fame.

The cook looks death in the teeth more often than the soldier.

We should pluck from the shadows this artist who exercises his truly divine talent in obscurity.

The effect of the French Revolution: In the past the cook's lot was an unassuming one. They were concentrated in a small number of opulent households, either at court, in high finance or in the world of the judiciary. They exercised their useful talents in obscurity while the number of capable judges of their worth remained small. By reducing the old landlord class to penury, the Revolution threw the best cooks out on to the streets. Since then they have employed their abilities by becoming merchants of good cheer with the name of restaurateurs. There were not above a hundred of these before 1789, there are perhaps five times as many now.

Once upon a time obscure skivvies, today almost millionaires.

Some people would have us believe that cooks are to butlers what apothecaries are to physicians. This comparison seems inapposite; for if it is true that apothecaries are essentially the doctors' cooks, it is not exactly the case that cooks resemble butlers' apothecaries.

A cook without faults is rarer than a great poet.

THE COUNTRY

One has a keener appetite in the country than one does in town.

ON THE DEATH OF DOCTOR GASTALDY,
PERPETUAL PRESIDENT OF THE JURY DÉGUSTATEUR

... he was helping himself to a dish of excellent salmon, which an otherwise benign Providence, sinister in this occurrence, had placed before him, when the Prelate [*the Archbishop of Paris*] caught sight of him and, scolding him tenderly for his imprudence, removed the offending dish from his reach ... Alas, it was too late; on returning home he lost consciousness.

DESSERT

When it comes to dessert ... [the gourmand] values little apart from cheeses and sweet chestnuts which, provoking thirst, are vehicles for the appreciation of the cellar.

The roast marks the end of the dinner for the gourmand; what he eats afterwards is for the sake of pleasing or being polite.

The dessert is to dinner what the *girandole* is to a firework display.

This is the brilliant part of the meal which requires a whole gamut of agreeable talents; a good pastry cook must be, all at once, an ice-cream maker, a confectioner, a decorator, painter, architect, sculptor and florist.

Without doubt the dearest course and that which demands the most care in preparation.

DIETS AND DIETING PEOPLE

Beware of people who don't eat; in general they are envious, foolish or nasty. Abstinence is an anti-social virtue.

Diets slow down the circulation of both blood and ideas and extinguish poetic vigour.

THE DIGESTION

Digestion is the stomach's business, indigestion the doctor's.

A gourmand should always avoid getting indigestion. It is even one of the great secrets of the profession.

DINNER

In contemporary Paris one dines a great deal later in the day than one took supper at the time of Charles VIII.

Dinner is the most interesting action of each day.

Few people other than fools and invalids would envy dinner the importance it deserves.

It is good to eat late, because it allows you to concentrate all your thoughts on your plate, forget your worries and think only about what you are eating and then retire.

THE LENGTH OF DINNER

Five hours at table are a reasonable latitude when the company is numerous and the cheer exquisite.

THE DINNER EMIGRATES – but is not Outlawed*

In one of the richest regions in France where the soil supports a continual activity, the churches' stipends and cures used to yield more than many a Provençal bishopric. The incumbents were, almost to a man, appointed by the local lords of the manor, who generally favoured their own relations. These priests, well adapted as they were to good living, regaled themselves with good cheer at the slightest pretext; and the feast of the dedication of their churches was an excuse for a rout.

It was on just such a day that the parish priest of Sainneville invited all his friends and colleagues to a feast. One person, however, was left out; the priest of the neighbouring parish, probably because, being at only half a league's distance, he thought he would always have time to invite him. In short, he was forgotten. The latter, in true Norman style, swore vengeance, and to that effect he visited the Amphitryon's house on the day of the dinner. He took care to arrive during the High Mass, knowing that he would find only the housekeeper in the presbytery.

The woman, believing this priest to be of the number, hastened to show him the spread. The latter affected an interest in everything he saw and reminded the woman that ordinarily the best cider was served with the first service, and that the priest had some excellent stuff. The servant agreed with him, and together they went to the cellar, which was at the extremity of the courtyard. The priest equipped himself with the necessary tools to pierce the barrel, which he did without further ado. Telling the housekeeper he was going to look for a tap or a plug, he asked her to stem the flow with her finger, and, despite the latter's protestations, he then made a similar hole in the next barrel, and asked the captive servant to plug this second leak with the index finger of her other hand.

Thus rid of the housekeeper, he quit the cellar, assuring her of his prompt return with the taps. But other cares preoccupied our wicked joker, and leaving the courtyard of the presbytery, he found his own servant, equipped with a horse and a number of baskets, which were rapidly filled with the dinner for which were being sung nearby such unctuous praises to the Lord. The thieving priest had the lot despatched to his house, following the tasty convoy with great haste.

After the High Mass was over, the Incumbent of Sainneville led his guests back to the presbytery, where he was angry to find that the places had not been laid for dinner in the dining-room. This wrath was as nothing compared to the emotion he felt upon entering the kitchen ... Oh woe! Neither pot not pan remained! And with them had gone the woman on whose cares the whole feast reposed. Her name was called in vain while a desolation entered the hearts of every diner. The master of the house was more greatly affected than anyone, having his losses, his hunger and that of his guests to manage. To calm the starving multitude, he proposed a collation of a crust of bread with a little wine, while he took stock of this lamentable situation. His guests assented. The priest ran to his cellar, which fortuitously lay alongside that in which he kept his cider and was where his unhappy servant was clamouring and bewailing her lot. Her master, hearing her cries, quickly released her from her frustrating labours. On her naming the culprit who had thus incarcerated her, every face beamed – the gaiety of that gentleman was well known in those parts – and no one doubted from that moment the identity of the person who had swiped the feast, nor did they doubt for an instant that the prank had been performed in order to lure the guests to his table.

Now, these gentlemen had legs no less proficient than their stomachs, and sped round to the neighbour's house, where he was expecting them. To appease their wrath, and to silence their complaints, he led them instantly into the pilgrims' hall, in other words, the dining-room, where an excellent dinner awaited them! 'O joy! What gentle intoxication.' What a delicious moment it was, and the best way of silencing all reproaches that might have uttered from their lips, while opening all the mouths of his honourable assembly to the succulent dishes on the table. Thus were satisfied the appetites doubled by fear and the recent run; the priest was absolved and the episode was found to be an excellent joke.

---

*Napoleon founded a commission to examine emigré cases, in March 1800. The findings allowed the greater number of the more liberal emigrés to return. An Order in Counsel of 11 April 1802 allowed the rest to come back under certain conditions, though about a thousand remained *proscrit* or outlawed.

ON THE DISPLAYS IN THE WINDOWS OF THE FOOD SHOPS

An almost superhuman virtue is required to face this new Tantalus, and to remain reasonably faithful to the Tenth Commandment of Our Lord.

DOGS

No one who knows how to behave at table ever brings a dog with him.

One must defend one's legs from its approach and one's plate from its voracity.

In many parts of the country, and above all in the Languedoc, the kitchen spit is turned by a specially trained dog shut in a hollow wheel. This performance has without doubt amusement value, but without dwelling on the unequal rotation or on the necessity of keeping an eye on an animal which allows the joint to catch by its standstills, one feels that a roast exposed to the caprices of a dog would be of uneven quality. One is at risk of forgoing it altogether should our modern Larido not be there when you need it or should the cook be forced to quit the kitchen to whistle his turnspit or to chase after it. Let us for the moment anyway be happy with our standard spits and cookers while we await their improvement by the march of mind.

THE EMPIRE

The number of Amphitryons, guests as well as true gourmands, not to mention the number of indigestions and physicians, has grown by an alarming proportion since the year 1803.

Gastronomic science is now all the rage ... and we are more than confident of seeing a chair of gastronomy set up in our *lycées* in years to come.

THE ENGLISH

As everybody knows, all the *regoûts* which bear the name of 'turtle' are of English origin. One could even say that with the exception of 'beaf's teak' (*sic*), pudding and chickens boiled in water, they are about all the English genius has created in the kitchen. It is a remarkable thing that these arrogant and greedy islanders, who persecute, destroy and despise all the other nations of Europe, have nothing to say for themselves when it comes to cookery. They know only how to half roast a joint: this scorching process owing rather more to the intense heat of their burning coals than to talent. Although their country is fertile and very well cultivated, abounding in fish and game of every sort, there is no other land where food is simpler, less inventive and less expert in its preparation. Only with the aid of French cooks do a number of lords maintain a good table in London. Though much more drunken than gourmand, they are, however no more knowledgeable when it comes to wine. The only thing they value in the drink is its strength and its spirit (a thing which must be distinguished from generosity). If that were not bad enough, their merchants cut with brandy almost all wines, be they from France or Portugal. With this land you are better off hitting hard than hitting accurately. Here in France it is quite the reverse. *Let's* get back to our turtle.

Ragoûts are practically non-existent when it comes to English cooking, which is limited to boiled chicken, a most insipid dish, and that thing which they call 'plump' [*sic*] pudding.

It is only through enlightened communication, and the mutual exchange of the results of experience, that the arts are respectively enriched by useful discovery. National pride must not be allowed to prevent us from learning from rival, or even enemy states, anything that might add to our pleasures or stimulate our sensuality; and even if it is true to say that French cooks are the greatest artists in Europe, they must not imagine that that permits them to rest on their laurels. Their art would never have achieved its present heights had they ever denied the contribution of more than one European gastronomy. Our own cuisine is made up of hordes of exotic *ragoûts*, which have been made native in the way that we have adopted and above all perfected them, something which has singularly contributed to the development of our national glory. Finally, if France has become the sovereign arbiter in matters of taste, it is to a great extent as a result of the care it takes not to reject any foreign discovery to which it is indebted.

England has never been famous for its *ragoûts*. There has never been any real reason for a gourmand to cross the Channel other than the desire to sample roast or grilled meats. This advantage is owed to the quality of the fuel, for coal produces a more ardent and aggressive heat than wood does, seizing the joint the moment it is put before it, closing the pores before the meat is cooked, resulting in the concentration of the juices rather than their evaporation. As soon as the crust formed by the furnace from the first rotations of the spit is removed and the joint is carved, it produces such a quantity of juice that it might be said to be a veritable deluge.

But it will be a long time before we shall see the triumph of the English in these matters, for not even every sort of roast responds to this treatment. Their method is viable only for the largest pieces of butchers' meat or game. It is quite clear that the intense heat required to seize a sirloin would char a chicken. When it comes to fowl, game, or little trotters, French roasters may still be assured of their superiority.

The tastebuds of these islanders are far less delicate than our own, and what would burn our mouths hardly even tickles theirs. It is for this very same reason that they prefer Port to Burgundy, and in general they show little enthusiasm for any wine which is not extremely strong and does not in some fashion rasp their throats.

Though the European country which buys the most expensive wines, it is most certainly the one in which it is the least agreeable for the connoisseur to drink.

ENTRÉE

The *piano nobile* and most important apartments of the feast.

ENTREMETS

Entremets may be compared to the airy attics which top the apartment of a town house or palace.

EMETICS

A true gourmand never ventures abroad without an emetic about his person; it is the quickest and safest way to avoid the aftermath of an indigestion.

FAUX PAS

The greatest outrage that may be perpetrated against a gourmand is to interrupt him in the exercise of his jaws.

It is an insult to your host to leave food on your plate or wine in your glass.

To fold your napkin at table is tantamount to inviting yourself back.

FEBRUARY

The salt-month.

FRY-UPS

The frying-pan is an excellent stock trader where Everyman comes to swop his old suit for a new one, or his ordinary apparel for a frock coat. Few people notice these metamorphoses; surely in this country they should be used to them. The genuine gourmand, whose tact is as certain as it is practised, is rarely taken in; even so he is quick to accept the metamorphosis if it is performed artfully and he is happy to be cheated as long as he is cheated well. In this last, he resembles many husbands.

FISH (various)

In Lyon: It is a principle that once out of water, a fish should never be put back in.

Turbot: An ocean-going pheasant.
        The King of Lent.
        A turbot in a *court-bouillon*: heroic simplicity.

Pike: The real Atilla of the fish ponds ... In his way a little crocodile.

Carp: The carp of the Seine are quite highly esteemed in the capital which goes to prove, despite the proverb, one is occasionally a prophet in one's own land.

Shad: A real aquatic hazelnut. At its happiest laid to rest with a good sorrel stuffing.

Sturgeon: Good Friday's roast.

Tunny: Carthusian veal. Still highly profitable to the medical profession as the source of a great many troubled digestions.

General: Once on the table a fish should never come into contact with iron; the dissection should be performed only by those metals worthy of the operation: gold and silver.

The Perch: The sick man's fish.

The Mackerel:*The more necessary he becomes to all of us the more welcome he becomes in every household.

Carp: This is a dish for a prince, or at the very least a *louche* Republican purveyor on his third bankruptcy.

Maquereau has a secondary meaning of pimp in French.

FOIE GRAS

These sumptuous morsels reappear without embarrassment until the last sliver has been polished off: like some new Pyrrhus they go from dinner to lunch and from lunch to dinner, just as that prince did 'from the daughter of Helen to the widow of Hector', they have too an advantage over that gentleman of being always well received. Really nothing surpasses an excellent *pâté de foie gras*; they have killed more gourmands than the plague. One knows as much, but the mere sight of this delicacy has the power to intoxicate; one tucks in with gay abandon without having the faintest idea how one is going to digest it. Our advice is to assist its dissolution in the stomach by grinding it right down with the help of crusts of bread and great libations of rum or Swiss absinthe ...

Strasbourg *pâtés de foie gras* seem heaven-sent to reconcile the Christians to the Jews, as it is said the latter are skilled in their manufacture.

The Goose: It would be an inhuman torture for it if the idea of its destiny did not offer some consolation, a prospect which allows it to face its sufferings with courage; when it reflects that its own liver, larger than the bird itself, stuffed with truffles and wrapped in pastry, will go to carry the glory of its name throughout Europe, the goose resigns itself to its fate and sheds not a single tear.

FORMALITY

All ceremony at table is to the detriment of dinner; the most important thing is to eat your food hot, cleanly, to eat a lot and at length.

FOWL (various)

Hen: The only place for the hen is the pot, where she may impart her strength to the stock.

Goose: An appetizing brunette.

Cursed be the man who plumps immediately for the wings; he will betray his lack of *savoir-faire* in polite society. First the breast of the goose should be sliced in the same way you would a duck. If the host accompanies these slices with a sauce made up of the juice of a lemon or a Seville orange, and a dash of virgin olive oil, he will have doubled his stock in the eyes of the connoisseurs.

GAME (various)

Fallow deer: ... this sort of dish is not at all democratic; only a few years ago it would have been sufficient to put an entire family in the dock of the Revolutionary Tribunal.

Teal: (*As a water fowl it could be eaten on both feast and fast days.*) Since the destruction of the French monasteries it has lost a little of its credit.

Lark: In the hands of a hungry man no more than a bundle of toothpicks, more appropriate to cleaning the mouth than to filling it.

Bartavelle:* One should speak of it only with respect and eat it only on one's knees.

---

*A breed of red partridge found in mountainous parts of France.

GAMING

There exists still in Paris a large number of households where, though decent in appearance, the cuisine is paid for by receipts at the gaming-table. In such places you are offered dinner only so that you might soon after pay four times its worth. These establishments are generally run by ancient dowagers or by loose women who have seen better days, assisted in the role of Alcmene* by pretty young girls who are easier on the eye. A delicate spirit should not set foot in this sort of household. But if he has committed the error of doing so, he may not decently refuse a hand. To do anything else would be tantamount to behaving like one of those rascals who make off from the taphouse without paying the reckoning.

*The wife of Amphitryon.

GARLIC

A number of Provençal *ragoûts* have become fashionable since the Revolution. Garlic was hardly tolerated in our kitchens before, cooks themselves only using it on the sly. The very name used to be sufficient to give the vapours to our little mistresses of the court and city. Since 1789 it has become an almost vulgar seasoning in Paris. Not only do cooks make no bones about using it but the most delicate of women do not scruple to partake of *ragoûts* where its taste is dominant. The freshness of their breath has undoubtedly changed, but as everybody is following the same diet no one is certain enough of him- or herself to offer any reproaches.

THE GASTRONOMIC ARTS

The gastronomic arts are a huge field, the borders of which are constantly being pushed back by every man who makes them the object of serious study or profound thought. These arts embrace all three realms of nature, and the four corners of the globe, all moral considerations and all social relationships. Everything comes within their scope in a more or less direct way and if they may seem superficial it is only to vulgar minds, who see no more to a kitchen than saucepans and no more to dinner than dishes.

GLUTTONY

M Barthe* the ingenious author of *Fausses Infidelités* and who was as egotistical as he was gourmand, had the habit of eating something from every dish on the table. His sight being poor, he suffered from the constant fear of having missed something; consequently he was forever turning to his servant and asking, 'Have I had any of that? Have I eaten any of this?' All of which was highly entertaining for the other diners. Barthe died from indigestion, exacerbated by a fit of temper; for he was irascible too. Had he only been a gourmand he might still be alive today, like his enemy, M Cailhava† of the Institut.

Let it be said that of all the Deadly Sins that mankind may commit, the fifth appears to be the one that least troubles his conscience and causes him the least remorse.

*Nicholas-Thomas Barthe (1734–85). Michaud states that he died as a result of a life of dissipation.
†Jean-François Cailhava de l'Estendoux (1731–1813).

GOING WITHOUT

Rarely in Paris is one forced to suffer going without. Because dinner is served at so many different times, a man with no household, and who is used to eating out, and who is acquainted with a large number of people, is almost certain of finding himself dinner any time between noon and seven o'clock in the evening.

GOOSE

The advantages of a roast goose extend beyond the dinner. The dripping it distils from an all-over cooking at a moderate temperature is a great resource in the kitchen for the seasoning of various vegetables, and above all spinach.

GOURMAND

(*Of frogs' legs*): A gourmand has no false delicacy; his first duty is to sample everything and to have an aversion to nothing.

A true gourmand is never late for dinner.

The gourmand is not just one who eats with depth, choice, reflection and sensuality; one who leaves nothing on his plate or in his glass, one who has never insulted his Amphitryon with a refusal nor his neighbour with a fit of sobriety. The gourmand must match his most strident of appetites with that jovial humour, without which the best of feasts is merely a gloomy rite. Always quick to repartee, he must maintain in a state of continual readiness every sense with which Dame Nature has endowed him. Finally his memory should be embroidered with a tapestry of anecdotes, stories and amusing tales which he is ready to retail in the interval between courses and the gaps between dishes to that sober folk might excuse the voracity of his appetite.

The artist of good cheer.

Never has there been a gourmand without plenty of wit.

If the *Dictionary of the Academy* is to be believed, *gourmand* is a synonym for glutton or greedy, as *gourmandise* is for gluttony. In our opinion this definition in inexact; the words gluttony and greed should be reserved for the characterization of intemperance and insatiability, while the word gourmand has, in polite society, a much less unfavourable interpretation, one might even say a nobler one altogether.

From forty to sixty years of age is the prime of a gourmand.

The desire to possess a good table is the driving force behind the ambitions of every Parisian. This has necessarily given birth to a new art.

A voracious appetite is all that is required to be a glutton. To merit the title of gourmand requires an exquisite judgement, a profound knowledge of every side of the gastronomic art, a sensual and delicate palate, and a thousand other qualities which are very difficult to find in the same person at the same time.

... it is essential to be able to tell the difference and not to try to judge a man by his external appearance. It should be clear that it is not appetite alone which gives the right to the title of gourmand. If that were indeed the case, the stoutest porter in the corn-market would have a greater claim than M d'Aigrefeuille.

GROCERS The Hôtel des Américains

Blessed with a cast-iron stomach and a vast appetite, happy the man who found himself incarcerated, imprisoned for life!!! O Utinam!

GUESTS

It should be unnecessary to say that they should always be dressed in clean linen; even the most mediocre of dinners is worth a shirt.

The invited guest, properly dressed, should arrive at the Amphitryon's house at the time indicated on the invitation. He should be equipped with an appetite equal to the reputation of his host's table and with his stomach, heart and mind wholly disposed to contribute their utmost to the charm and pleasure of the proceedings.

He should avoid being late at all costs. In this base world a dinner is the thing which least tolerates delay.

Invitations should be answered within twenty-four hours of receipt.

GUINEA FOWL

Their aggressive and quarrelsome nature renders them anti-social. They are generally regarded by other species of fowl to be the scourge of the farmyard.

HABITUÉS

The Revolution, by bringing in the new order, redistributing fortunes, killing off the old *rentier* class as well as robbing nine-tenths of the former landlords, has all but annihilated this old breed of scavengers. The *nouveaux riches* are less credulous, less self-confident and less polite than their forerunners were. They know better the value of coinage than praise. Pimps are more likely to be well received in their households than adulators. The only place where one might catch a glimpse of this breed of parasites is in the homes of a handful of female zealots and one or two illustrious antique dowagers who have safeguarded their kitchens from the general shipwreck and who are happy to be robbed and bullied by sheer force of habit, finding it gentler coming from flatterers than from domestic servants.

Men of letters and artists form a class of people who do not eat at home. This sort respond only to regular, formal, written invitations and pay the reckoning with anecdotes, witticisms, stories, ingenious repartee, amusing quotations, comic tales, bawdy songs, party games, bacchic couplets, light-hearted dalliance, etc.

HORS D'OEUVRES

A grand dinner with no hors d'oeuvres would be about as improbable as a pretty woman not wearing rouge.

If we accept that the entrées are like the lovely rooms which constitute the *piano nobile* of a town palace, the hors d'oeuvres should be seen as those little offices and boudoirs: retreats that add immeasurably to the beauty of the layout, setting off the principal rooms and completing the elegance of the apartment.

Or, if you prefer, hors d'oeuvres resemble those entresols, dignified lodgings that, though betokening a lesser opulence of show than an apartment on the first floor, demand as high a rent and boast furnishings as costly.

Women have great fondness for these trifles.

HOTHOUSES

Hothouses produce, artificially and at great expense, fruit and vegetables without flavour to supply the lavish tables of the modern Lucullus.* These false creations might well satisfy one's vanity, but they will never please the palate.

*'A rich Roman soldier, noted for his magnificence and self-indulgence ... On one occasion a very superb supper was prepared, and when asked who were to be his guests the "rich fool" replied, "Lucullus will sup tonight with Lucullus."' (Brewer, *Dictionary of Phrase and Fable.*)

ICES

Talented ice makers are almost as rare as good roasters.

OF THE INGRATITUDE OF GUESTS

All Amphitryons should unite to put these offenders on a diet.

INVITATIONS

In *gourmandise*, to break off an engagement is to break a promise, throw a dinner into disarray, to inject trouble and dismay into the heart of an honest Amphitryon, and to proffer him one of the most deadly insults. What is more, it is to expose oneself to being never again invited by the latter, for it requires a supernatural degree of indulgence to convoke anew the dishonest guest who has ever dared to break his word.

The gravest of illnesses, a fractured limb, imprisonment or death, only these may excuse a cancellation, and make it, if not admissible, legitimate at least. But even so, the first two cases will require a duly certified affidavit, attesting the state of the invalid; in the third instance, the duplicate of the order submitted to the turnkey and in the last, the death certificate should be attached to or take the place of the letter of cancellation.

An Amphitryon who cancels an engagement, even if it is a woman, a pretty woman, or even a pretty actress (that is the *nec plus ultra* of people to whom one offers everything), will be for ever more dishonoured in the eyes of a gourmand. That person deserves, from that point onwards, to have all his or her invitations refused, that not even a glass of water be acceptable from that hand; were he or she to have a cook of the stature of Morillon, Robert, Méot or Philippe*, the result would still be the same; one must condemn them for the rest of their days to a solitary dinner which, for an Amphitryon, is a sort of civil death.

Dis-engagements and dis-invitations are the greatest scourge that exists in this base world after diets and dinners 'among friends'.

It is rare that a real gourmand sleeps in any bed but his own; invitations can be delivered during his absence and it is essential to the progress of the art that he should refuse none. Seldom it is that one learns nothing from a meal and in this honourable profession one should never pass by an opportunity to educate oneself.

... The only acceptable invitations are those which fix a day.

---

*Morillon, cook to Grimod *père*. Robert, inventor of the sauce of that name, replaced Laguipière as the cook to Prince Murat after the latter died before Vilna on the Russian campaign. Méot was one of the most famous cooks of the revolutionary period whose restaurant has now been replaced by buildings of the Banque de France. Philippe: creator of the culinary glories of Chartres.

JAM

What a pity the name of the inventor of jam has been lost to us!

He deserves a statue made out of sugar candy and we would lick our lips in mentioning his name.

JOURNALISTS

They are recognizable by their apoplectic throats, their bushy moustaches and their puffy bibulous visages.

JULY

Quails ... a good plump quail on a spit, dressed up in a morning coat of fat bacon and an overcoat of vine leaves, is the most exquisite roast of the season. In its delicacy it is worthy of the table of the Gods.

KITCHENS

It is as difficult to put together a kitchen as to create a library.

LENT

The happy Carnival is already on the wing, the obsequies of Shrove Tuesday have finished and Ash Wednesday, that sad precursor and element of Lent, has already lowered its funereal veil over the horizons of the gourmand. Its appearance is the signal for all fur and feather to scurry and fly away. Farewell then Cotentin beef, Pontoise veal, Pré-Salé, Cabourg and Ardennes mutton, nutritious pork, the skittish fallow deer, the valiant wild boar, the timid fawn and the melancholic hare, yet more timid and no less agile, such bliss to fix on the spit. If the law of Lent is for us a time of penitence, for them it is a period of jubilation. Where we shiver in sackcloth and ashes, they gambol about returning our hungry stares and insulting our appetites; for a while they need not look to protect themselves from our pursuit. Swelling, reproducing, getting fat and enjoying themselves are now their entire preoccupations, while we gloomy children of the Church, we do precisely the reverse.

But comfort yourselves, brother gourmands; the Church is not calling for the death penalty, it is seeking only to reform the sinner. If it is asking us to fast for forty days, it allows us at least a pause on Sundays, and on that day we can eat ten meals without causing offence to Heaven. If it forbids us lunch, it permits us a cold collation. These cold dishes may not include quadruped or bird, but in all security of conscience one may summon up pâtés made up of tunny, sturgeon, red mullet or eel, pickled sardines, Fréjus anchovies, pickled oysters from Granville, an infinite number of dried fruits from Touraine and Provence, appealing dainties which seem made for Lenten collations, and which we would value more highly if we could learn to wait till Lent each year to renew acquaintance.

LIQUEURS

It would be unthinkable to invite guests to the simplest of meals were there not two or three liqueurs flanking the coffee pot.

LUNCH

Lunch is an inconsequential meal, ideal for a man anxious to conceal his fortune, for a bachelor without staff or for an unassuming gourmand who may safely receive without shocking his neighbours or causing tongues to wag.

Since we have begun to dine in Paris at eight o'clock in the evening (with dire consequences when it comes to wit, gaiety or conversation), we sup no longer. We have therefore been obliged to transform lunch into some sort of meal, and though the tablecloth is not laid, in the majority of rich households the meal is of an altogether respectable solidity.

It could be said that, with the exception of the tablecloth, the soup and the roast, they are veritable morning dinners.

It is not possible that even the toughest stomachs can resist a comparable régime for long. Even the best designed man is not capable of doing justice to more than one good meal a day, and eating one in the morning necessarily detracts from the evening repast. In the old days, those who dined copiously supped but little, and veritable 'suppers' (if we can excuse the word) hardly ever dined. The solid Midases of our day lunch majestically, and dine on no lesser a scale. Now this régime has its attractions, but sensible men should limit themselves to admiration without seeking emulation, for if they do so, it will be at the expense of their minds, their health and their very existence even.

LYON

The lowliest Lyonnaise housewife could usefully instruct the majority of the great artists of the capital.

MADEIRA

The greater part of the wine made in Madeira is shipped to Great Britain.* The English [sic] are singularly fond of it, and after Port, it is the wine they drink the most. However, either to make it suit their bizarre tastes and blasé palates, or to allow it to bear quite a lengthy sea voyage, it is cut with a sizeable quantity of French brandy. Only in that sophisticated state is it allowed to leave the ports of the island. This explains why in peacetime innumerable shipments of brandy leave the ports of Bordeaux and La Rochelle destined for Madeira.

*Grimod was mistaken. The greater part of the wines of the island were, in fact, shipped to the American colonies, and later to the United States. This was due to a loophole in commercial legislation which, classing Madeira as a part of Africa, did not require merchants to ship it through the mother country.

MAY

Herbs are at the height of their power, butter too is at its best. Peas in pods, peas shelled. The song of May.

MILLE-FEUILLE

Such a cake should be sired by a man of genius and demolished in the most able hands.

MONEY

Why in this perverse century, when it comes to the fair sex, should Plutus* be the most powerful of the deities? Cashmere, gold and diamonds make a greater number of conquests and triumph over many more stubborn hearts than does love or wit.

*The God of Riches.

MONKFISH

Monkfish livers in a pastry case, what a delicious concoction! One would be enough to make a gourmand die a thousand times on the bed of honour.

MORALITY IN THE KITCHEN

Neither Nicole,* Pascal,† La Rochefoucault‡ or La Bruyère§ would ever have suspected that such an abundant source for moral observation could have been provided by the nineteenth-century kitchen.

*Pierre Nicole (1625–95), author of *Essais de Morale*.
†Blaise Pascal (1623–62). His *Pensées* were published posthumously.
‡Duc François de La Rochefoucault (1613–80). *Maximes Morales*, 1665.
§Jean de La Bruyère (1645–96). *Les Caractères*, 1688.

MUSTARD AND VINEGAR

M Maille is the Corneille of mustard. When it comes to vinegar it has to be said M Maille is the Corneille, Racine and Crébillion all in one.

... to sharpen the appetite, to conceal the cook's mistakes, finally to honour everything it is served with.

Without it, pigs' trotters *à la* Sainte Ménéhoult [*sic*] would be only an epigram without salt.

MUTTON

It is a great deal easier to find a sensitive lady than a tender leg of mutton.

NOUVEAUX RICHES

They have shown themselves anxious to walk in the footsteps of those who preceded them down that path [of *gourmandise*] ... The dawn of the summer days of good cheer was not slow to shine.

It was with a view to offering these worthy neophytes some useful guidelines that we first became involved in the wholesale trade and later went over wholeheartedly to gastronomic literature, which until that time we had hardly even embraced *in petto*.*

Those who once supped off nothing but cheese now regale themselves with truffles and ortolans.

The upheaval that has taken place in the distribution of wealth as a necessary result of the Revolution has transferred old riches into new hands. As the mentality of the majority of these overnight millionaires revolves around purely animal pleasures, it is believed that a service might be rendered them by offering them a reliable guide to the most solid part of their affections. The hearts of the greatest number of rich Parisians have been suddenly transformed into gullets, their sentiments are no more than sensations, their desires appetites; it is therefore with the idea of most usefully serving them that we give them in these few pages, the best possible means of drawing the greatest profit for their penchants and their pockets.

*In Italian in the text.

NOVEMBER

All those who belong to the honourable class of gourmands find themselves reunited from Martinmas onwards.

For healthy men it is the season of emetics and enemas.

OF THE OLD SERVICE AT TABLE

It is in the very nature of this service to throw guests into a confusing *embarras de choix* which is always detrimental to the appetite. The action of tasting must be successive to be enjoyable, which makes the service of dishes one by one the method which best stimulates and satisfies the appetite. It is comparable to a Sultan who, surrounded by fifty *odalisques* and not knowing which one to tip the wink, feels his desires ebb away.

ORTOLAN

Happy the palate that engulfs it!

PALATE

Coffee should be taken burning-hot and soup boiling. Happy the man possessing a delicate palate and a cast-iron throat.*

*'Every palate [in Paris] seems to be lined with mosaic work or to be endowed with the faculty of the incombustible Spaniard.' (*Travels from Berlin through Switzerland to Paris in the year 1804*, Augustus von Kotzebue, 3 vols., London 1804.)

PARASITES

The members of this profession are generally proletarians who, possessing no household of their own, would eat for twelve sous in a soup kitchen had they not wormed their way to some opulent table. They eat voraciously, monopolize the conversation by recounting the day's news (always of doubtful authenticity from their lips), secondhand stories and meaningless theories. Their impudence is equalled only by their avidity. Base flatterers, vile toadies, witless adulators, joyless jokers, graceless courtiers, they have little to offer but their effrontery, loquaciousness and dexterity. And if the Amphitryon does not take care they will make off with all his food and reign in sovereign state at his table.

... One of these domestic robbers had already diverted several pieces of food into a pocket lined with tinplate and consecrated to this sort of 'fencing', when he was spotted by the Amphitryon. As the man was not far away, the latter took advantage of the situation and, choosing a moment when the scavenger had his head turned in another direction, all the while exposing the mouth of this new-style larder, the Amphitryon poured in a carafe full of water, exclaiming with not a little *sang-froid*: 'It has eaten enough to deserve a drink.'

... Because in the past there used to be many more dinners than diners, there was nothing humiliating about being a parasite. Today the reverse is true; a man of reduced means who retains some dignity, prefers to fast at home than to expose himself to an indigestion, which is all the more shameful when one reflects on the majority of places one might contract one. Besides, is it becoming to frequent those people one despises? That unholy alliance of thieves and their dupes, of executioners and their victims? Is it not better to hang on to one's honest sentiments amid this poverty and prevent the Revolution from robbing one of both one's pride *and* one's fortune?*

... Parasites have existed since time immemorial. They were

---

*'There are presently in Sirap [Paris] more dinners than diners, something which has greatly reduced the number of parasites. One sees hardly any these days except courtiers.' (*Lorgnette Philosophique. Trouvée par un R.P. Capucin sous les Arcades du Palais Royal & Presentée au Public par un Célibataire* [i.e. Grimod de La Reynière], London 1785.)

known to the Egyptians, the Greeks and the Romans as well as every modern civilization. But it is in France today that they exist in the greatest abundance, for it is here that one eats the best ...

PARIS

In Paris four o'clock means five; four o'clock precisely means four-thirty and four o'clock *very* precisely means four.

If there is no town on earth that consumes as much wine as Paris, there is no other where so much of the wine sold is adulterated. Its wine merchants deserve even more than the ancient Romans the epithet the good Horace gave them of *'perfidus hic caupo'*.* Now he was an excellent toper and must have known his stuff.

... the city both the most gourmand and the most magnificent in Europe, the place where the opulence of the table is carried to the highest degree, where all the elements of good cheer have evolved to their loftiest state, finally, where the great art of eating has been hoisted to perfection ...

The truth obliges us to say that the gastronomic art of the capital has never been at a higher stage of development than that which it has achieved today.

*'treacherous innkeeper'

PARSLEY

Parsley is the culinary abc, and the lucky charm of the novice cook.

PASTRY COOKS

Good pastry cooks are almost as rare as great orators.

A PERTINACIOUS PRIEST

The ladies who lived at the Château de *** wanted to commit a little act of vengeance on the local incumbent (a man renowned for his *gourmandise* throughout the province), or simply amuse themselves at his expense, and dreamt up this little prank. The priest, who had refined tastes, was more enthusiastic about subtle and delicate foods than he was about more rustic cheer. However, being a prodigious eater, he was not difficult when obliged to opt for the latter. The ladies decided to base their naughtiness on that premise. The priest was invited to dinner and found the table groaning with huge dishes, vulgar meats and healthy *entremets*, etc., nothing more. He therefore placed himself in the hands of his appetite and, taking his time, consoled himself over the lack of ortolans with the presence of the sirloin. The ladies hardly ate at all, but that worried him but little. But what is this? Instead of dessert a second dinner is laid out on the table, made up of delicate entrées, game and little trotters, all cooked according to the grand principles of the art. Our priest, who had gorged himself, became furious at this scene, was very short with the ladies, and rising from the table, left in high dudgeon, hearing no entreaties and entertaining no requests to remain. As soon as he left, the ladies began to reproach themselves for having pushed the joke too far, when suddenly the priest reappeared, feigning good humour, sat down again and ate for four. One can guess what he must have done during his short absence ... but what is less certain is that these mystified pranksters understood, in their turn, that one must never attack a genuine gourmand on the subject of good cheer.

PHEASANT

The most solid treasure that the Argonauts brought back from the conquest of the Golden Fleece.

All things considered a genuine gourmand will opt for a good capon from the Maine in the place of the most brilliant and tenderest of pheasants.

Though it was one of the first victims of the democratic system of government adopted in France since 1789, it is however still possible to find the odd one that has escaped from the clutches of Revolutionary justice.

Of the hanging of pheasants: As long as it takes for a man of letters who has never learnt the art of flattery, to receive a pension.

A pheasant hung up on Shrove Tuesday is ready for the spit on Easter Sunday.

PHYSICIANS

No doctors preach from their own example. If they forbid the use of sauces to their *clients*, even when they are in good health, never do they themselves abstain. Proportionally speaking, this profession is, without a shadow of doubt, that in which is found the greatest number of gourmands, all of which does prevent them from seeing a profit in their profession.

It is other people's indigestions which prevent them from having to diet themselves.

THE PIG

The gourmand's God, the encyclopaedic animal.

The pig is the civilized version of the wild boar, or rather that which has been reduced by castration and slavery. But that humiliation is to the advantage of our sensuality; and the peace-loving, sociable qualities of the one seem, in the kitchen at least, far preferable to the wild, republican virtues of the other.

The King of Base Beasts.

Ingratitude has been pushed to such extremes in his case as to make the name of the animal most useful to man into a vulgar insult.

Without it no fat and therefore no cooking; without it no ham, no sausages, no *andouilles*, no black puddings and as a result no pork butchers.

If two of the best pork butchers in Paris, Messrs Corps and Duthé, owe their fortune to its flesh, the bristles on its back were the first instrument of Raphael's glory, and they were not exactly useless to Rameau.

As one knows, a gourmand never speaks of this animal without respect.

So disdained and despised during its life, once the pig dies the position is reversed and his passing over spurs into activity the talents of a great number of artists, each and every one studying to vary the innumerable preparations which the animal's flesh sacrifices to *gourmandise*, metamorphosing this precious beast into puddings and *andouilles*, sausages and brawn, stuffed trotters, simply done or *à la* Sainte Ménéhould*, gammons and cutlets, hams, etc., etc., for another four pages, etc., etc.,...

Whosoever seeks to study closely the behaviour of this animal will find a great resource of philosophy in all its habits. From Saint Anthony's pig and the hogs of Epicurus, through to those of whom we have the honour to be contemporaries, and who turn up *en masse* every Monday at the Market in Saint Germain-en-Laye to supply the capital, there has not been one that was not in its lifetime an example of stoicism, impassiveness, egoism and good appetite, qualities which have been recognized in every time since the dawn of man, and above all in our own.

---

*Sainte Ménéhould in the old province if Champagne has always been famous for its recipes. The trotters are cooked in breadcrumbs and served with a variant on a Sauce Robert. These trotters were so esteemed both then and now, that Camille Desmoulins put it about that the very gourmand King Louis XVI would never have been caught at Varennes had he not stopped at Sainte-Ménéhould for a plate of trotters.

PIGEON

The pigeon awaits the return of the peas to be at its best.

PILAU

An Ottoman *ragoût* worthy of French citizenship.

PISTACHIO NUT

One of the most exquisite sweets that might perfume the taste buds of a delicate tongue.

PLUM PUDDING

A rather bizarre and indigestible mixture; as a preparation, neither sagacious nor salubrious.

PLATES

To leave anything on them is to insult the master of the house in the person of his cook. This duty is no less obligatory for ladies than it is for men, and we will here warn those little mistresses who think it good manners to do otherwise that it is better to accept nothing at all or very little, and that way finish everything you are given. This rule is *de rigueur*.

THE POTATO

Almost unknown to our tables forty years ago, this vegetable owes a greater part of its celebrity to M Parmentier. Its virtue is to offer the poor a healthy staple, both nutritious and ensuring their eternal protection from want; for the rich it has the advantage of providing the most delicate and varied pleasures.*

---

*The potato made a late entry on to the French gastronomic scene in the years immediately prior to the Revolution. Its apostle was Antoine-Auguste Parmentier (1737–1813), though the root had been used in other parts of France before the late eighteenth century (notably Franche-Comté). It was Parmentier who first advocated the potato at court and who cultivated it on a plot of land at Neuilly outside Paris. In 1785 the vegetable was presented at court, Parmentier being rewarded by the honour of kissing Marie-Antoinette's hand. Parmentier is honoured in a number of dishes bearing his name, all containing potatoes. At the end of his life the agronomist was in correspondence with Grimod.

PUNCTUALITY

In the houses of real gourmands one sits down to dinner at the stroke of the clock, and that is the moment for the sporting of the oak.

RAMS' TESTICLES

There is good news for the ewes; these highly prized delicacies have entirely gone out of fashion.

READINESS

It is proven that all things here below want to be served, gathered or eaten at their apogee; from the maiden who has but an instant to show us her beauty in all its freshness, and her virginity in all its lustre, to the omelette which demands to be devoured on leaving the pan.

RECONCILIATIONS

One is never properly reconciled to someone until there has been a mutual sacrifice to the God Comus; an indigestion acquired in common is the most sacred seal that can be put on the patching up of a quarrel. In a phrase, the table is for two gourmands who have fallen out, what the conjugal bed is for two momentarily warring spouses; sulking is no longer permitted once people have dined or slept together.

RED PARTRIDGE

Other game birds are rarer, more expensive, more welcome for the sake of vanity, prejudice or fashion, but the red partridge, beautiful in itself, whose qualities are divorced from fantasy, which unites in its person all that may enchant the eye, delight the palate, stimulate the appetite and revive the spirits, is not for an age but for all time; it will be the crowning glory of all feasts in every guise it wears.

THE REVOLUTION

Had the reign of the vandals lasted longer we should have lost even the recipe for chicken fricassée.

The Jacobins and the Directoire put us on a three-year diet.

The memory alone sticks in the gourmand's throat.

... If the French Revolution had a detrimental effect on almost all the arts this was not the case with cooking; far from having suffered as a result, it has the Revolution to thank for its rapid progress and motive force.

The Revolution reduced by so many the number of Amphitryons that we must now labour to re-create the species.

Never has there been less liberty or equality in France as now when the words are scrawled on every wall.

... former marquises, high court attorneys become masters of chicanery, the majority of the wealthy are lacking education and polite usage, the women want wit or upbringing; soon we will know *politesse* and respect only by name.

The dukes and peers of the monarchy were a great deal more polite than the bankers and racketeers of the republic.

The shock would have totally unseated the polite arts, which in our society have taken three centuries to achieve this degree of perfection, and would have returned them to a primitive condition had it not been for certain right-thinking gentlemen of the ancient mode who have meticulously preserved the tradition.

... One has no idea of the amount of brigandage which has been carried out by carriers on land and water since the Revolution, and this is also true of those employed to man the *octrois*. This criminal activity is directed towards the transport of wines, and takes place both *en route* and on their arrival. All along the road, these trustees dip into the casks, refilling with water. When they carry vinegar from Orléans or Saumur, as they cannot drink it, they swop it for wine with the innkeepers by the roadside, thus hiving off several litres in such a way as to guarantee the non-reliability of these liquids. All these crimes are committed quite unabashed and with total impunity, which is truly scandalous. The use of double barrels provides an imperfect remedy. It is high time the authorities tightened up when it comes to this sort of theft; it was practically unknown before 1789.

RICE

The most honorable mausoleum in which one might bury a chicken fricassée.

ROASTS

There are a thousand people who can cook well to one who knows how to dress the roast.

The roast is like the drawing-room, the main feature of the house, which, all things considered, shows off the pride of its owners because it is the room furnished with the most care, as it is designed to hold the greatest number of guests and as its decoration was the most expensive.

It is even rarer to find a man who can dress a joint well than to meet a great cook.

If it is mean, burnt or tough, all the excellent dishes that preceded it are forgotten and a dismal silence reigns throughout the course. Diners lower their gaze or hold their tongues and the embarrassed and perplexed Amphitryon can make amends only by producing some exquisite *vins d'entremets*.

SALAD

It is above all the ladies who are most fond of this, and those of them who possess a pretty hand never avail themselves of forks to eat it with.

SAUCES

Sauces may be compared to the furnishings which adorn the apartments of some splendid edifice ... Without sauces ... a dinner would be as bare as a house which had just passed through the hands of the bailiffs.

... the last brush stroke of the painter, the final adjustment to a beautiful woman's toilet.

SEPTEMBER

Oysters: neither fresh nor fat enough to excite the sensuality of a gourmand.

SERVANTS

Their ears pricked up, their eyes on stalks, their bellies empty, all go to make their labours a real torture for dinner guests and for themselves ... The sight of their long faces and hungry mouths is enough to paralyse the appetite of the staunchest of trenchermen.

Valets have become successively betrayers, judges, and executioners of their masters. Most of the denunciations filed during the Terror were their work.

An Amphitryon should allow himself to be robbed a little by his servants in order to be better served.

Generally speaking servants are both more difficult and more demanding than their masters.

... The practice of keeping the wine on the sideboard at the disposition of valets, depending on them when a drink is required, is tantamount to risking death by thirst if you do not have some great rascal planted behind your chair throughout the meal.

The presence of valets at table is the greatest scourge that can be inflicted on a meal. Their eyes avidly devouring all the dishes, their ears mopping up all the opinions, and as for their tongues, always ready to denounce their masters, or at the very least to vilify them, they know only too well how to profit from them.

SILENCE

Silence in guests is a mark of strong disapproval.

SINGING AT TABLE

The habit of singing at table, abandoned by everyone else, is still common among the lower orders. But patriotic songs have replaced those pleasant, sensitive or tender couplets that used to exist; veritable cues for carnage, cannibal chants, terrible invocations alternating with horrifying blasphemies, smiting the ear of the peace-loving citizen who, having no love for any party, wishes only for a little rest while enjoying his meal, and who believes that rest dearly paid for by the loss of his entire fortune.

SOUP

The *porte cochère* of a well-structured meal.

The soup is to dinner what a portico or peristyle is to an edifice.

A good soup is the poor man's ordinary, a pleasure often coveted by the opulent.

Like the overture of a comic opera it should announce the subject of the work.

Good soup is rarely found in great kitchens because the stock is constantly being dipped into to moisten the *ragoûts* and then being topped up with water.

As for Potage *à la* Necker,* it is so named without doubt in an attempt to deride the man, or to create his very antithesis, for it is excellent. That vain and hypocritical old man was the prime mover in all the ills that have befallen France these last fifteen years. He certainly could not have sired anything good.

---

* Jacques Necker (1732–1804). Principal minister of Louis XVI. Madame de Staël was his daughter.

SPICES

Spices are the soul, the hidden spirit of good cookery.

STIMULANTS

Many is the time when a lover or a gourmand would be seriously unequal to their reputation were it not for art coming to the aid of nature.

STOMACH

Treat it with care, and remember, a gourmand who has lost the use of his stomach is as useful as a Grenadier in the Invalides.*

The stomach of an authentic gourmand should be like the casemates of a fortified town, i.e. bomb-proof.

A true gourmand must labour to elect his stomach to the Godhead. Sacrifices and libations must be multiplied on the altar of this guardian deity rather than the smoke of some sterile incense. Indeed, for a gourmand it is not a viscera but a divinity. Cursed be all those who take offence at our religion, and treat us as idolators! They will henceforth be seen as unworthy to approach a saucepan or to shake out a napkin.

*The equivalent of Chelsea Hospital.

STRAWBERRY

Just like a timid virgin it defends itself against the profaning hand; it must be plucked from its stem which all too often follows it on to the table where, bathed in pools of milk or champagne, it drinks of a liquor more gentle than the dew.

THE SUBTLE CAPUCIN

One day some youthful rascals decided to amuse themselves at the expense of a Capucin father whom they had invited to dinner. A ravishing spit-roast sucking pig was being served, and the monk was asked if he would perform the honours. As he seemed fully disposed to do so, the burliest of the youths said to him, 'Reverend Father, for Heaven's sake take care! For we have already decided among ourselves that whatever you do to that animal, we will do the same to you, and you may count on it, that should you lop off a limb, or the head, the very same will happen to you that instant. Never will the law of retaliation be so rigorously obeyed.' The Capucin, quite unruffled, performed the same manoeuvre on the pig as we have suggested as a means of determining whether young turkeys are worthy of purchasing or not.* He then addressed the company. 'Gentlemen,' he said, 'I heartily beg of you to carry out your menaces; as you see, you do not frighten me.' Who was then the dupe? The pranksters themselves. Thus will be treated all whose who seek to rag a gourmand.

---

*He stuck his finger into the pig's anus, breathed in deeply and then sucked it.

SUCKING PIG

If the pig provides little or nothing in the way of good roasting meat, this is not the case with his heir.

On Carving a Sucking Pig: Without wasting a minute you must first of all take courage and with one single blow from your well-sharpened knife, chop off his head. This is the only way of eating the crackling crunchy, otherwise it becomes flabby, and there is nothing that is more insipid than limp flesh and flabby skin.

SUMMER

The summer is the worst season for fine food and above all for good meat. During this season all species reproduce and it is important not to disturb them in an industry from which we ourselves will reap the principal fruits. Hot weather frequently prevents fresh fish from reaching the Paris markets. The prime resources are therefore found in the fruits and vegetables, and so it is that *entremets* and desserts outshine all other dishes in this season at the expense of the other services. One must add that it is the season in which one gives the fewest formal dinners; Amphitryons rest, cooks meditate, and diners not possessing suitably equipped households, eat, often in memory alone.

SUPERSTITION

There are people who fear an upturned salt cellar or thirteen at table. You should be frightened of this number only when there is enough food just for twelve; as for the knocked-over salt, the most important thing is that it should not end up ruining a good dish.

SUPPER

If lunch is the meal of friendship, if dinner is that of etiquette and tea, children, then supper belongs chiefly to love.

Women are kinder at supper-time than at any other moment of the day; one might say that the more imminent the moment of their inevitable empire, the more seductive and tender they become.

THE TABLE

The table has become, in our time, the pivot of all political, literary, financial and commercial dealings. There are no promotions, no academic laurels, no business and no markets which are not awarded at table.

TEA

Tea is an aid to digestion and those who sit down to lunch would be well advised to use it in place of wine. Their minds would be in a keener state for business and their appetites for dinner.

TEAS

You will find neither conversation, nor entrées, no wit or roasts; on the table only huge cold joints which are hardly less difficult to swallow than the fat Midases seated around it.

TEETH

Teeth are the gourmand's most important possession; he should spare no effort to ensure their preservation as they are keys to his profession.

A gourmand should respect his jaws as an author his talent.

THE TERROR

The ghastly Terror would never have happened if the honest folk had had one-tenth of the audacity of the cowards.

THREE THINGS TO AVOID

'A little wine which I bought directly from the grower'..., a dinner which is described as '... just among friends', and amateur musicians.

THRUSH

A thrush in a juniper dressing ... When this little *ragoût* has been well made, you will want to suck your fingers to the marrow; one would eat one's own father in this sauce.

TOKAY

Like many people of our acquaintance, the great reputation which is enjoyed by this wine seems unjustly acquired. The difficulty procuring any, the great distance the wine needs travel, its nobility, etc., etc., all contribute to the maintenance of a favourable prejudice towards this wine. But connoisseurs are little impressed by these considerations, and see in a wine only its innate qualities. Thus a painter strips beauty of all its ornaments, even of all its veils, in order to judge it in the apparel of the

Graces. In the same way, if a wine is suspicious, cloudy, thick and vile-tasting, a real connoisseur will never furnish his cellar with it, were it to come direct from those of Prince Estherhazy himself.

THE TOURING GOURMAND

They visit markets instead of libraries, and they are keen to bring home to their native land the knowledge of some new dish in the same way as it was the custom in former times to return with a sketch of an antique monument.

TRUFFLE

I regard this root as a foretaste of paradise.

We eat truffles for only four months a year, and spend the other eight regretting the fact.

Truffles are one of the greatest benefits that Providence in its immeasurable liberality has deigned to grant us gourmands.

TURKEY

The first turkey cock to visit these shores arrived in 1570 and was dished up at the nuptials of Charles IX. It is known that we owe it to the Jesuits for having assured the naturalization of this precious animal just as we must be grateful to them for the first shipments of quinine. Both should be equally treasured, one for calming the appetite, the other for curing the fever ... but the turkey has become so common of late that no one dares serve it at table unless it has arrived directly from the Périgord and has been stuffed with several pounds of truffles.

If the turkey is a local bird and served without this dressing, it is talked of with nothing but abuse, our contemptuous little mistresses dismissing it with the name of 'the cobbler's lark'.

We have no intention of allowing this insulting epithet to pass.

True gourmands rise above prejudice, especially that which has no other foundation than a ridiculous vanity. Both things and animals they prize at their real value and not from vain renown. A simple turkey from the Gâtinais or from Orléans, when the flesh is good and white, young, tender and delicate, is in their eyes preferable by far to the Périgourdine, which is often dry and tough despite its rich sauce. It is thus with a little common girl, who, when she is blonde and fresh, dressed in the simplest of clothes, will appear highly appetizing in the estimation of the connoisseur. She will always be a better bet than some rich old dowager, dripping with pride and brilliants.

St Martin's bird.

Nobody who likes baby turkey (and who in the world does not?) could possibly hate the Jesuits; for it is said that we owe it to these good fathers (themselves no turkeys) for having introduced the bird to France ... Ah! What in Heaven does it matter where it came from, as long as it is tender?

Method of Knowing They are Young and Tender: You should put your index finger into the anus of the animal and suck it immediately afterwards, at the same time breathing in heavily. This trick never fails.

It is said that eating the feet helps you to sleep; but you sleep extremely well anyway in the company of baby turkeys.

THE USELESS SOLDIER

In his time M de L* R******* was the most illustrious gourmand in Paris, and it is not an idle boast. As a rich financier he had need of nothing more than a vast appetite to satisfy his needs. The pigeon-holes of his office and the drawers of his desk were stuffed with everything that France produced of the best at the time, which presented him with no problem, for as a result of his position he had every mail coach in the land at his command. He chomped away at a pâté de foie gras as if it were a *brioche*, swallowed truffles like cherries and his bread rolls were no less than huge *cervelats*. His wife, however, who was perhaps frightened of widowhood, never let up scolding him for his passions and he was obliged to retreat behind locked doors for the full and free exercise of his tastes. Then one day he fell ill, and the first remedy that a physician prescribes a gourmand is dieting. For our hero, it was the worst punishment imaginable, and would have been doubtless very poorly kept had it not been for the vigilance of Madame de L* R*******, who made off with all the keys and taking on the role of sicknurse, put him wholly under her régime which, of course, is always the case when a man is forced to take to his bed. The cures worked, and M de L* R******* began his convalescence. Finally he was given permission to take solid food, but the doctor, who knew the weakness of his patient, was scrupulous in the prescription of the quantities allowed, which consisted, for that first meal, of a single fresh egg, accompanied by one solitary soldier. M de L* R******* would have liked that egg to have been laid by an ostrich rather than a hen, but he made up for it by the soldier. He sent out for the longest loaf of bread that could be found in Paris. The result was a soldier measuring more than an ell and weighing upwards of a pound. Madame tried to remonstrate, but she was on shaky ground, for the prescription had been followed to the letter. The egg was brought on in great pomp, and a place set on the sick man's bed, who was inclined to dine in the style of a true convalescent; but in sucking the milk of his fresh egg, he sucked so hard that he swallowed the yolk at the same time! Oh horrid fate, that deplorable haste which rendered the soldier useless! Madame de L* R******* had it carried off with the empty shell. M de L* R******* almost fell ill again in despair. He was not consoled until his first indigestion.

This was the same man, who, when his physician in similar circumstances had allowed him, and this again in writing, a *cuisse de poulet*,* added to the prescription *d'Inde*†, which, as you may imagine, solidly alters the state of things.

---

* Chicken leg
† Turkey leg

TO THE SHADOW OF VATEL* Dedication of the eighth year of the *Almanach des Gourmands*

The first martyr of the Gastronomic Arts. Never was a suicide more excusable, more honourable, than Vatel's. He is the first

Saint in the Butlers' Calendar, and we owe him an homage that doubtless even M d'......... [Aigrefeuille‡] would be happy to share with him.

Let his generous example forever inspire the emulation of other butlers, for now and in times to come! And should they fail to achieve his glorious suicide, let them ensure, at the very least, that they rally all their human resources to guarantee that fresh fish will never be absent from our tables.

---

*Fritz-Karl Vatel (*d.* 1671), a Swiss, was butler first to Fouquet and later to the Great Condé. The traditional interpretation of his suicide, and that on which Grimod relied, is given in a letter from Madame de Sévigné to her daughter, Madame de Grignan, dated 24 April 1671: 'Finally Vatel, that great Vatel...a man of a distinguished capacity, whose excellent mind was capable of running a state, this man I knew, seeing at 8 a.m. that no fresh fish had been delivered, was unable to bear the thought of the opprobrium he would have to face and, in a word, he stabbed himself.' It seems, however, that Vatel's mind had been troubled for some time, and he was experiencing some stress, occasioned by Louis XIV's visit to Chantilly.

Though often described as one of the forefathers of the table, it seems that Vatel was never a cook. A three-year stint in London, however (1661-4) did inspire him to pen a book on carving entitled *L'Art de l'Escuyer Tranchant, Utile à tous les Gentilshommes de cet Emploi.*

‡Butler to the *Archichancellier* Cambacérès.

VEAL

If the calf is not altogehter the son of the ox everyone will agree that he is the nephew at least.

A fattened pullet on four feet.

THE VALUE OF WALKS

He who travels without tears arrives without appetite.

It is a proven fact that all centenarians have been prodigious walkers.

A morning constitutional of four or five leagues is one of the best ways of seasoning the dinner that greets you on your arrival. A similar walk back has a singular faculty of aiding the digestion.

WINE

'It is better to be drunk on wine than ink; it is less morbid' (M Aze).

'There is too much wine in the world for the Mass and not enough to turn windmills; it should therefore be drunk up' (Procureur of the Abbaye des Chanoines Reguliers de Domèvre).

Our life's companion, our consolation in sadness, the ornament of our prosperity, the principal source of our true sensations.

The milk of old people, the balm of adults and the vehicle of gourmands.

Cursed be the man, though he be in the throes of a gentle intoxication, who forgets that a dining-room is in no way a boudoir.

Wine has less power to turn the head of someone whose stomach is largely staunched.

The best meal without wine is like a ball without an orchestra.

WINE MERCHANTS

...public poisoners, the police couldn't possibly watch them too carefully.

The majority of Burgundy, Champagne and claret wholesalers traffic the wine themselves before releasing it on to the market. Wines should be carried off as they leave the vat, just as in the good old days young girls were abducted from the convent gates.

Nothing in this world is rarer than a pure wine or a wholly innocent maiden.

WINTER

For a gourmand winter is the season *par excellence*, for it is not only that in which markets and tables are in the greatest abundance but it is also when one dines the best and the most frequently. From All Saints' Day to Easter Sunday, there is not one feastday in those hazy five months which is not the epoch, the occasion or the signal for a gastronomic assembly. Patronal festivals, solemn festivals, gastronomic feasts, formal dinners, family reunions. You may choose your moment on any day from Martinmas* to mid-Lent. What of Christmas night? The Epiphany? The Feast of Saint Charlemagne?† The Carnival? The Feast of Saint Anthony?‡ etc., etc. One is all at sea with these feasts! For a lover of good cheer it is a succession of indigestions or rather one long one lasting five months. Amphitryons, cooks, physicians, apothecaries, guests and grave-diggers, never do they have a dull moment in that happy time; they no longer know whether they are coming or going.

---

*11 November
†28 January
‡17 January

WOMEN

Their feeble appetite is more suited to sucking and nibbling than to the ingesting of big chunks.

It is very rare that one invites ladies to lunch. If one makes exceptions in certain cases it is only for loose women or those who are very understanding when it comes to questions of etiquette. This is because a lunch can never be pleasant unless one has banished all forms of trouble, and it is for the very same reason that valets are equally *personae non grata*.

Our vaporous little mistresses were laid to rest with the Ancien Régime. The robust beauties of the present day can hold their own against the most vigorous of trenchermen, breakfasting off chicken wings and slices of ham with as much dispatch as their forerunners sipped herbal teas.

Little dishes divert them, giving them the chance to show off their pretty fingers, delighting their appetites without encumbering their stomachs.

... Though everywhere else the most charming element of society, women are out of place at a gourmand's dinner, where the attention of the assembled company, inaccessible to distraction, is directed towards that which is on the table, not those who are seated around it. On these important occasions the stupidest goose takes precedence over the most delightful woman. But after the coffee has been served the fair sex wins back all its rights and some make out that it has then an even greater allure than it had before the meal began.

Women have ceased to be seductive because they have ceased to be modest. Prudishness is the food of desire; one wants nothing from the woman who no longer cares to conceal anything.

Is there a woman, no matter how pretty you assume she is – were she to have the head of Madame Recamier,[1] the deportment of Mademoiselle Georges Weimar,[2] the enchanting graces of Madame Henri Belmont,[3] the sparkle and appealing plumpness of Mademoiselle Émilie Contat,[4] the smile and mouth of Mademoiselle Arsène,[5] etc., etc. – who could rival those admirable partridges of Cahors, the Languedoc and the Cévennes, the divine aroma of which dwarfs in its magnitude the perfumes of Arabia? Could you compare her to those fat goose- and duck-liver pâtés to which the cities of Strasbourg, Toulouse and Auch owe a greater part of their fame? What is she beside the stuffed tongues of Troyes, the Mortadelles of Lyon, Parisian brawn, Arles or Bologna sausage, foods which have won so much glory for the person of the pig? Could you enter some painted pretty little face in competition with those admirable sheep of the Pré Salé,[6] Cabourg, the Vosges or the Ardennes, which melting in the mouth become the most delectable of meats? Who would dare prefer a woman to the indescribable calves, weaned by the riverside at Pontoise or Rouen, the whiteness and tenderness of which would make the very Graces blush? Where is the gourmand so depraved who would opt for some sickly, scrawny beauty rather than one of those enormous succulent sirloins from the Limagne[7] or the Cotentin, which drench the carver, and cause those who eat them to faint from the very taste? Incomparable roasts! In your vast flanks is the source of all vital energy and genuine sensations; there, the gourmand derives his very being, the musician his talent, the lover his tenderness and the poet his creative genius! Would you rather have some attractive but irregular face than a Bresse pullet, a capon from La Flèche or Le Mans, a virgin cock from the Caux, the beauty, finesse, succulence and plumpness of which exalt all the senses at once, marvellously seducing the nervous crests of a delicate palate? And gentlemen, you will note that in my arguments I do not allude to the lark pâtés of Pithiviers, the duck pâtés of Amiens, the dotterel pâtés of Chartres; robin redbreasts of Metz, the partridges of Carhaix, geese from Alençon, smoked tongues of Constantinople, the smoked beef of Hamburg, Ostend cod, oysters of Marennes, Dieppe, Cancale and Etretat; I haven't even mentioned Breton, Isigny or Prevalaye butter, or delicious Sotteville cream; who could waver at the steely force of arguments of a sweeter or more sugary nature? I shall pass in silence over crystallized walnuts, apple jelly from Rouen, prunes from Tours, Rousselet pears, fresh or preserved,[8] gingerbread and *nonettes* from Rheims,[9] Metz *mirabelles*, redcurrants from Bar [le-Duc], the Cotignac of Orléans,[10] the Epine-Vinette of Dijon,[11] Roquevaire preserves, Malaga grapes, the excellent figs of Olioules, the dried figs of Brignoles, the muscat grapes of Pézénas, royal prunes or candied orange blossom from Agen, sugared almonds, rose and vanilla pastilles from Montpellier, apple and apricot paste from Clermont [-Ferrand], fruit pastes from Beaucaire and Béziers,[12] etc., etc. I shall not speak, knowing the weight they would lend to my argument, of Bordeaux *anisette*,[13] Hendaye liqueur,[14] Danziger Goldwasser,[15] Phalsbourg Kernel liqueur,[16] aniseed oil and Kirschwasser from Verdun,[17] Mocha cream from Montpellier, Colladon water from Geneva, Rose oil from Cette [*sic*],[18] Jasmin oil from Marseille (the best of all indigenous liqueurs),[19] cherry Ratafia from Louvres and Grenoble,[20] Liqueur Saint André,[21] the fine liqueurs made by M Noël de la Serre or M Folloppe, Arabian Cream produced by M Le Moine, M Tanrade's syrops,[22] and lastly that human balm, crème de menthe, sandalwood and other Martinquais liqueurs, etc. Be grateful then gentlemen for my silence on the matter, and see if you can establish any comparison between these delicious foods and drinks and the caprices of a women, her moods, her sulks, and, let us not be frightened to say, her fleeting favours! Think about the dishes I have enumerated first, prepared by the cooks of our modern France, basted by the roasters of Valogne [*sic*],[23] and finally carved by German butlers, and will you still hold your original position?...

Let us conclude then: accept that the pleasures a rich gourmand procures from the table are the greatest that exist, and a great deal longer-lasting than those one tastes in breaking the sixth commandment of the Decalogue. They lead to no languors, no disgust, no fears, no remorse; the sources of these pleasures never cease to renew themselves, without ever drying up. Far from fraying the nerves or weakening the brain, these pleasures become the happy foundation of a robust health, brilliant ideas, and the most vigorous sensations. Further, far from engendering regrets or fostering hypochondria, something which finishes by making a man intolerable even to himself, and all too frequently to others, these joys are quite the reverse; we owe to them the face of jubilation, the distinctive mark of all the children of Comus,[24] and how different that is to the pale and washed-out visage which is the ordinary guise of the bashful lover.

1: Great society beauty, wife of the banker from Lyon, Mistress of Chateaubriand.
2, 3, 4, 5: Actresses in the contemporary Parisian theatre.
6: Pastures where the sheep develop a salty flavour from their proximity to the sea.
7: Possibly Limogne in the Lot.
8: 'The genuine Rheims rousselet. Famous for its pronounced musky scent, it was a little pear, of which the skin, green mottled with grey, became yellowish at the end of August. Once ripe, the side exposed to the sun took on a brick red colour. The watery consistency and very rapid ripening of the fruit made keeping impossible. As soon as they were picked, the pears were dried in the oven to make *poires tapées*, which, once bottled, could be kept for a long time without their losing their exquisite flavour.' Now a thing of the past (Sarazin: *La France à Table*). In England it is called the 'Katherine Pear', cf., Suckling: 'A Ballad upon a Wedding' – 'For streaks of red were mingled there/Such as are on a Katherine pear [the side that's next the sun].'
9: Glazed gingerbread made in the local convents before the Revolution. Hence the name.
10: Quince paste much loved by the infant Balzac.
11: I can find no trace of this today.
12: *Patissoun*: little lemon pastes eaten hot, sprinkled with sugar.
13: Then and now made by the firm of Marie Brizard.
14: Even the locals have lost all knowledge of this liqueur.
15: Spirit flavoured with orange peel and herbs. Distinctive for the small gold flakes which float about when the liqueur is poured.
16: From Alsace but, it seems, no longer produced.
17: Vespetro, an aniseed liqueur, used to be made in nearby Metz. Kirsch is now made chiefly in Alsace, the Black Forest and Switzerland.
18: Sète is now only famous for vermouth.
19: No longer made.
20: Liqueur de Cérise. It used to be a cottage industry. An almond liqueur called Mérisette de Grenoble was also made.

21: I can find no trace of this.
22: All Parisian distillers and merchants.
23: Cf. Lesage, *Turcaret*, 1709 – '*Vive Valognes pour le rôti!*'
24: The God of Revelry.

WOODCOCK

There is something of the Great Lama in this bird; everything which emanates from it is treated with the utmost reverence and solemnity.

In parts of the country where there is an abundance of woodcock, a purée is made from their pounded carcases which serves as a base for a number of entrées like little mutton cutlets or chicken wings, etc. This purée is one of the most delicious things that can be brought into contact with the gourmand's palate, and he who has never eaten it may be assured that he has never known the joys of an earthly paradise. A well-made woodcock purée is the *nec plus ultra* of human pleasures. One should greet one's Maker straightway afterwards as all other experiences will seem insipid from then on, that is without excepting even Périgourdine turkeys stuffed with truffles or Abbéville sturgeon pâtés prepared by the celebrated Richard.

The Queen of the Marshes.

It used to be a dish for a bishop; Lord knows who eats it now.

YOUNG WILD BOAR

Hyppolitus* in the kitchen.

The heir apparent to the King of Our Forests.

Despite its wild and noble ancestry, the young wild boar is not really worth the expense of an upset stomach.

A wild Republican.

*Hyppolitus was unjustly accused of violating his mother.

Le lever d'un gourmand

Notes

Le plus mortel ennemi du dîner

The Makings of a Gourmand (pp. 1-27)

1. Prince de Soubise (1715–87). An ill-starred general. It is quite possible that Grimod's grandfather supplied his armies, but he was never a pork butcher.

2. 1721–94. He was executed as Louis XVI's defender. Walking from his prison to the tumbril, his foot hit a paving stone: 'A Roman in my place would have gone back home.'

3. Stephanie-Felicité du Crest de Saint Aubin, Comtesse de Genlis (1746–1830). Suzanne-Elisabeth had been her benefactress, which made her attacks all the more shameful. 'I don't know why Madame de Genlis forgets a trait in my character which no one should remember as well as she, that is that the financier's wife had at one time pushed insolence to the degree of giving dresses to a well-born lady whom she counted among her friends. It must be added that the lady in question was known at the time only for her pretty voice and her talent for the harp.'

4. Author of *Mémoires d'un bourgeois de Paris* (1853–5). Physician and director at the Opéra.

5. Charles-Louis Clérisseau (1720–1820)

6. Marquis d'Aigrefeuille (*c.* 1745–1818). Former Procureur Générale to the Cour des Aides in Montpellier, in which town he kept open house. Cambacérès was received there and recognized his generosity by making him his steward once he had been made Second Consul. D'Aigrefeuille can be held responsible for injecting a certain amount of Ancien Régime *ton* to the court of the Empire.

7. Julien-Louis Geoffroy (1743–1814).

8. René Alissan de Chazet (1774–1844).

9. André Marie de Chénier (1762–94). A poet, he was guillotined on 17 July 1794, two days before the end of the Terror. Marie-Joseph de Chénier (1764–1811). Playwright.

10. The brothers Trudaine, both executed the day before the end of the Terror. They were the sons of Jean-Charles Trudaine de Montigny, Intendant-Général de Finances. They sympathized with the Revolution and were friends and patrons of David.

11. Louis-Sebastien Mercier (1740–1811). In 1811 he published the first parts of his *Tableau de Paris*, which caused his exile from the city. He fled to Switzerland, where he met Lavater. Grimod later followed his example. A Conventionel, he voted for the death of Louis XVI. In 1795 he became a member of the Cinq-Cents. A Member of the Institute, he was described as the *singe de Jean-Jacques* on account of his philosophical views.

12. Comte Alphonse-Toussaint-Joseph-André-Marie-Marseille de Fortia de Piles (1758–1826). Born in Marseille, Chevalier de Malte. He emigrated from 1790–2, when he travelled extensively in the north of Europe. In 1801 he inherited a Papal Duchy from his grandfather.

13. Hector Soubeyran de Saint Prix (1756–1828). Conventionel, Député de l'Ardèche.

14. Jean Mauduit de Larive (1744–1827). Tragedian, Member of the Institute.

15. Comte Louis de Narbonne-Lara (1755–1813). Minister of War under Louis XVI.

16. Pierre-Augustin Caron de Beaumarchais (1732-99).

17. Espirit-Boniface-Henri de Castellane (1763–c.1835). Knight of Malta, royalist, he escaped from the prison in the Luxembourg palace, thus evading certain death. Lived an intensely dissipated

life, keeping many mistresses among whom was numbered the Princess of Salm-Dyke, the 'ex' of Carnot.

18. Tragedy by Phillipe Quinault.

19. In the rue de L'Ancienne Comédie. Now a tourist restaurant.

20. Chevalier de Champcenetz (1759–94). One of the most elegant young men of the capital. Sentenced to death under the Terror, he asked Fouquier-Tinville if it were like the *sections*, i.e. if he could name a replacement.

21. François-Marie Neveu (1756–1808). Landscapist. Taught at the École Centrale.

22. Dazincourt, Joseph-Jean-Baptiste-Albouy (1747–1809). Born in Marseille, specialized in portraying valets. Imprisoned for eleven months by the Revolution. Professor of Declamation at the Conservatory, Director of Entertainments at the Court of Napoleon.

23. Marie-Emilie-Guillaume Duchosal (1763–1806). Lawyer, first in Bordeaux. Author of satires, *Les Exiles de Parnasse* (1783), etc.

24. Joseph Joubert (1754–1824). Conseilleur de l'Université, friend of Chateaubriand.

Exile: the Political Education of a Gourmand (pp. 29-41)

1. Jean-Gaspard Lavater (1741–1801). His *Essais Physiognomoniques* were published in Zurich from 1775.

2. Marquis de Villevieille.

3. Lucullus, see p. 190; Sardanapalus, King of Nineveh and Assyria 'noted for his luxury and voluptuousness' (Brewer).

4. Robert Pons, *dit* de Verdun (1794–1844). Lawyer. In the Revolution became public prosecutor. Conventionel, voted for

the death of Louis XVI. Responsible for voting in the law exempting pregnant women from execution, thus saving many lives during the Revolution.

5. The Marquis de Condorcet (1743–94). He cheated the scaffold by poisoning himself in prison.

6. Camille Desmoulins (1762–94).

A Gourmand in Paris (pp. 43–95)

1. The Public Prosecutor of the Revolutionary Tribunal (1747–94).

2. Phillipe-François Fabre d'Eglantine (1755–94). Actor. Having won a prize at the Jeux Floraux de Toulouse, he added Eglantine or 'dog-rose' to his name.

3. Jacques-René Hébert (1755–94). After a pre-Revolutionary career as a ticket-seller and domestic servant, became a successful journalist and editor of the *Père Duchêsne* during the Revolution. Upset Robespierre by his passionate atheism.

4. Pierre-Gaspard Chaumette (1763–94). One of the Revolution's greatest fanatics, even to the degree of encouraging the people to wear clogs and plant the Tuileries with potatoes. In private life an advocate of the wines of Aÿ, i.e. Champagne.

5. Victor Louis (1736–1802). Prix de Rome 1755. Responsible for a number of buildings in Bordeaux including the public theatre.

6. François-Marie Mayeur de Saint Paul (1758–1817). Actor and playwright. On stage he specialized in lovesick and naïf roles.

7. Antoine-Pierre-Augustin de Piis (1755–1832), *chansonnier* and regenerator of vaudeville. His father was a Chevalier de Saint Louis; a cousin, Antoine de Piis, lost his life in the Terror in Bordeaux.

8. Pierre Musson (b.1739). Court painter to Louis XVI, specialized in miniatures and pastels.

9. Pierre Laujon (1727–1811).

10. Stanislas Maillard (dates unknown). Before the Revolution a *laquais* and a bailiff. Played an important rabble-rousing role in the storming of the Bastille and the Women's March on Versailles. Changed his name after the September atrocities.

11. Comte Louis de Barras (1755–1829).

12. Gabriel-Julien Ouvrard (1770, died in London 1846).

13. Theresia Cabarrus (1773–1835), married first Devin de Fontenay, secondly Jean-Lambert Tallien, and finally the Prince de Chimay; in between, mistress of Barras, Ouvrard, etc.

14. Jeanne-Françoise-Juliette-Adelaide Bernard, Madame Recamier (1777–1849).

15. Marie-Jean Herauld de Séchelles (1760–94). From a distinguished family of the Robe, *avocat général* in the Paris Parlement, a position he owed to the protection of his cousin the Duchesse de Polignac. Dantoniste.

16. Baron Johan-Baptiste 'Anacharsis' Clootz (1755–94). A Prussian, and the richest of the 'Sans Culottes'. Regicide.

17. Jean Baptiste de Belloy (1709–1808).

18. Emmanuel de Haller (1745–c.1820). The son of the poet and scholar Albert. Born in Berne, he associated with the Catholic banker Le Couteulx in Paris. This Calvinist, having robbed the Jacobin state, fled to Genoa but refound favour under Napoleon. Told by Pius VI, whom he pillaged for his own ends, that he wished to die in Rome, Haller replied: 'People die everywhere, and if you will not be convinced by gentle means there are others at my disposal.'

19. Claude-Louis Marquis de Saisseval (1754–1820). Author of several works on finance.

20. A. M. Lafortelle, vaudeville playwright.

21. Francis, pseudonym of Marie-François-Denis-Thérèsa Leroy, Baron d'Allarde (1778–1840). A prolific playwright who dissipated a family fortune in high living. Among his most famous lines were:

> *Faisons sauter le champagne,*
> *Et nos femmes tour à tour.*

22. Yves Barré (1749–1832). Ex-lawyer, founded the Théâtre de Vaudeville with de Piis in 1792. Monarchist.

23. Jean-Baptiste Radet (1752–1830).

24. Guillaume-François-Fouques Deshayes, *dit* Desfontaines, (1733–1825).

25. Armand Gouffé (1773–1845).

26. Marc-Antoine-Madeleine Désaugiers (1772–1827). *Chansonnier*.

27. François-Guillaume Ducray-Duminil (1761-1819). Novelist.

28. *Representative en mission*. Those despatched by the Convention to deal with provincial towns unsympathetic to the Revolution in Paris.

29. Jean-Antoine Chaptal, Comte de Chanteloup (1756–1832). Chemist and politician, inventor of the process of sugaring wine musts named after him.

30. Marshall Duroc, Duc de Frioul (1772–1813). Killed by a cannonball.

31. Augustus von Kotzebue (1751–1819). Dramatist, killed by Sand, a nationalist fanatic.

32. *Splendeurs et Misères des Courtisanes.*

33. Joachim Murat (1768–1815). King of Naples.

34. Horace 'Carle' Vernet (1758–1836).

The Eclipse of a Gourmand (pp. 97–108)

1. Marie-Marguerite Dreux d'Aubray married the Marquis Goblin de Brinvilliers in 1651. From her lover Sainte-Croix she learnt the secrets of poisons and promptly killed her two brothers, a sister and the Lieutenant Civil. She also poisoned paupers with spiked biscuits in the Hôtel Dieu hospital. After a number of other similar crimes she fled to England and thence to Liège whence she was lured back into France. She was decapitated and burned in 1676.

2. Anne-Françoise-Hyppolyte Mars (1778–1837).

3. Joris-Karl Huysmans (1848–1907). *A Rebours* (*Against Nature*) 1884.

4. Markus Sittikus, Graf Hohenems, Prince Archbishop of Salzburg (1612–19).

5. Charles Nodier (1783–1844). *Trilby* 1822.

6. Léonce Thiessé (1793–1854), lawyer and journalist.

7. Horace-Napoléon Raisson (1798–1854). Author of a *Code Gourmand* and a *Code Conjugal*. Balzac was a close collaborator at this time and it is tempting to believe that the novelist had a hand in the *Nouvel Almanach des Gourmands*.

8. Born 1755.

9. Marie-Antoine Carême (1784–1833). Thrown out on to the street by his father at the age of ten, he went to work for the *patissier* Bailly in the rue Vivienne, where he learnt to build

works of architecture out of pastry. Also worked for the Csar, the Prince Regent and Baron James de Rothschild.

Grimod's Food (pp. 109–58)

1. Prince Alexander Kourakin (1752–1818).

Bibliographical Note

None of Grimod's books has so far been translated into English, though there exist modern editions in French. The principal work is obviously the eight volumes of the *Almanach des Gourmands* (1803-13). The first year of the Almanach has been reprinted twice in recent years, once in 1973, with an introduction by Robert Courtine (who as 'La Reynière' writes food commentary for *Le Monde*), and also in 1978 with an introduction by Jean Claude Bonnet, who has also produced an edition of the *Manuel des Amphitryons*. Grimod's other works are of less interest. The theatre criticism refers to a period when French theatre was not going through one of its moments of glory while the earlier 'philosophic' works are essentially derivative. A great loss is that he never completed his *Culinary Dictionary*, an idea which was later taken up by Dumas *père*.

As for biographical information, the principal source for the writer's early life is his letters, as published in the 'novels' of his friend Rétif de La Bretonne. The letters are started in *Les Contemporains* and are continued in *Le Drame d'une Vie*. One of the most sympathetic of the later biographies is that written by Charles Monselet (no mean gourmand himself) and published in 1857 in a collection entitled *Les Oubliés et les Dédaignés*. This was later reprinted in a collection called *Gastronomie*. In 1877, a full-length biography was published by Gustave Desnoiresterres (pseudonym of Le Brisoys). This has been largely superseded by the excellent 1983 biography by Ned Rival – *Grimod de La Reynière, Le Gourmand Gentilhomme*. M Rival's extensive work in archives has closed the door to further Grimod research for the time being.

Index

Academy of the Arcades 13
Adèle et Théodore 6
Aigrefeuille, Marquis d' 16, 38, 92, 93, 94-5
Alembic Littéraire 63
Alexandre, Monsieur 78
Almanach der Leckermauler 65
Almanach des Gourmands 23, 63, 65-6, 71-2, 76-80, 108; attack on 99-100; dedication 93-4; extracts 83-4, 86, 161-223; food featured in 116, 118, 128, 134, 144; parodies 70-1; piracy of 65, 105-6; settling old scores in 76-8
Almanach des Pauvres Diables 70
Anchovy Sauce (recipe) 132
Annales de l'Inanition pour Servir de Pendant à l'Almanach des Gourmands 70-1
aphrodisiacs 17, 158, 164
Arléquin Gastronome 73
Artichokes à la Grimod de La Reynière (recipe) 144
Asparagus Tips à la Pompadour (recipe) 144-5
Aubray, Antoine d' 100
Aze, Jean-Baptiste-Philippe 18-19, 23, 48, 66, 69, 70, 130

Bal des Victimes 60
Baleine, Alexis 83-4, 101
Balzac, Honoré de 71, 82, 87-8, 106, 108, 161
Barras, Comte Louis de 60, 88
Barré, Nicolas 9
Barré, Yves 73
Barthe, Nicholas-Thomas 186
Barthe (secretary) 31, 35

Beauharnais, Madame de 34
Beaumarchais, Pierre-Augustin Caron de 18, 27, 32, 60
Beausset, Chevalier de 39, 60
Beausset, Comte de 103
Beausset, Comtesse de (aunt) 37, 38, 94, 125
Beauvilliers, Antoine 50, 52
Beef (recipes) 130-1
Belloy, Cardinal Jean Baptiste de 67
Belmont, Madame Henri 69
Berchoux, Joseph 62, 65
Bercy 87, 126
Bessi, Angélique de 14, 15
Béziers 37, 38-9
Bibliothèque de la Cour et de la Ville 6
Biennait, Monsieur 77-8
Biré, Edmond 51
Biron, Armand-Louis, Duc de 91
Bishop (recipe) 157
Bloated Herrings à la Dublin (recipe) 124-5
Bocuse, Paul 119
Boeuf à la Mode (restaurant) 88
Bonaparte, Joseph 95
Bonnet, Jean Claude 235
Bordin, Madame 101
Borgne, Marie-Charlotte 7
Bouchée (chef) 91-2
Boulanger, Monsieur 50
Brandade de Merluche (or Morue) (recipe) 125-6
breakfast club 17-18
Breteuil, Bailli de 8, 11, 13, 35; acting against Grimod 14-15, 26, 27
Brillat-Savarin, Anthelme 106, 108, 150, 166
Brinvilliers, Marquise de 100

Cadran Bleu (restaurant) 86
Café Anglais 87, 89
Café Conti 87
Café de Foy 53, 88
Café des Aveugles 89
Café du Caveau 88
Café Egyptien 89
Café Hardy 86, 111
Café Mécanique 53
Café Riche 86-7
Cailhava de l'Estendoux, Jean-François 186
Cambacérès, Jean-Jacques-Régis de 16, 77, 86, 88, 90, 91, 92-5, 167; description 94; Grimod's praise of 94
Camerani, Bartolomeo-Andrea 119
Capelle, Monsieur 84
Cardon-Perrin, Madame 101
Carême, Marie-Antoine 90, 92, 93, 108
Carnival 167-8
carving 75, 168
Cases, Monsieur de 20
Castanier, Doctor 24
Castellane, Esprit-Boniface-Henri de 18
Caze, Monsieur de 8
Censeur Dramatique 59-63
censorship 61-2
Chagot, Monsieur 67-8, 101
Champcenetz, Chevalier de 24, 33
Chardon-Perrin, Madame 87
Château, Monsieur 58
Chaumette, Pierre-Gaspard 52
Chazet, René Alissan de 16, 55-6, 72, 112
Cheeses 150-1
Chénier, Andre Marie de 18, 60
Chénier, Marie-Joseph de 18, 60
Chevet, Madame 77
Chicken (recipes): *Chicken Bayonnaise* 136; *Poularde à la Grimod* 137; *Sauté à la Suprême* 142
Clause, Jean-Pierre 4
Clavaux, Monsieur 18
Clérisseau, Charles-Louis 9
Clootz, Anarcharsis 60
Cod-liver Canapés (recipe) 127-8

Collège de Reims 10-11
Collège du Plessis 10-11
Collège Louis-le-Grand 11
Collin (bookseller) 95
Collot d'Herbois, Jean-Marie 35-6, 46
Comédie Française 59
Condorcet, Marquis de 40
Contades, Maréchal Marquis de 4
Corcellet 77
Corrazu (café) 88-9
Courtine, Robert 235
Cussey, Marquis de 69, 101, 105, 122, 135-6

Danton, Georges-Jacques 52
Dazincourt, Joseph-Jean-Baptiste-Albouy 23, 24, 68-9
Debauve 77
déjeuners à la fourchette 111
Désaugiers, Marc-Antoine-Madeleine 74, 108
Desbordes, Madame 69
Desfontaines (Guillaume-François-Fouques Deshayes) 73
Desmoulins, Camille 41, 53
Desnoiresterres, Gustave 12, 235
Desserts (recipes) 148-51
Dictionnaire de la Cuisine 74, 161
Dieulafoy, Monsieur 69
Dinaux, Arthur 55
Dîner des Mystifications 54
dining clubs 16-17, 54-6
Divoff, Madame 58
Domèvre-sur-Vezouse 27, 31-4, 36
Dronsart, Jean-Charles-Baptist 101
Du Harme, Monsieur 87
Dubois, Urbain 115
Duchosal, Marie-Emilie-Guillaume 26
Ducray-Duminil, Anne-Victoire 101
Ducray-Duminil, François-Guillaume 70, 74
Dugazon 59
Dumas, Alexandre (*père*) 161
Dupuis, Rose 69, 101

Ecole des Gourmands 16, 66-7, 108, 112
Euphratis, Father 162

Fabre d'Eglantine, Philipe-François 52
Fanchons and Fanchonettes (recipe) 148-9
Ferrière, Madame 69
Feuchère, Adelaide 36, 46-7, 57, 63, 100, 103, 107
Fish 182-3; *Fish Stew, Madame Guichard's* (recipe) 126-7
Fly-Catchers' Club 54-5
Foie Gras 183
Fortia de Piles, Comte de 18, 24, 31, 69, 101, 138-9
Fouché, Joseph 46, 71
Fouquier-Tinville, Antoine-Quentin 45
Francis (Baron d'Allarde) 72
Fruit (recipes) 149-50

Game: *Sauté à la Suprême* (recipe) 142
Garbure (recipe) 121-2
Gastaldy, Doctor 66-7, 174-5
Gault and Millau 66
Gaxotte, Pierre 47
Gay (factotum) 45, 48
Genlis, Stephanie-Felicité, Comtesse de 6, 22, 33
Geoffroy, Julien-Louis 16, 74, 101, 103
Gibbon, Edward 11
Gilbey, Walter 153
Gouffé, Armand 74
gourmands: thoughts on 187-8
Grec, Monsieur 76
Grimod, Antoine (great-grandfather) 3
Grimod de La Reynière, Alexandre-Balthazar-Laurent: ancestry 3-4; birth 3, 7, 46; deformities 7; memories of childhood 10; schooling 10-11; amorous encounters 11, 14; legal studies 11-12; thoughts of becoming a monk 11; views on women 11, 14, 33, 59-60, 219-23; passion for theatre 12-13; theatrical critiques 12-13, 59-63; crisis between mother and 13-15; pranks 13, 26, 102-3, 454; profession of celibacy 14; membership of dining clubs 16-18, 54-6;
represented on stage 16, 72-3; changing views on Revolution 19-20, 37-8, 39-41, 61, 205-6; curious appearance 19-20; repartee 19; fighting duel 20; famous supper 21-6; mistresses 21, 35, 36, 46; dislike of servants 23, 53, 69, 207-8; exile 26, 27, 31-6; imprisonment 26, 27, 31-4; mentality 27; letters to Rétif 31, 235; legal career 32; political views 33-4, 37-8, 39-41, 61; travels under *lettre de cachet* 34-6; daughter by mistress 36; enjoying food in Lyon 36; eroticism 36; reconciliation with parents 36-7; in business with father 37; enjoying food in Béziers 37, 38-9; views on religion 40; return to Paris 45; 'gastronomic voyeurism' 46, 48; saved during Revolution 46; journal 47; relations with mother after father's death 57; selling off effects 58; undeveloped palate 63-4; on Jury Dégustateur 66-70, 101, 115; sorting out tangled finances 68; love of animals 69, 105; opinion of Emperor 71-2; magazine articles on food 73-4; views on English 75; settling old scores in *Almanach* 76-8; establishments praised by 77; paying for pear for Cambacérès 95; marriage 100; adopting daughter 101; 'funeral' 101-2; selling Hôtel de La Reynière 103; obsession with pigs 104-5, 201-2; retirement 104-7; in local politics 105; views on restoration of monarchy 105; in old age 106-7; food featured by 111-58; comments on English food 119-21, 131, 179-81; death 102, 107-8
Grimod de La Reynière, Françoise-Thérèse (aunt) 5
Grimod de La Reynière, Gaspard (grandfather) 3-5
Grimod de La Reynière, Laurent (father): career 3; artistic interests 4; birth 4; fear of thunder and lightning 4, 224; fortune 4; gourmandise 4-5; marriage 5-6; escaping

from wife 8-9; collection of paintings 9; self-effacing character 22-3; paying to save son's name 26; in business with son 37; business deals 45; death 45; will 45; wine left in cellar 57, 152

Grimod de La Reynière, Suzanne-Elisabeth (mother): family 5-6; marriage 5-6; dissatisfaction with marriage 6-7; birth of child 7; lovers 7-8; entertaining friends 8; locket left to son 10; crisis between son and 13-15; arrest 45; release from prison 48; relations with son after husband's death 57; selling off husband's effects 57-8; becoming devout 58; taking lodgers 58; refusing son's marriage request 100; death 103

Grimod de Verneuil (cousin) 47, 67
Guichard, Madame 87, 126
Guillard, Nicholas-François 78

Haller, Emmanuel 68
Ham, Spit-roast (recipe) 135-6
Hardy, Madame 86, 111
Harleville, Collin d' 78
Hébert, Jacques-René 52
Herrings (recipe) 124-5
Hervey, Madame 101
Hoaxers' Dining Club 54
Hopkins, Madame 69
Hôtel de La Reynière 9, 103-4
Hôtel des Americains 77
Hugo, Victor 60

Incomparable Roast (recipe) 138-40

Jarente de la Bruyère, Monsignor Louis Sextius de (Abbé) 6, 27
Jarente de Sénar, Suzanne-Françoise-Elisabeth de, *see* Grimod de La Reynière, Suzanne-Elisabeth
Jarente family 5-6
Jefferson, President Thomas 38
Joubert, Joseph 27
Jourgniac de Saint-Méard, Monsieur 54-5, 69

Journal des Gourmands et des Belles 55, 73-4, 117, 146
Jury Dégustateur 66-70, 101, 115

Kotzebue, Augustus von 81, 84, 90, 93
Kourakin, Prince Alexander 115

La Salle, Marquis de 26
La Tuilerie, Château de 8-9
La Vallée 80
Labègue, Agnes 46
Labouchère, Monsieur de 103
Lafortelle, A.M. 72
Lamb à la Serviette (recipe) 132-4
Larive, Jean Mauduit de 18
Laujon, Pierre 55-6, 84
Lauzun, Armand-Louis, Duc de 91
Lavater, Jean-Gaspard 35
Le Doyen (restaurant) 86
Le Gacque (restaurant) 16, 85-6, 142
Le Moine, Monsieur 79
Lebrun, Monsieur 24
Lecocq, Monsieur 68
legitimations 70, 74
Lent 192; revival 79
Les Halles 79-80
Little Fingers à la Trappiste (recipe) 146
Lorgnette Philosophique 18, 19, 21
Lorraine, Stanislaus, Duke of 31
Louis XV: statue 10
Louis XVIII 105
Louis, Victor 52
Loyson, Jeanne-Renée-Françoise, *see* Nozoyl, Madame de
Lugeac, Marquis de 8
Lyon 35-6, 46

Mackerel (recipe) 128
Maillard, Stanislas 59
Maille 77
Malesherbes, Chrétien-Guillaume de Lamoignon de 5, 7, 26-7, 37, 60
Manuel des Amphitryons 74-6; extracts 161-223; food featured in 116, 135
Maréville 33
Marmite Perpetuel (restaurant) 80, 87

Mars, Anne-Françoise-Hippolyte 69, 101
Matelote (recipe) 126-7
Mayer de Saint Paul, François-Marie 54
Mayonnaise Sauce (name) 136
meals: dishes served at 112-15; presenting dishes separately 115; times of 111-14
Ménéstrier, Augusta 69, 101, 148
Ménéstrier, Minette 69, 70, 101, 148
Méot (chef) 52
Méot (restaurant) 85
Mercier, (Louis)-Sebastien 18, 25, 27, 31, 32, 39, 60, 85
Mézeray, Josephine 59, 69, 101
Michiels, Alfred 131
Mitoire, Charles 14
Mme Guichard's Fish Stew (recipe) 126-7
Mock Turtle Soup (recipe) 119-21
Monselet, Charles 235
Monsieur Nicolas 17-18
Musson, Pierre 54
Mutton Cascalopes in Oil (recipe) 134
Mutton Leg Club of Caen 67

Napoleon Bonaparte 71-2, 75, 89, 90, 92, 96, 105, 178
Narbonne-Lara, Comte Louis de 18
Necker, Jacques 209
Neveu, François-Marie 24, 65
Nichole, Monsieur 78
Nicolai, Monsignor de, former Bishop of Béziers 37, 38-9
Nodier, Charles 103
Noël (notary) 95
Nozoyl, Madame de 21, 46
Nuits de Paris 50-1
Nuptial Wine (recipe) 158

Onion Soup à la Cussy (recipe) 122
Ourches, Comtesse d' 45, 48
Ouvrard, Gabriel-Julien 60, 103
Oysters 152-3

Palais Royal 52-3, 87-9
Parc d'Etretat (restaurant) 84-5

Paris: Allied occupation 103; effects of Revolution on 47, 48-53
Parmentier, Antoine-Auguste 203-4
Pasta, Vegetable (recipe) 123
Pâtés, Vegetable (recipe) 123
Peacock, Thomas Love 92
Peas (recipe) 145
Philippe-Egalité, Duke of Orléans 52
Physiologie du Goût 106, 108
Pigeons as Turtles (recipe) 137-8
Piis, Antoine-Pierre-Augustin de 54, 74
Pilau Rice with Saffron from the Gatinais (recipe) 147
Pons de Verdun, Robert 39
Potage à la Camerani (recipe) 118-19
Poularde à la Grimod (recipe) 137
Punches (recipes) 157-8

Quails à la d'Egmont (recipe) 138
Quinault, Mademoiselle 12, 22

Radet, Jean-Baptiste 73
Raisson, Horace-Napoleon 105-6
Récamier, Madame Jeanne-Françoise-Juliette-Adelaide Bernard 60
recipes 117-58
Reichhardt, Monsieur 93
Remuzat, Monsieur 80
restaurants 49-53, 81-9
Rétif de La Bretonne, Nicolas-Edmé 10, 24-5, 34; anger with Grimod 46; depicting Grimod in works 14-15, 17-18; descriptions of restaurants 50-1; during Revolution 37-8; fixation with anniversaries 34; letters from Grimod 31, 235; prank played on 54; revenge on Grimod for un-Revolutionary critiques 40; writing about Grimod 19
Reveillère, 'Gastermann' 74
Revolution 34, 37-8, 61; effects on eating times 111-12; effects on Paris 47, 48-53; end of Terror 47; thoughts on 205
Richelieu, Duc de 117
Rival, Ned 235
Rivarol, Antoine de 24, 33

241

Robert (restaurant) 85
Robespierre, Maximilien de 47, 52
Rocher de Cancale (restaurant) 55, 74, 83-4
Ronay, Egon 66
Roques, Dr 105, 106, 122, 123, 136
Rouget (pastry cook) 68, 101, 148
Rouvière, Dr 69
Ruty, Claude 7

Sade, Marquis de 54
Saint Prix, Hector Soubeyran de 18
Saint-Ange, Fariau de 26
Sainte-Beuve, Charles-Augustin 4
Saintonge, Joseph de 31
Saisseval, Claude-Louis Marquis de 68
Salads (recipes) 117-18
Salmis of the Benedictine Dom Claudon of the Abbey of Haute-Seille (recipe) 141
Salmon in Champagne à la Grimod (recipe) 129
Salt Cod Brandade (recipe) 125-6
Sauté à la Suprême (recipe) 142
Séchelles, Marie-Jean Herauld de 60
Sélis, Nicolas 54
Sittikus, Markus 102
Skate-liver Canapés (recipe) 127-8
Société de Gobes-Mouches 54-5
Société des Dîners du Vaudeville 55, 73, 84
Société des Mercredis 16-17, 54, 69, 86, 142
Société du Gigot de Caen 67
Soubise, Maréchal Prince de 3
Soups (recipes): *Garbure* 121-2; *Mock Turtle Soup* 119-21; *Onion Soup à la Cussy* 122; *Soup à la Camerani* 118-19
Spit-roast Ham (recipe) 135-6
Stanislaus, King, Duke of Lorraine 31
Stuffed Tomatoes à la Grimod (recipe) 123
supper: given by Grimod 21-6
Switzerland 11, 34-5

table d'hôte system 48-9
Tailleur, Monsieur 152
Talleyrand, Charles-Maurice de 90-2, 151
Tallien, Madame Theresia Cabarrus 60
Talma 59, 84, 101
Taurès, Monsieur 53
tax farmers 3
theatre: actors first dining on stage 73; representations of Grimod 16, 72-3
Thiers, Adolphe 9, 125
Thiessé, Léonce 105-6
Tiberius, Emperor 36
Tourton, Monsieur 152
tradesmen: criticized by Grimod 76-8; praised by Grimod 77
Trois Frères Provençaux (restaurant) 88, 118, 125
Trudaine brothers 18, 25
Turkey 214-15; *Turkey Legs Sauce Robert* (recipe) 143; *Turkey of the Société des Mercredis* (recipe) 142

United States Embassy 9, 104

Variétés Gourmandes 161
Vatel, Fritz-Karl 216-17
Veal (recipe) 134
Vegetable Pâtés and Pasta (recipe) 123
Vegetables (recipes) 144-7
Vernet, Horace 88
Veron, Doctor 9
Véry (restaurants) 52-3; 81-2
Vigée, Monsieur 24
Villain (restaurant) 16
Villevieille, Marquis de 38, 92, 95
Villiers-sur-Orge 100, 102-3, 104-5

Wattelier, Basile 103
Wellington, Duke of 103
Werdet (publisher) 82
Whiting Fillets à la Cussy (recipe) 129
wines: Champagne 169; *coup de milieu* 156-7; differences between French and English tastes 153; Grimod's choices 151-8; in Grimod's father's cellar 57, 152; Madeira 194; Punches (recipes) 157-8; serving with meals 153-7; thoughts on 218; Tokay 213-14
women: views on 11, 33, 59-60, 219-23

Grenetier
haricots de Soissons
pommes de terre
Au Boisseau
il faut Manger pour Vivre